ALSO FROM
VISIBLE INK PRESS

HANDY TITLES:

The Handy Bug Answer Book
The Handy Dino Answer Book
The Handy Earth Answer Book
The Handy Gardening Answer Book
The Handy Geography Answer Book
The Handy Physics Answer Book
The Handy Science Answer Book
The Handy Space Answer Book
The Handy Weather Answer Book

SPORTS TITLES:

The Hockey News Hockey Almanac
Inside Sports Golf
Inside Sports NASCAR Racing
Bud Collins' Tennis Encyclopedia

THE
HANDY
SPORTS
ANSWER
BOOK

THE
HANDY
SPORTS
ANSWER
BOOK™

Roger Matuz

VISIBLE
INK
PRESS

Detroit • New York • London

THE HANDY SPORTS
ANSWER BOOK™

Copyright ©1998 by Visible Ink Press

Published by Visible Ink Press™
a division of Gale Research
835 Penobscot Building
Detroit, MI 48226-4094

Visible Ink Press is a trademark of Gale Research

Most Visible Ink Press™ books are available at special quantity discounts when purchased in bulk by corporations, organizations, or groups. Customized printings, special imprints, messages, and excerpts can be produced to meet your needs. For more information, contact Special Markets Manager, Visible Ink Press, 835 Penobscot Bldg., Detroit, MI 48226. Or call 1-800-776-6265.

Art Director: Michelle DiMercurio
Typesetting: The Graphix Group

ISBN 1-57859-065-5

Printed in the United States of America
All rights reserved
10 9 8 7 6 5 4 3 2 1

Library of Congress Cataloging-in-Publication Data

Matuz, Roger

The handy sports answer book / Roger Matuz.
    p.   Cm.
Includes index.
ISBN 1-57859-065-5 (alk. Paper)
    1. Sports—Miscellanea.   I. Title.
GV706.8.M37   1998   98-16994
796—dc21   CIP

*This book is dedicated to my father, mother, and brothers:
their encouragement in sports and to search for answers
led to this and many other good things.*

Contents

BASEBALL . . . 3

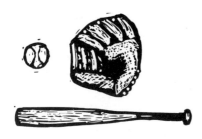

Origins and History . . . Equipment and Measurements . . . The World Series . . . Hall of Fame . . . Outstanding Individual Feats . . . Pitching . . . Hitting . . . All-Star Game . . . Change, Innovation, and Money . . . Baseball and Race . . . Changing the Rules . . . Financial Concerns . . . Odds and Ends . . . Amateurs and the Draft . . . All in the Family . . . Bar Bet Winners

BASKETBALL . . . 57

Origins and History . . . Women's Basketball . . . Techniques, Rules, and Equipment . . . Players . . . Pro . . . College and Amateur . . . Teams and Coaches . . . Odds and Ends . . . Game Time

SOCCER . . . 279

Origins and History . . . World Cup . . .
Leagues and Tournaments . . . Players . . .
Off-Field Concerns

OTHER SPORTS . . . 295

Off to the Races . . .Footracing . . . Horse
Racing . . . Auto Racing . . . Tennis . . . Men's
Tennis . . . Women's Tennis . . . On Water . . .
Boxing . . . Freestyling: General Things to
Know

Introduction

Sporting competitions are much more than trivial pursuits for participants and fans. As well as exercising the body and mind, sporting competitions offer rewards, lessons, and insights—from the perseverance that results in individual achievement to the selfless teamwork necessary for group accomplishments. Sports have always been a distinctive part of civilization, and many of the sports we play and watch have ancient antecedents: as cultures spread, so too did the games people played. Today, sporting events are routinely televised internationally and sports that used to be considered a national pastime of a certain country—baseball in the United States, hockey in Canada, for example—have become more dynamic through international participation and attention.

In *The Handy Sports Answer Book*, we have strived to cover sporting competitions as more than trivial pursuits and to go beyond facts and statistics—delving into history and development, techniques on which athletes are judged and those they use to excel, and the stories that personalize amazing achievements, as well as odd and amusing information just for the sport of it. Readers can trace a sport's history, use the book as a reference while watching a sporting event, and test and expand their knowledge of rules and memorable performances. In many cases, we've gone beyond your basic trivia questions and answers—beyond "Who was the first amateur to win golf's U.S. Open" to why it was such a remarkable achievement; beyond the question of "who invented the game of baseball" to how the sport developed; beyond "what is basketball's triple-double" to finding the most amazing accomplishment associated with that single-game statistic (how about someone *averaging* a triple-double for an entire season!).

To help you find information easily, *The Handy Sports Answer Book* is divided into eight chapters and includes an expansive index for quick reference. The eight chapters cover questions relating specifically to baseball, basketball, football, golf, hockey, the Olympics, soccer, and miscellaneous sports (tennis and racing, for example). Each chapter is subdivided into thematic clusters (origins, individual accomplishments, for example) for further ease of use.

This book came about through the efforts of two teams—Manitou Wordworks, Inc. and Visible Ink Press, one handling research and development, the other editing and fine-tuning. It began with a trivia question: what player achieved baseball's Triple Crown twice but was not voted the league's Most Valuable Player for either season? Hitting the right answer, Ted Williams, after several at-bats, was a start—like getting on base. But we needed to know why it happened that someone could be the most productive player by far during a season and not win a league's MVP. And that is what this book is about—scoring by going beyond facts and statistics to more in-depth information and answering questions asked by rookie and veteran sports fans. The MVP for those two years Williams did not win the award, by the way, went to Joe Gordon and Joe DiMaggio, respectively, each of whom had great years while leading their Yankee teams to the World Series.

Ted Williams, the Splendid Splinter, amassed 2,654 hits, 521 home runs, and had a hit about every 3.5 at bats while striking out only about once each 11 at bats, but there's much more to him as a baseball player than mere statistics. Among other things—like the fact that he twice interrupted his career for military service—Williams was interested in the "science" of hitting a baseball and wrote a book about it. Basic to his scientific approach is to look for a pitch in a certain spot—reducing the strike zone to the hitter's area of strength—and hitting the ball hard when it is pitched there.

A similar approach guided *The Handy Sports Answer Book*. We listened to and asked and looked for questions basic to understanding the history, rules, and equipment of sports and amazing athletic achievements. Once a question was pitched into that defined zone, we hit information sources hard for answers, verification, and related items of interest and amusement. A team was established through Manitou Wordworks to seek out questions people want answered about their favorite sports and those other sports they can't quite understand (yes, we've even tackled Australian Rules football). Team meetings at the Atwater Block Brew Pub and Caribou Coffee, over the phone and the Internet, at Detroit Red Wings and Detroit Tiger games, and ongoing play-by-play helped uncover nearly 600 questions—from basic to esoteric, and from serious to just for the fun of it—about games people play. The result is *The Handy Sports Answer Book*, which we hope you find as informative and fun reading as we did in playing and working on it.

Roger Matuz, Manitou Wordworks, Inc.

Acknowledgments

This book is the result of the hard work and talent of two groups of people: Visible Ink Press and Manitou Wordworks, Inc. At Manitou, Dean Dauphinais, Jay Dooley, Dan Fricker, Peter Gareffa, Allison Jones, Kelly Judsen, Ralph Primo, Mary Ruby, Les Stone, and Bill Szumanski, as well as their respective sports connections, teamed with me to compile this book. We executed the game plan, challenged each other, and completed what we set out to do; if you find yourself returning to this source time and again, we will have achieved our goal.

At Visible Ink, editors Jim Craddock and Brad Morgan kept everything running smoothly despite several hurdles. Christa Brelin provided wise counsel and insight throughout the process. Michelle DiMercurio and Cindy Baldwin contributed Herculean efforts on the page and cover designs. Sarah Chesney handled photo acquisition, and Randy Bassett, Robert Duncan, and Pam Reed tackled the imaging process. And of course, Marco Di Vita at the Graphix Group typeset this tome in record time. We can't forget the people who brought the project into being; Martin Connors, Julia Furtaw, Roger Janecke, and Brian St. Germain.

Photo Credits

Wayne Gretzky and Stanley Cup courtesy the Hockey Hall of Fame.

Mark McGwire, Bobby Orr, Satchel Paige. Arnold Palmer, and Pele courtesy of Archive Photos, Inc.

Wilt Chamberlain/Bill Russell and Julius Erving courtesy of Corbis Corporation.

Joe Dimaggio, Elizabeth I, Vince Lombardi, Babe Ruth, and John L. Sullivan courtesy of the Library of Congress

The early football team and Lee Trevino are courtesy of the National Archives and Records Administration.

The photos of the Chicago White Sox and Patrick Ewing are in the public domain.

NASCAR pit stop courtesy W. Dennis Winn.

Lee Petty/Richard Petty courtesy Al Pearce.

All others courtesy of AP/Wide World Photos.

BASEBALL

PLAY BALL!

ORIGINS AND HISTORY

What are the **origins of baseball**?

People have been playing stick and a ball games since the early days of civilization. On that premise, baseball can be traced back to games played in ancient Egypt, China, and Persia. But if we recognize baseball as a game played with four bases in a diamond configuration and a few other definite particulars, the organized sport we recognize as baseball began on June 19, 1846, on the Elysian Fields in Hoboken, New Jersey. Two amateur teams of nine players played a game umpired by Alexander J. Cartwright, a surveyor and athlete, who established guidelines for a game that most closely resembles modern baseball.

Games somewhat similar to baseball were played before that date in North America. The English sport of Cricket was played in the early 1800s, but another game brought over from England called Rounders is even more similar to baseball. In Rounders, a batter strikes a ball and runs around bases. Balls caught on the fly are outs and fielders can put runners out by hitting them with the ball as they run between bases. Clubs began forming to play this game, which they called baseball, based on those rules.

3

When did professional baseball begin?

By the 1850s, baseball parks were rented to clubs and teams would collect donations from fans to cover costs. The National Association of Base Ball Players (NABBP) was formed in 1858. After restricting members from taking payment for playing baseball, even though ballpark owners earned profits by renting the field and by selling food and beverages, the NABBP changed its policy in 1868. The first professional baseball team, the Cincinnati Red Stockings, began play in 1869.

Legend has it that Abner Doubleday invented baseball in Cooperstown, New York, in 1839. However, while several varieties of baseball were played then and prior to 1846, and though Doubleday helped popularize them, there is little evidence that his game resembles baseball as we know it, even though a baseball-type game thrived in Cooperstown, which became the home for baseball's Hall of Fame.

Alexander Cartwright is recognized as having founded the first true organized baseball club, the Knickerbocker Base Ball Club, in 1842 in New York City. Cartwright and his Knickerbockers developed a set of 20 rules in 1845: the rules called for nine-player teams and a playing field with a home base and three additional bases set apart at specific distances (42 paces, later standardized to 90 feet); instead of hitting runners with the ball, they introduced the new rule of having fielders tag runners or being able to force runners out by tagging the base a runner has to advance to after a batter puts the ball in play; and they created foul lines that marked a distinct field of play, differing from the Rounders and Cricket format where the ball can be hit anywhere.

The Knickerbocker-styled game (popularly called the New York Game) began spreading. During the Civil War, Union soldiers from New York City introduced the game in places they were stationed, and by 1865 the game with the Knickerbocker rules had become the most popular style of baseball.

When were the Major Leagues formed?

In 1900, Ban Johnson, president of the minor league Western League, renamed the organization the American League and teams began play the following year. Along with the already-established National League, which had begun play in 1876, they became recognized as the Major Leagues, ushering in the modern era of baseball.

What were some of the **first teams and leagues**?

The Cincinnati Red Stockings barnstormed around the country in 1869, winning 60 games without a loss. In 1871, The National Association of Base Ball Players (NABBP) became the National Association of Professional Base Ball Players, representing players from 10 clubs that made up the first professional baseball league. The teams played each other and the best teams met for a championship series. In 1876, the National League of Professional Base Ball Clubs, known as the National League, was created with teams in Boston, Chicago, Cincinnati, Hartford, Louisville, New York, Philadelphia, and St. Louis. The rival American Association was founded in 1882. In 1883, the two leagues formed an agreement that included playing exhibition games between the leagues' best teams following the regular season and adopting the reserve clause, which required players to obtain permission from their club's owner before joining another club. The American Association folded after the 1891 season and its four best teams joined the National League. Before it went defunct, the American Association was considered a Major League.

What important **records** predate Major League baseball?

The top four season averages of all time, led by Hugh Duffy's .438 in 1894, and the most runs scored during a season (196 by Billy Hamilton in 1894) are among the enduring season records established before the turn of the century. Pitching records include Amos Rusie's 52 games started; 50

When did the 7th inning stretch originate?

According to baseball legend, the 7th inning stretch originated when President William Howard Taft attended a game in 1910. Between the top and the bottom of the 7th inning, Taft stood up to stretch his legs; the crowd, thinking he was getting up to leave, also stood up as a show of respect. Taft then sat down, and the crowd followed. Since that time, the story goes, the tradition of stretching began, and many teams have taken the opportunity to invite the crowd to sing, "Take Me Out to the Ballgame" during the 7th inning stretch.

Taft was also the first president to throw out the ceremonial first pitch at the beginning of the baseball season. That also happened in 1910. His vice-president, James Sherman, was hit that day by a foul ball off the bat of the Philadelphia Athletics' Frank "Home Run" Baker and knocked unconscious.

complete games, 482 innings pitched, and 218 walks—all in 1893. Cy Young earned 289 of his 511 career victories (the most ever) before 1900. The great Cap Anson amassed over 3,000 hits in 22 seasons before 1900.

What is the **Dead Ball era**?

From roughly 1900 through the end of World War I, home runs were rare, ERAs were minuscule, and the preferred style of play was "scientific" baseball (what today would be called "small ball.") During this era, pitchers were discovering and mastering new trick pitches. Spitballs were not yet illegal, infields were in poor condition, and the ball was not as lively as in later years. Home run titles were won with totals as low as eight, and most of those were probably of the inside-the-park variety. This caused teams to play for one or two runs at a time, instead of playing for the big inning. A premium was placed on contact hitting, moving runners along with sacrifices, bunting, and speed.

Four developments ended the Dead Ball era: The Black Sox scandal of 1919, the rise in popularity of the home run (personified by Babe Ruth), the outlawing of the spitball, and the new composition of the baseball. The new, cork-centered ball became the baseball of choice in the 1920s, as Ruth's popularity grew with each home run. The owners needed a popular figure in 1920 to distract the public from the growing scandal of the 1919 World Series, when eight White sox players were accused of conspiring to "throw" the Series. Pitchers must've felt like there was a conspiracy against *them* when, along with all the other changes, the spitball was outlawed. A few pitchers who were at the end of their careers and relied on the spitter were allowed to throw it until they retired.

EQUIPMENT AND MEASUREMENTS

What makes a **curveball** curve?

To throw a curveball, the pitcher presses his middle finger against the outside seam of the ball and releases the ball with a snap of his wrist (a clockwise twist for righties, counterclockwise for lefties), creating top spin. As the ball moves toward the plate air streams by on either side. The raised seams of a spinning baseball passing through the air disrupts the wake in the air created by the ball's movement. One side of the ball is spinning in the same direction as the streaming air, the other is spinning against the air; the ball curves in the direction of least resistance. A curveball can make as many as fifteen revolutions before passing over the plate. A righthander's curveball will move away from a right-handed batter.

Making the ball curve in the opposite direction—the pitch called a screwball—requires the right-handed pitcher to twist his wrist in a counterclockwise manner, the lefty to twist his wrist in a clockwise manner, a maneuver that puts tremendous strain on the forearm and elbow. Compare the difference between throwing a curve and a screwball by lifting your arm and dropping it forward while twisting your wrist toward your body, and then do the same while twisting it away from your body.

While the curve and screwball have topspin, a slider has sidespin. The pitcher grips the ball as he does with a curveball but does not snap his

7

How do you figure out a pitcher's earned run average?

The total number of earned runs a pitcher has allowed is multiplied by nine and divided by the number of innings a pitcher has pitched. For example, a pitcher has given up five earned runs over 20 innings: 5 x 9 = 45; 45 divided by 20 = 2.25.

Earned runs are all the runs scored against a pitcher by base runners who reached base without the aid of an error. Runs that score because of an error are called unearned runs and not charged against the pitcher; if a batter reaches base on error with two outs already recorded in an inning, his run and all subsequent runs are considered unearned, because the inning would have been over without the error and shouldn't victimize the pitcher. Earned runs are multiplied by nine in the equation because there are nine innings in an average baseball game.

wrist, relying for spin instead on the pressure of his finger against the seam. The slider is faster and curves less, but it begins to curve later—closer to the plate—making it more difficult for the batter to pick up and judge the ball's movement.

Pitchers throwing fastballs and fielders making a play place their index and middle fingers on the seams or across the seams to avoid top or side spin and achieve maximum velocity.

How do speeds in **fast-pitch softball** compare in speed with baseball pitches?

The softball is larger—between $11\frac{7}{8}$ and $12\frac{1}{8}$ inches in diameter—and weighs $6\frac{1}{4}$ to seven ounces. Many leagues use a kapok ball or a solid polyurethane sphere that is anything but soft. But it is fast: Michele Granger, college softball's sultana of strikeouts, has an underhand "riseball" that blasts over home plate somewhere in the mid-70s. The pitch-

Where is the sweet spot on a baseball bat?

The sweet spot is usually located six to eight inches down from the end. You'll know it when you hit the ball there—your hit will feel as effortless as running a hot knife through a stick of butter, and you'll cream the ball. There is no sting in the sweet spot, "the center of percussion." To find the sweet spot, hold the bat off the ground by the knob and tap it up and down gently with a hammer: when you don't feel a vibration, you've found the sweet spot.

ing rubber in softball is closer to the plate (46 ft.) than it is in baseball (60 ft. 6 in.); Granger's pitch, adjusted to distance, is somewhere in the neighborhood of a 96-mph major league fastball.

What are baseball **bats** made of?

White Ash. The tree is felled when it reaches a foot in diameter (when it's about 60 years old) and cut into 40-inch cylinders, called "billets." The average 60-year-old White Ash will yield about 60 billets, of which about six or seven are generally considered good enough to make bats. The billets are aged for two years, then dried, sorted by weight, and graded.

Billets have been carved into bats by lathe since about 1884, when a teenager named Bud Hillerich carved a bat for Pete Browning of the Louisville Eclipse—thus, the Louisville Slugger was born. Almost three decades later, Hillerich formed a partnership with Frank Bradsby, a salesman, and the batmakers Hillerich & Bradsby was born.

After the billets have been aged, those that pass inspection are carved by a lathe that has 28 knives and can be adjusted to over 200 different shapes. The process takes 15 seconds. The bat is then branded with the trademark, sanded, and either dipped into one of six finishes or briefly roasted over flame, depending on the specifications of the order.

What are baseballs made of?

From the inside out, a baseball consists of a cork core within a rubber ball that is a little smaller than a golf ball. The rubber is surrounded by woolen yarn topped by a thin layer of cotton string. The cotton and yarn are wound tight—by machine—to precisely $8\frac{1}{2}$ inches in circumference, $4\frac{1}{8}$ ounces before the cover is added. The leather cover—made from cowhide, which replaced horsehide in 1974—is tanned, cut, punctured with holes along the edges, and stamped. The cover is then sewn on with red cotton thread, a process that takes a skilled sewer about 15 minutes.

Speaking of specifications, Ted Williams once returned a shipment of bats because the grip "just didn't feel right." The bats were remeasured and found to be .005 of an inch thinner than Williams had specified.

Why is the "ping" of an **aluminum bat** more powerful than the "crack" of a wooden bat?

Aluminum bats are made of a seamless tube: the hollowed bat is lighter than a similarly-sized wooden bat, allowing the batter to swing faster. The weight of aluminum bats is more evenly distributed and the sweet spot is larger, since the quickness of the swing brings the center of gravity closer to the body. Balls fly off aluminum bats as much as four mph faster than they do off of wooden bats, which increases potential distance by as much as 10%. This differential works well enough in little league, and aluminum bats last longer and are cheaper investments. They work equally well in college, but at that level there is concern about the dangerous speeds the ball reaches off the bat, as well as the inflated offensive potential. Some great college players have had trouble adjusting to wooden bats in professional baseball. Considering that a baseball is crushed by up to 8,000 pounds of force by a full swing (which

What are the dimensions of the baseball diamond?

The bases are spaced 90 feet apart (someone once said that if first base were 89 or 91 feet away from home plate there would be fewer close plays). The pitcher stands 60 feet, 6 inches away from home plate, a distance standardized in 1893. Home plate (pentagon shaped and resembling a house) is 17 inches wide, 17 inches high (8½ on the side and another 8½ inches tapering to the point at the top). Batters stand in a 6 ft. long batters box (centered in relation to the plate) that is four-feet wide. The pitcher's plate, better known as the rubber, is two-feet long and six inches wide. The pitcher must keep one foot on the rubber while delivering a pitch. The distance of the outfield walls varies from ballpark to ballpark, but has become somewhat standardized in recent years.

compresses the baseball as much as half of its original diameter upon impact), the concerns of danger and inflated statistics are very real. Besides, few things are as sweet to hear as the crack of wood launching a baseball, at least for the hitter.

How did **catcher's** equipment evolve?

Catcher's equipment has been referred to as "the tools of ignorance" (and that by a catcher—Bill Dickey, one of the greats of the position), but think of being a catcher without that protection: so it was in the early days of baseball. It wasn't until 1875 that catchers and the other fielders began wearing padded gloves. The catcher's mitt, with extra padding in the pocket, was designed by Harry Decker in 1889 (for a while catcher's mitts were called deckers). The catcher's mask was invented in 1876 by Frederick Winthrop Thayer, captain of Harvard's baseball team. The chest protector came along in the 1880s, and catcher Roger Bresnahan (a future Hall of Famer whose nickname was The Duke of Tralee) introduced shin guards in the early 1900s. Since then

11

Who is the smallest player ever?

Eddie Gaedel, at three feet, six inches, was the smallest player ever to appear in a major league game. He led off a game in 1951 for the St. Louis Browns, who were owned by Bill Veeck, a showman not afraid to bring novel approaches to the game and its marketing. Gaedel walked on four pitches (he was ordered not to swing)—getting on base like a good lead-off man should—and was promptly replaced by a pinch runner. The catcher, crouched on his knees, was taller than Gaedel.

there have been subtle variations—the chest protector today is lighter and no longer has a seam running down the center, changes that have increased mobility and made throwing easier. In the early 1980s, Steve Yeager popularized the neck guard, a flap of metal or hard plastic that hangs from the chin pad of the mask and protects the throat. Yeager, a catcher for the Dodgers who played on four World Series teams, had suffered a serious injury when part of a shattered bat punctured his throat, but the incident occurred while he was in the on deck circle, waiting to bat, not when he was catching.

How can a batter **strike out** against a pitcher he never batted against?

Remember that a pitcher brought into a game must pitch to at least one batter and a hitter cannot be pinch hit for once he has two strikes.

In a minor league game in 1997, a right-handed batter was ejected from the game by the umpire for arguing a strike call. He had two strikes on him. The batter was replaced by a left-handed batter, and the opposing manager changed pitchers, bringing in a lefty. The second pitcher struck out the second batter.

Because the first batter had accumulated two strikes, the out was charged to him. Because the second pitcher was on the mound when the out was made, he gets credit for the strikeout.

Satchel Paige, legend of the Negro Leagues, helped the Cleveland Indians over the top in 1948, and pitched for the Kansas City A's at the age of 59 in 1965.

During a baseball game, when may a **stadium's lights be turned on**?

Before the game or between completed innings. Neither team should gain an advantage because of the lights.

Who is the **youngest player** ever to appear in a Major League baseball game?

Joe Nuxhall was 15 when he made his debut as a pitcher for the Cincinnati Reds in 1944. He pitched in one game, lasting ⅔ of an inning while

13

walking five, allowing two hits, and giving up five runs. He didn't make it back into the majors until 1952. Nuxhall won 17 games in 1955 at the ripe old age of 27, and 15 in 1963. He retired after the 1966 season and became a popular broadcaster of Reds games.

More auspicious debuts were made by Bob Feller (aged 17 when he played for Cleveland in 1936), who had over 100 wins by the time he was 23, and Mel Ott (aged 17 when he played for the New York Giants in 1926), who went on to play 22 years for the Giants and slugged 511 home runs. Al Kaline was 18 and straight out of high school when he debuted for Detroit in 1953, and he won the batting title two years later with a .340 average. David Clyde was the most recent player to go from the Prom to the Show, pitching for Texas in 1973 at the age of 18. Clyde pitched five years and lost almost twice as many games as he won. With the tutoring and experience available at the college, rookie league, and the minor league levels these days, players are more likely to have to pay their dues before breaking into the Bigs.

Who is the **oldest player** ever to appear in a Major League baseball game?

Satchel Paige. He made his Major League debut in 1948 after he turned 40, delayed only by the color barrier. The legend of the Negro leagues posted an impressive 6-1 record with a 2.48 ERA in 1948 for Cleveland. Paige retired in 1953 at age 47, then returned in 1965 at age 59. He pitched three scoreless innings for the Kansas City A's, giving up one hit and striking out one.

Minnie Minoso was 58 when he got in for two at bats for the Chicago White Sox in 1980, marking the fifth decade in which he played in a Major League game. A native Cuban, Minoso batted over .300 in eight different seasons. Knuckleball pitcher Hoyt Wilhelm was the oldest to play regularly, pitching in 16 games for the Los Angeles Dodgers in 1972 at the age of 49. Wilhelm pitched in more games (1070) and won more games in relief (123) than any other pitcher, and he earned 227 saves before the advent of the closer.

The 1919 Chicago White Sox. The Sox lost the 1919 World Series to the Cincinnati Reds amid allegations that eight players had conspired with gamblers.

THE WORLD SERIES

What was the **Black Sox scandal**, and who were the eight players implicated?

In 1919, the Chicago White Sox ran away with the American League pennant and were heavily favored to win the World Series against the Cincinnati Reds. The early betting lines reflected the general prediction of a Chicago rout. As the Series was about to get underway, however, the odds started shifting toward the Reds. At the time, the phenomenon was dismissed as optimism on the part of Reds fans. Later on it was viewed as another piece of damning evidence.

Late in the 1920 season, the story broke that eight Chicago players had, indeed, conspired with gamblers to "throw" the Series for $10,000 each. The eight implicated were first baseman Chick Gandil and shortstop Swede Risberg (the supposed ring leaders), ace starting pitchers Eddie Cicotte and Lefty Williams, outfielders "Shoeless" Joe Jackson and

15

Happy Felsch, third baseman Buck Weaver, and backup infielder Fred McMullin.

Amid numerous double-crosses and changes of heart, it is believed that only Cicotte and Jackson ever received anything close to what was promised. Weaver argued his innocence until his death, proclaiming that he was at the meeting where the "fix" was discussed but never participated in the scheme. His Series performance would seem to verify his story. In 34 at-bats he collected 11 hits (four of them doubles) for a .324 average. He also played errorless ball at third. McMullin, a reserve, didn't have much effect on the outcome. He just happened to overhear a conversation and wanted to cash in by promising to keep quiet. The level of participation of Gandil, Risberg, Felsch, Williams, and Cicotte is pretty undeniable. Risberg hit .080 with four errors, Gandil hit .233 with an error, while Felsch contributed two more errors and a .192 average. Williams had a 6.61 ERA to go with two losses, and Cicotte contributed two losses (aided by two errors of his own). Cicotte did win Game 7 (it was a best-of-nine Series that year) after the players had decided to go ahead and try after being double-crossed by the gamblers. Jackson's role is a little harder to decipher. He admitted in an affidavit (later stolen) that he was involved, but he led the team with a .367 average, 12 hits, five runs, and six RBI.

All eight players were indicted and tried in court. The key evidence, signed confessions of the players, turned up missing during the trial. Without these documents, the prosecution's case collapsed and the eight players were acquitted. It has been hypothesized that the disappearance of the confessions was the work of Arnold Rothstein (the gambler who had financed the fix) and Charles Comiskey, the tightwad owner of the White Sox who didn't want to lose his team.

After the acquittal, Judge Kenesaw Mountain Landis, who had been appointed Commissioner of Baseball in the wake of the scandal, disregarded the verdict and banned all eight players from baseball for life.

To learn more about the Black Sox, read Eliot Asinof's excellent book, *Eight Men Out*. The book was faithfully adapted into a movie by John Sayles in 1988.

What teams have made **the most World Series** appearances?

The Yankees lead by far with 34 and are the only franchise to have won more than nine times, sporting a 23–11 record. The Dodgers rank second with 18 (6–12 overall, 3–8 vs. the Yankees), followed by the Giants (16, 5–11), the Cardinals (15, 9–6), and the A's (14, 9–5). The Cubs haven't won a Series since 1908, but they've been to the Fall Classic 10 times, ranking sixth in appearances while sporting a 2–8 record.

How many **World Series** have been canceled?

The World Series has been played during World Wars, the Great Depression, and an earthquake, but on two occasions baseball officials have allowed their concerns to become bigger than the game.

The 1904 Series was canceled because New York Giants owner John T. Brush refused to allow his team to play against a representative of the upstart American League. The American and National Leagues had joined to form the Major Leagues in 1901, and the first World Series was held in 1903. The agreement between the leagues placed a franchise in New York—the Highlanders, later to become the Yankees—which competed for fans with Brush's Giants. Brush had other grudges, including the fact that the American League had consistently raided players from the National League.

Joe Carter watches his Series-winning homer leave the yard in the ninth inning of Game 6 of the 1993 World Series.

There have been several subway series, but has one ballpark ever hosted all the games of a single World Series?

Before the completion of Yankee Stadium, the New York Yankees and the New York Giants both played in the Polo Grounds. They met in the 1921 World Series and took turns being the home team.

In 1944, The St. Louis Cardinals and the St. Louis Browns played all six of their World Series games in Sportsman's Park. It was the Cardinals's third straight Series appearance and the Browns' first (and only) one before moving to Baltimore in 1954 to become the Orioles.

As early as August of the 1904 season Brush announced that his team would not participate in the World Series. The Highlanders were likely to win the American League pennant, especially after a mid-season deal that brought them outfielder Patsy Doughtery from the defending champion Boston Pilgrims (later the Red Sox). The deal was pushed along by American league president Ban Johnson, who wanted a strong presence in the country's largest market.

Even though Boston won the American League pennant (the pennant-clinching run scored on a wild pitch by the Highlanders' great Jack Chesbro, who had 41 wins that season), Brush stuck to his guns, and the series was canceled. A New York newspaper cartoon depicted him as a rat scurrying down a hole. Brush later apologized and even helped formalize the seven-game World Series format, which was put in place in 1905. That Series was won by his Giants.

Labor/management problems led to the cancellation of the 1994 Series. The Players Association had gone on strike in August, and with no agreement in sight, the Series was canceled on September 14.

Gene Tenace is one of only two players to hit a home run in each of his first two World Series at-bats.

Reggie Jackson connects for the first of his three homeers in Game 6 of the 1977 World Series.

How many **World Series have ended on a home run**?

The two most famous world championship-winning hits were home runs. Bill Mazeroski led off the bottom of the ninth of Game 7 for Pittsburgh in the 1960 World Series with the score tied 9–9: he hit the second pitch delivered by the Yankees' Ralph Terry over the left-field fence for a game winning homer, finishing one of baseball's great games. The Pirates had scored two runs in the first and second innings, but the Yankees rallied back and led 5–4 after six innings. They scored two more in the top of the eighth to make it 7–4, but a bad hop in the bottom of the eighth on a sure double-play grounder kept a Pirate rally alive and they ended up scoring five runs, for a 9–7 lead. The Yankees didn't die: they scored twice more in the top of the ninth, saved by an alert base running move by Mickey Mantle. Mantle was on first when the batter hit a grounder to the first baseman, who touched first and threw to second base to complete a double play: but Mantle stopped running and returned to first safely (the rule on force outs is explained below) to keep the rally alive. Then Maz ended it all.

Another wild ending occurred in 1993. The Toronto Blue Jays led the Series three games to two and had a 5–1 lead in Game Six after six innings. But the Philadelphia Phillies rallied for five runs in the top of the seventh and held the 6–5 lead going into the bottom of the ninth. Rickey Henderson led off the bottom of the ninth with a walk, Paul Molitor followed with a single, and Joe Carter then sent a low slider into the leftfield seats for a Series-winning three run homer.

What is the rule on **force outs**?

Force outs occur when a runner must leave a base about to be occupied by the batter or by another runner. A runner on first must run for second, for example, after a batter puts the ball in play and the ball will not be caught in the air. If there are runners on first and third, the runner on third is not being forced to move because there is no runner on second.

A runner is no longer forced to leave a base if the runner behind him is retired. For example, a runner is on first and the batter hits a grounder to the first baseman, who touches first and retires the batter. The runner who had occupied first must then be tagged out to be retired, since he is no longer being forced.

When was the designated hitter first used in the World Series?

In 1976. The Cincinnati Reds, with Dan Driessen as the National League's first-ever designated hitter, swept the Yankees for their second straight world championship. Driessen contributed a .357 average in the Series.

Starting with the 1976 Series, the DH was used in even-numbered years. In the 1990s the format changed to allow the DH in every World Series, but only in the home park of the American League champ. Pitchers still bat when the NL team hosts a Series game.

Who are the only two players to hit **home runs in their first two World Series at-bats**?

In 1972, Oakland's Gene Tenace homered in his first two World Series at-bats. He went on to hit two more homers and become the World Series MVP.

Andruw Jones went deep in his first two World Series at-bats in 1996, becoming an instant celebrity in the process. Jones' feat wasn't enough to bring the Braves a title, however, as the Yankees overcame a two games to none deficit to beat Atlanta in six games.

Which two players have hit **three homers in a World Series game**?

Reggie Jackson did it in 1977, on three consecutive pitches off three different Dodger pitchers (Burt Hooten, Elias Sosa, and Charlie Hough). Babe Ruth did it twice, in the 1926 Series, which the Yankees lost to the Cardinals, and in 1928, when the Yankees defeated the Cardinals. In the 1926 Classic, Ruth also made headlines by making the last out of the Series while attempting to steal second base.

Has there ever been a **World Series no-hitter**?

Yes. Don Larsen not only threw the only World Series no-hitter, he threw a perfect game: 27 batters up, 27 batters down, and not one reached base in Game 5 of the 1956 Series. The first hit of the game didn't happen until the bottom of the fourth, when Mickey Mantle hit a homer off the Brooklyn Dodgers' Sal Maglie.

Larsen had developed a no-windup pitching style during that 1956 season, in which he won a career-high 11 games (against 5 losses). Larsen's perfect game put the Yankees ahead three games to two in a Series they went on to win 4–3. In Game 2 of that Series, the Yanks staked Larsen to a six-run lead (one in the top of the first, five runs in the second inning), but he couldn't hold it and was knocked from the game after walking four batters during a six-run Dodger rally in the second inning. Considering his Game 2 performance, the fact that Larsen had lost 21 games (winning 3) two years earlier, and sported a lifetime record of 81–91, his perfect achievement is all the more remarkable. The image of Yogi Berra running up and jumping into Larsen's arms after the final out is one of the great shots in sports history. That last pitch, Larsen's 97th of the game, was a called strike on the Dodgers' Dale Mitchell. "I thought it was outside, but what's the difference," said Mitchell. "I couldn't hit the strikes he threw me anyhow."

What pitcher recorded the **most strikeouts in a single World Series**?

In 1968, Bob Gibson of the St. Louis Cardinals struck out 35 batters in a seven-game series with the Detroit Tigers. In Game 1, he set the single-game Series record with 17 K's.

In his three World Series (1964, 1967, 1968), totalling 81 innings pitched, Gibson struck out 92 batters.

Who is the only manager **to win World Series titles in his first year with two different teams**?

Bucky Harris took over the Washington Senators (and played second base) at the age of 27 in 1924. The Senators beat the New York Giants four games to three in the World Series for their first world championship.

Babe Ruth was a member of the Hall of Fame's first induction class in 1936.

Who was the last player-manager to participate in a World Series?

Lou Boudreau was the Cleveland Indians' everyday shortstop and manager in 1948. That year, his club met—and beat—the Boston Braves in the World Series. Boudreau, who had four doubles in the Series, had been the Tribe's manager since 1942.

In 1947, Harris, now retired as a player, led the Yankees to a Series title by beating the Brooklyn Dodgers four games to three in his first season as Yankee skipper.

Approximately how much higher is the **players' share** of a seven-game World Series than a four-game World Series?

There is no difference: the players' share is frozen to prevent foul play.

Who was the only **president** ever booed while participating in a World Series ceremony?

Herbert Hoover was booed because of his support of Prohibition.

What was baseball's **"Shot Heard 'Round the World?"**

On October 3, 1951 the New York Giants' Bobby Thomson hit three-run home run in the bottom of the ninth inning of the third playoff game to decide the National League pennant.

In an era before the League Championship Series, the Brooklyn Dodgers and New York Giants needed a three-game playoff to decide the pennant after a furious race in the last weeks of the regular season. Brooklyn had led most of the year before a late-season collapse.

After splitting the first two games, the two teams returned to the Polo Grounds to finish the series. Don Newcombe of the Dodgers took a 4–1 lead into the ninth but tired. Giants' shortstop Alvin Dark opened the ninth with an infield single, followed by Don Mueller's single. After Monte Irvin popped out, Whitey Lockman doubled Dark home. Mueller went to third, breaking his ankle on the slide (Clint Hartung ran for him). Charlie Dressen, the Brooklyn manager, brought in Ralph Branca to pitch to Thomson. On Branca's 2–1 pitch, Thomson deposited the ball into the Polo Grounds' cozy (256 ft.) Left-field corner stands.

The World Series, which that year seemed a bit anti-climactic, wasn't as kind to the Giants. They were beaten by the powerhouse Yankees. That Series did mark the World Series debuts of Willie Mays (who was on deck when Thomson hit his blast) and Mickey Mantle, however.

Branca was also the losing pitcher in the first playoff game ever. In 1946, the Dodgers and St. Louis Cardinals ended the season deadlocked. Branca started and lost Game 1, 4–2.

THE HALL OF FAME

When was the **Hall of Fame** established?

The Baseball Hall of Fame was established in 1936 for two purposes: to honor the greatest players of the past, and as part of the celebration of baseball's upcoming "centennial." The first induction class of Ty Cobb, Christy Mathewson, Honus Wagner, Babe Ruth, and Walter Johnson was elected in 1936, none unanimously. The 1937 class consisted of Cy Young, Tris Speaker, and Nap Lajoie. The Hall itself didn't open formally until 1939.

Why is baseball's Hall of Fame in **Cooperstown**?

Cooperstown was chosen as the site for the Baseball Hall of Fame because that is where Abner Doubleday, according to the officially sanctioned myth, "invented" baseball in 1839.

Ty Cobb was a member of the Hall of Fame's first induction class in 1936.

Who entered the Baseball Hall of Fame
the soonest after playing his last game?

Roberto Clemente was killed in a plane crash after the 1972 season, while on a humaitarian mission of bringing supplies to earthquake-ravaged Nicaragua. Clemente was a cinch for the Hall, having compiled 3,000 hits and leading the Pittsburgh Pirates to the 1971 World Championship. The standard five-year wait after a player's retirement was waived. The annual Roberto Clemente Award honors players for community service.

In the early part of the century, a patriotic nation needed American origins for its National Pastime. A.G. Spalding, a former player and owner of the White Sox, as well as owner of a rather famous sporting goods company, formed a blue-ribbon panel to find baseball's American origins. Based on the barest of circumstantial evidence, the panel rubber-stamped the story of Abner Doubleday laying out the diamond and setting out the rules of baseball in a cow pasture near Cooperstown, N.Y.

The debate raged on, however, as historians persisted in pointing out baseball's origins in the English games of Cricket and Rounders. The Doubleday myth was finally put to rest for good in the 1960s.

Doubleday had been a Union officer in the Civil War—he was present at Fort Sumter when the first shots were fired. But he could not count inventing baseball among his accomplishments. He was a cadet at West Point in 1839. The only connection he could claim is that, as a participant in the Civil War, he probably played baseball and helped spread its popularity at his various posts.

Cooperstown, already known as the birthplace of James Fenimore Cooper, is a picturesque setting, and is representative of the area where baseball evolved and gained its popularity in America.

What does it take to get elected into the **Baseball Hall of Fame**?

An outstanding career and a little help from the baseball writers. The members of the Baseball Writers Association of America (BBWAA) elect the Hall of Famers. To be eligible for the Hall of Fame, a player must have played at least 10 years in the Major Leagues and be retired for five years. Once he is on the ballot, he needs to be named on 75 percent of the ballots cast to be elected. If he falls below that, he remains on the ballot unless he recieved less than 5 percent of the ballots cast. A player can remain on the ballot for 15 years as long as he stays above 5 percent. After 15 years, players are taken off the ballot and can no longer be considered for enshrinement by the BBWAA. The Veterans Committee can then consider them. The 15-member Veterans Committee is made up of five Hall of Famers, five members of the baseball media, and five members who have been involved in the game in a capacity other than playing or covering it (such as managers, team executives, etc). The Veterans Committee can consider anyone who appeared on at least 60% of the BBWAA ballots cast when he was eligible. As with the writers' voting, a candidate must receive support from 75% of the Veterans Committee to be enshrined.

What is the only **father-son tandem in the Hall of Fame**?

Larry and Lee MacPhail. Larry MacPhail served as President of the New York Yankees and Brooklyn Dodgers. Lee MacPhail was General Manager of the Yankees, where he developed the talent that provided nine pennants and seven World Championships in ten years, and Baltimore Orioles. In Baltimore, MacPhail put together the team that would win the franchise's first world championship in 1966. For this he was named 1966 Executive of the Year. He worked in the Commissioner's office as chief administrative assistant to William Eckert after leaving Baltimore. From 1974–1983, Lee MacPhail served as American League President, where he preserved the designated hitter, helped settle the 1981 strike, and presided over the first expansion of the AL since 1969.

Lee's son Andy is president of the Chicago Cubs, and his grandson, Lee, is the scouting director for the Cleveland Indians.

> ## What active major league baseball player was the first to win the Cy Young Award four times in a row?
>
> **A**tlanta Braves pitcher Greg Maddux. His first came in 1992 with the Chicago Cubs. After joining the Braves via free agency, Maddux continued his dominance of the National League in 1993 and the strike-shortened seasons of 1994 and 1995. Twice during that span his ERA was under 2.00 (1.56 in 1994 and 1.63 in 1995). His record for the four years was an amazing 75–30.

OUTSTANDING INDIVIDUAL FEATS

PITCHING

Who pitched the only **back-to-back no-hitters**?

Several pitchers have hurled two no-hitters during a single season, but Johnny Vander Meer of the Cincinnati Reds is the only pitcher to throw no hitters back-to-back. They came on June 11 (winning 3–0 against the Boston Braves) and June 15, 1938 (winning 6–0 against the Brooklyn Dodgers). Vander Meer was 23 at the time and only in his second big league season. Some feel his accomplishment is the one baseball record that will never be broken, considering it will take three consecutive no-hitters to beat it.

Who are the two most recent pitchers to hurl **two no-hitters during a single season**?

Nolan Ryan pitched two no-hitters in 1973 for the California Angels and Jim Maloney tossed two in 1965. Maloney's no-hitters were excruciating: he lost the first one 1–0 and gave up a hit in the tenth inning (which reflects the fact that a no-hitter covers nine innings), and he won

31

the other game 1–0 in ten innings. Sandy Koufax pitched a perfect game that year and he, too, won a 1–0 battle.

Has anyone ever pitched a **no-hitter on Opening Day**?

Yes. Bob Feller blanked the White Sox 1–0 in Chicago on April 16, 1940.

Mike Witt of the California Angels pitched a perfect game on the last day of the season in 1984.

Who threw a **no-hitter to clinch a division title**?

Mike Scott clinched the NL West Division Championship for the Houston Astros on September 25, 1986. Scott's 2—0 mastery of the San Francisco Giants included 13 strikeouts and eliminated the Cincinnati Reds.

Cy Young won the most games (511), but which pitcher **lost the most games** in baseball history?

None other than Denton True (Cy) Young, who lost 316. At 511–316, though, his winning percentage was still over .600. Pud Galvin was the second biggest loser, but he, too, posted a winning record (361–308). Same with Nolan Ryan, who ranks third with 292 losses. In fact, only

32

one pitcher in the top 15 in career losses sported a career losing record—Jack Powell at 245–256—proving you have to be darn good to lose so often.

How many pitchers were used by both sides combined in the **longest major league game** ever played, 26 innings, in 1920?

Two: Leon Cadore pitched for Brooklyn, Joe Oeschger for Boston.

HITTING

What is the **Triple Crown**?

The Triple Crown—one player leading his league in home runs, batting average, and runs batted in—has been accomplished 14 times. Paul Hines (Providence, 1878) and Hugh Duffy (Boston, 1894) accomplished it before the turn of the century. The last player to do it was Boston's Carl Yastrzemski in 1967. St. Louis' Joe Medwick was the last National Leaguer to turn the trick, in 1937.

Pitchers have a less-recognized but equally impressive Triple Crown to shoot for—leading the league in wins, earned run average and strike-outs. Roger Clemens of the Toronto Blue Jays was the last to accomplish this feat, in 1997. Winning this Triple Crown usually adds up to a Cy Young Award, as it did for Clemens.

How many players are in the **30/30 club**?

The 30/30 club is made up of players who have stolen 30 bases and hit 30 home runs in a single season. There are 36 members through 1997. Ken Williams of the St. Louis Browns was the first to do it, slugging 39 homers and stealing 37 bases in 1922. No one else did it until Willie Mays hit 36 homers and stole 40 bases in 1956, then the Say Hey Kid did it again in 1957 (35 HR, 38 SB). Jose Canseco was the last American Leaguer to do it, in 1988. The 30/30 club was expanded 23 times in the National League during the 1990s. Twenty-eight National Leaguers and eight American

> ## How many people have hit safely in at least 40 consecutive games?
>
> **O**nly six players have had 40-game hit streaks, led by Joe DiMaggio at 56 in 1941. He broke Willie Keeler's 44-game hit streak of 1897, and Pete Rose tied Keeler at 44 in 1978. Bill Dahlen of the 1894 Cubs (42), George Sisler of the 1922 Cardinals (41), and Ty Cobb of the 1911 Tigers (40) are others with hit streaks of 40 games or more. Paul Molitor had a streak of 39 in 1987.

Leaguers have reached the 30/30 plateau. In 1997, four players joined (or renewed membership in) the club: Raul Mondesi of the Los Angeles Dodgers, NL MVP Larry Walker of the Colorado Rockies, Jeff Bagwell of the Houston Astros, and Barry Bonds of the San Francisco Giants. Bonds joined his father Bobby Bonds as the only five-time members.

Has anyone ever gone **40/40**?

Jose Canseco did it in 1988 (42 HR, 40 SB) and Barry Bonds in 1996 (42 HR, 40 SB): they are the only two members of the 40/40 club.

Cal Ripken broke Lou Gehrig's streak of consecutive games, but whose **streak did Gehrig break**?

The Iron Horse passed Everett Scott, a shortstop who played for Boston and New York in 1,307 straight games from 1916 through 1925; interestingly, his streak stopped on May 5, 1925, and Gehrig's started a few weeks later on June 1, 1925. Scott was traded from the Yankees to the Senators on June 17th. Joe Sewell, of Cleveland, had a streak of 1,103 games from 1922 to 1930, running ahead of Gehrig for five years, but Gehrig went on to play through to 1939.

Has a player ever won the Triple Crown and not been named the league's Most Valuable Player?

Ted Williams won the Triple Crown twice, in 1942 and 1947, but was not voted the MVP for either season. In 1942, the Baseball Writers Association of America voted the Yankees' Joe Gordon MVP. Gordon's statistics pale against Williams' (he hit .322, with 18 homers and 103 RBI, compared to Williams' .356, 36, 137), but Gordon was a key member of the pennant winning team that year. In 1947 Williams' .343 average, 32 home runs, and 114 RBI were not enough to sway voters from Joe DiMaggio's stats (.315, 20, 97) for a pennant winner. Williams did win the MVP twice, though, in 1946 (.342, 38, and a league-leading 142 RBI) and 1949 (.343 average, and league leader in homers with 43 and RBI with 159; for good measure, he also led the league in 1949 in runs with 150, doubles with 39, and walks with 162).

Even though Cal Ripken's streak continues on into 1998 from May 30, 1982 and has passed 2,500 games, he still hasn't reached the top 20 all-time in games played. Gehrig isn't in the top 20, either. In fact, no player who appeared in over 1,000 straight games (there are six) is in the top 20 in career games played, which shows the value of an occasional day off. George Brett is 20th, by the way, at 2,707 games played, and Pete Rose is first at 3,562.

Who won a major league batting title in 1972 **without hitting a single home run** during the season?

Rod Carew won the first of his six batting titles with a .318 average in '72. Of his 170 hits, none were home runs, and only 27 of them were for extra bases.

That season wasn't out of the ordinary for Carew. His highest single-season home run total was 14 (in 1975 and 1977), and of his 3,053 career hits, only 92 were dingers.

35

JOE DI MAGGIO
Salutes His Bat

© 1941..The Sporting News Pub. Co.

Joe Dimaggio has the longest hitting streak in major league history. He hit in 56 straight games in 1941. After the streak was ended in Cleveland, he promptly started a 17-game streak.

Has a player on a first-year expansion team ever won a batting title?

Yes. In 1993, first baseman Andres Galarraga hit .370 to win the NL batting crown while playing for the Colorado Rockies.

The only other first-year expansion team member to lead the league in a positive stat was the Washington Senators' Dick Donovan, who led the American League in ERA with a 2.40 mark in 1961.

Who is the only **rookie to win a batting title** in baseball's "modern era" (since 1900)?

Tony Oliva of the Minnesota Twins hit .323 to lead the American League in 1964. He also led the league in hits (217), doubles (43), and runs (109) that year. Throw in 32 home runs, 94 RBI and 161 games played, and he was a shoo-in for AL Rookie of the Year.

Who is the only player to be named **Most Valuable Player in both leagues**?

Frank Robinson. In 1961, Robinson took NL MVP honors by hitting .323 with 37 home runs and 124 RBI, scoring 117 runs, and leading the Cincinnati Reds' charge to the National League pennant.

After the Reds, considering him "old" at 30, traded him to Baltimore after the 1965 season, Robinson had a career year in 1966. That year he hit .316, with 49 home runs and 122 RBI to win the Triple Crown. He also led the league with 122 runs scored and a .637 slugging percentage. He again led his team to a pennant (and a World Championship) and was the easy choice for AL MVP.

37

How many at-bats did it take Pete Rose to set the record for most career hits?

It took Rose 14,053 at-bats (number one all time) to compile 4,256 career hits. He compiled a .303 career batting average, had ten 200-hit seasons, and led his league in hits seven times.

Rose added 35 post-season hits in 130 at-bats for a .269 average in October.

Who was the only **rookie to be named Most Valuable Player**?

Fred Lynn of the Boston Red Sox hit .331 with 21 homers and 105 RBI, led the league in doubles (47), runs (103), and slugging percentage (.566), and stole ten bases to lead Boston to the pennant and earn AL Rookie of the Year and MVP honors in 1975.

Who was the first player to collect **500 hits with four different teams**?

Rusty Staub had started with the Houston Colt .45s/Astros, where he collected 792 hits. He then went to Montreal, where, in the first of two tours with the Expos, he had 508 hits. New York was another two-time destination (1972–1975 and closing out his career from 1981–1985), where he tallied 709 hits. In Detroit from 1976–1978, he added 524 more safeties. Staub ended up with a career total of 2,716 major league hits.

What baseball great holds the record for **most career walks**?

Babe Ruth holds the career record at 2,056. He led the league in walks 11 times during his career, with a high of 170 in 1923.

Mark McGwire posted back-to-back 50-homer seasons in 1996–97. In 1997, he smashed 58 homers while switching leagues after a mid-season trade.

What former major league player holds the career record for **most strikeouts as a batter**?

Hall of Famer Reggie Jackson struck out a record 2,957 times. Reggie led the league in strikeouts five times (one more time than he led the league in homers).

As is typical of power hitters of his era, Jackson surpassed 100 K's in 18 different seasons. Babe Ruth, by contrast, had no seasons above the century mark. His single-season high was 93.

What player hit **the most grand slams in one season**?

In 1987, Don Mattingly of the New York Yankees hit six grand slams to set the single-season mark.

What National Leaguer holds the record for the most **home runs hit after his fortieth birthday**?

Stan Musial, who hit 46 dingers from 1961 to 1963.

Who are the only two players to have **back-to-back 50-homer seasons**?

Babe Ruth and Mark McGwire. Ruth smashed 54 home runs in 1920, then followed that up with a 59 homer season in 1921. He also had 54 homers in 1928, the season after he set the record with 60.

McGwire posted 52 round-trippers in 1996, followed by his 58-homer performance for the A's and Cardinals in 1997.

How many players **homered on the first pitch in their first major league at bat**?

Seventy-two players have hit a home run in their first at bat through 1997, 11 on the first pitch. Chuck Tanner (1955), Bert Campaneris (1964), and Jay Bell (1986) are the best-known, and Jay Gainer in a 1993 game for Colorado was the last to do it.

Who hit the first All-Star Game grand slam?

In the third inning of the 1983 All-Star Game at Chicago's Comiskey Park, Fred Lynn of the California Angels came to the plate with the bases loaded and a 5–1 lead. Lynn drilled Atlee Hammaker's 2–2 delivery into the right field seats, scoring Cleveland's Manny Trillo, Angel teammate Rod Carew, and Milwaukee's Robin Yount ahead of him. The AL went on to win 13–3, breaking the NL's 11-game winning streak.

THE ALL–STAR GAME

When was the **first All-Star Game**?

The first All-Star Game was part of Chicago's Century of Progress Exposition in 1933. It was founded by *Chicago Tribune* sports editor Arch Ward as the featured sports event for the celebration. Comiskey Park was the host park.

Ward went on to create the Chicago College All-Star Football Game in 1934, and the All-American Football Conference (AAFC) in 1946.

Who is the only **manager to suffer All-Star Game losses in both leagues**?

Cincinnati's Sparky Anderson was the NL manager in the 1971 classic at Detroit's Tiger Stadium for the NL's only loss of the decade. Five future Hall of Famers homered (and 11 future Hall members played) in the 6–4 AL victory.

Anderson's other All-Star loss came in 1985, 6–1. Anderson, now Detroit's skipper, faced Dick Williams, who had three previous All-Star losses as an AL manager.

Who was baseball's first Rookie of the Year?

Jackie Robinson batted .297 and led the league in stolen bases during his rookie year of 1947, helping lead the Dodgers to the World Series and becoming the first Rookie of the Year. The first two Rookie of the Year awards were given to one major league player; in 1949, awards went to the best rookie in their respective leagues, as voted by the Baseball Writers Association of America. Two years later, Robinson won the MVP award. The Rookie of the Year Award now bears the name of its first recipient.

What are the only days of the year on which **none of the four major sports leagues (NBA, NHL, NFL, and Major League Baseball) have any games scheduled**?

There are no regular-season or playoff games for any of the four major sports on the day before (Monday) and the day after (Wednesday) Major League Baseball's All-Star Game. Baseball is the only one of the four that's in season in July.

CHANGE, INNOVATION, AND MONEY

BASEBALL AND RACE

Who were the first players to break the **color line**?

In 1884, African-American brothers Welday and Moses Fleetwood Walker played for Toledo of the American Association, which was at the time considered a major league. No African-American played Major League Baseball again until 1947.

Jackie Robinson broke the color barrier in 1947 with the Brooklyn Dodgers. He led the Dodgers to the NL pennant and was named the first Rookie of the Year.

Who was the first
black manager in the Major Leagues?

Frank Robinson made history when he was named player-manager of the Cleveland Indians for the 1975 season.

Robinson again made history when he became the first black manager in the National League by taking over the San Francisco Giants in 1981.

Larry Doby, the second African-American *player* in the majors, was also the second African-American to manage in the bigs, taking the helm of the Chicago White Sox in 1977.

In 1947, Jackie Robinson became the first African-American to play Major League Baseball. Playing for the Brooklyn Dodgers, Robinson debuted in April of 1947. Larry Doby broke the American League color line with the Cleveland Indians on July 5th of that year.

After Jackie Robinson broke the color barrier, how long did the **Negro Leagues** survive? Did they produce any additional major leaguers?

The integration of Major League Baseball in 1947 took its toll on the Negro Leagues quickly. By the early 1950s, the Negro Leagues were little more than a stopover on the way to the majors. By the early 1960s, they were gone completely.

Many of Robinson's contemporaries followed quickly after he opened the gate. On the Dodgers alone, he was quickly joined by Joe Black, Roy Campanella, and Don Newcombe. Larry Doby's debut in Cleveland later in 1947 made him the first African-American to play in the American League, where he suffered many of the same hardships as Robinson in relative anonymity. Early in 1998, Doby joined Robinson in the Hall of

When were the first
radio and television broadcasts of baseball games?

The first radio broadcast of a baseball game was during the 1922 World Series. Postseason games were broadcast regularly after that, but it wasn't until the '30s that owners (who feared that radio would affect gate reciepts) finally realized that radio could be a revenue producer and allowed regular-season contests to be aired.

The first televised baseball game came in 1939. The Brooklyn Dodgers hosted the Reds, as well as over 33,000 paying customers. At the time, New York City had about 500 TV sets.

Fame, elected by the Veterans Committee. Stars such as Monte Irvin of the New York Giants and Luke Easter of the Indians came later in the decade.

Some of the biggest stars of the '50s and '60s served brief apprenticeships with the fading Negro Leagues in the late '40s and early '50s. Hank Aaron, Ernie Banks, and Willie Mays were all signed out of the Negro Leagues.

Satchel Paige, legendary for his skill and showmanship in the old days, arrived in Cleveland in time to help the Indians to a pennant in 1948, though he was way past his prime. He made another appearance for Charlie Finley's attention-starved Kansas City A's in 1965.

CHANGING THE RULES

When was the first **night game** played?

Although suggested as early as the 1880s, night baseball didn't make its Major League debut until May 24, 1935 at Crosley Field. The Cincinnati

How much did the Red Sox get for Babe Ruth?

In 1920, Harry Frazee, cash-strapped owner of the Boston Red Sox, sold Babe Ruth to the New York Yankees for the then-unheard-of sum of $125,000. Frazee needed the money to finance a theatrical venture. The play closed shortly after it opened. Ruth led the Yankees to seven AL pennants and four World Championships. The Red Sox didn't return to the post-season until 1946, and they're still awaiting their first post-Ruth Series title.

Reds hosted the first night baseball game in major league history, defeating the Philadelphia Phillies.

Falling attendance due to the Great Depression was one of the main reasons for night baseball. Owners figured that the novelty, plus the fact that people who *were* working would be able to attend more games at night would make the experiment a success. Eventually they were proven correct and now a weekday (or even Saturday) afternoon game is a rarity.

The first night-time World Series game was Game 4 of the 1971 Classic. Many purists took this as a sign of the coming apocalypse

When was the **save** added as an official statistic?

1966. Although players and management had been keeping unofficial count of saves since the 1950s.

Who was the first **designated hitter**?

Ron Blomberg of the New York Yankees. On April 6, 1973 Blomberg came to bat in the first inning with the bases loaded and walked.

The idea of the designated hitter had been around for a while—early proponents included Connie Mack—but it wasn't until the American

League (in a quest for more offense) decided to give it a three-year trial, that it actually reached the majors. The "experiment" stuck, and now the National League is the only league in organized baseball that still lets the pitcher bat.

What is the **"ten and five rule"**?

The clause is part of the Basic Agreement between the players' union and the owners which stipulates that a player with ten or more seasons in the majors and five consecutive years of service with one team has the right to refuse to be traded. This clause was part of the contract signed between the owners and players in February of 1973. On December 5, 1973, Ron Santo, a lifelong Chicago Cub, was the first to exercise his veto right when he refused to be traded to the California Angels. A week later, Santo approved a trade to the Chicago White Sox.

In March of 1973, Jim Perry, who had been in the majors since 1959, and had been a member of the Minnesota Twins since 1963, accepted a trade to the Detroit Tigers, waiving his veto right.

FINANCIAL CONCERNS

Who formed the **$100,000 infield**?

Connie Mack's Philadelphia A's of the 1910s boasted a veritable All-Star team, especially in the infield. The "$100,000 infield," so named because their combined salaries added up to that sum, consisted of "Stuffy" McInnis at first base, Eddie Collins at second, Jack Barry at shortstop, and Frank "Home Run" Baker at third.

By 1915, spiraling salaries caused by the Federal League forced Mack to break up his dynasty, and the A's sank to the second division until the late 1920s.

Who holds the record
for the most strikeouts in the College World Series?

Carl Thomas struck out 64 batters over the course of three years (1954–56) while playing for the University of Arizona.

Who was the first player to earn **$1,000,000** for a single season?

In 1980, Nolan Ryan left the California Angels for the home cookin' of his native Texas and the $1,000,000 per season that the Houston Astros offered him.

ODDS AND ENDS

AMATUERS AND THE DRAFT

What player was drafted out of college by the Utah Stars (ABA), the Minnesota Vikings (NFL), **and the San Diego Padres (NL)**?

Dave Winfield. He chose the Padres, which turned out to be a good choice. Winfield had a Hall of Fame career with the Padres, Yankees, Angels, Blue Jays, Twins, and Indians.

Which teams have won **multiple college baseball championships**?

Through 1997, the University of Southern California has won the College World Series 11 times. Arizona State (five) and Texas (four) are next; Arizona, Cal State Fullerton, Louisiana State, and Minnesota have won three, California, Miami of Florida, Michigan, Oklahoma, and Stan-

48

What father-son tandem is the first to be drafted in the first round of the free-agent draft?

Tom and Ben Grieve. Tom was the Washington Senators' first round pick in 1966. Ben, chosen second overall, was the first choice of the Oakland A's in 1994.

After a nine-year career, Tom Grieve served as the Texas Rangers' general manager. Ben Grieve impressed many in his brief stay with the A's in 1997, and is being counted on as a major part of Oakland's rebuilding project.

ford have won twice. Florida Southern has been the Division II champion eight times.

ALL IN THE FAMILY

What **brother combination** has hit the most home runs?

Between them, Hank and Tommie Aaron smacked 768 homers. Hank, of course, is the all-time leader with 755. Tommie, who played on the same Milwaukee and Atlanta Braves teams as Hank from 1962 to 1971, contributed 13 dingers to the total.

What **father-son duo** has recorded the most hits?

Bobby and Barry Bonds and the Griffeys, Ken Sr. and Jr., are closing in, but Gus and Buddy Bell lead with 4,337 hits combined. The Roses, Pete Sr. and Jr., rank second, with father Pete collecting 4,256 and son Petey adding one in 1997. Through 1997, the Bonds have bonded for 3,614.

49

Hank Aaron connects for one of his 755 home runs. He and brother Tommie lead all Major League brother acts in homers with 768.

The Griffeys rank fifth with 3,351 through 1997, soon to pass the sizzlin' Sislers (George and Dick), who accumulated 3,532.

Who made his major league debut by **pitching against his brother**?

Pat Underwood beat the Toronto Blue Jays—and brother Tom—1–0 in his first major league start. Pat went $8\frac{1}{3}$ innings and gave up only three hits. Older brother Tom went the distance, allowing six hits, one of which was a Jerry Morales home run.

Who are the only two major leaguers to **play each of the nine positions in a single game**?

Bert Campaneris and Cesar Tovar. Playing for the Kansas City A's against the California Angels on September 8, 1965, Campaneris played all nine positions before leaving the game after a home plate collision in the ninth inning. Campaneris started the game at shortstop (his natural position), moved to second base, then third, then proceeded around the outfield—moving from left field to right—to first base before taking the mound in the eighth. Campaneris finished up behind the plate, where the aforementioned collision ended his night. Jose Cardenal, Campaneris' second cousin, played in the game for California.

Tovar matched Campaneris' feat, ironically against Campaneris's A's, on September 22, 1968. Tovar started the game on the mound, where he faced—and retired—lead-off man Campaneris. Tovar's Twins won the game 2–1.

BAR BET WINNERS

What franchise has had the **most Rookies of the Year**?

The Brooklyn/Los Angeles Dodgers have had 16 Rookie of the Year winners, beginning with the first-ever Rookie of the Year recipient: Jackie Robinson in 1947. Dodger rookies have had four- and five-year winning streaks: From 1979–82, pitchers Rick Sutcliffe, Steve Howe, and Fernando Valenzuela, as well as second baseman Steve Sax, brought the award back to Los Angeles. Dodger kids also dominated from 1992–96, when Eric Karros, Mike Piazza, Raul Mondesi, Hideo Nomo, and Todd Hollandsworth took the hardware.

Other Dodger rookie winners are Don Newcombe (1949), Joe Black (1952), Jim Gilliam (1953), Frank Howard (1960), Jim Lefebvre (1965), and Ted Sizemore (1969).

The only other franchise to have more than two consecutive winners is the Oakland A's, who had Jose Canseco, Mark McGwire, and Walt Weiss win from 1986–1988.

The New York Yankees lead the AL with eight winners.

Have **non-playing managers ever been traded**?

Yes. On August 3, 1960, the Detroit Tigers and Cleveland Indians traded managers. Tigers skipper Jimmy Dykes jumped two places in the stand-

Who is the only player to play
for both the Seattle Pilots and the Seattle Mariners?

Pitcher Diego Segui helped usher in both Major League Baseball eras in Seattle. In 1969 (the Pilots' only year of existence before moving to Milwaukee to become the Brewers), Segui went 12–6 with a 3.35 ERA. In the Mariners' debut season of 1977, Segui, at the end of his career, compiled an 0–7 record with a 5.68 ERA. He is the father of first baseman David Segui, who recently signed as a free agent with…Seattle.

Lou Piniella was an original member of the Pilots, but was traded to fellow expansionists Kansas City during spring training of 1969. He is currently the Mariners' manager, and led them to their first post-season appearance ever in 1995.

ings when he took over the fourth-place Indians. Joe Gordon moved from Cleveland to Detroit, and settled in at sixth place.

What is the **Mendoza Line**?

The "Mendoza Line" signifies a batting average at or around .200 (a mark that usually sends a player to the bench or back to the minors). It's named after Mario Mendoza, an infielder for the Pittsburgh Pirates, Texas Rangers, and Seattle Mariners in the '70s and early '80s. Mendoza's career average was .215 and only four times in his nine-year career did he surpass the barrier that bears his name. George Brett is said to have coined the phrase.

Rumor has it that Mendoza's not too pleased with his unique celebrity, and a case could be made in his defense. He had a good glove, and there were plenty of players before him who didn't measure up with the bat. One such player was Bob Uecker, a backup catcher in the '60s with the St. Louis Cardinals, Milwaukee Braves, and Philadelphia Phillies who finished his career with a lifetime batting average of exactly .200. Uecker

Who was the first player to have a candy bar named after him?

Reggie Jackson—the Reg-Gie Bar. The Baby Ruth was not named for Babe Ruth but rather for President Grover Cleveland's granddaughter. In a self-fulfilling prophesy he made while playing for Oakland, Jackson had predicted that if he ever played in New York, they would name a candy bar after him.

later became a broadcaster and actor, and used his self-effacing humor to turn his on-field inadequacies and clubhouse clowning into a career as a professional celebrity. Maybe they should call it the Uecker Line.

What are **Blue Darters**?

Blue Darters was a term Shoeless Joe Jackson used to refer to hard hit line drives that fall in safely for hits. They are more impressive than Texas Leaguers—lazy fly balls that fall in between infielders and out-fielders.

The name of what slugger is on the **bat Jack Nicholson wields menacingly** at Shelley Duvall in *The Shining*?

That would be Yaz—Carl Yastrzemski, the Red Sox slugger who was the American League MVP in 1967.

BASKETBALL

ORIGINS AND HISTORY

Who invented **basketball**?

Basketball was created by Canadian James Naismith in early December 1891 during his tenure as an instructor at the School for Christian Workers, which trained leaders for the Young Men's Christian Association (YMCA). Luther Gulick, chairman of the physical education department at the School (now Springfield College) in Springfield, Massachusetts, suggested to Naismith that he devise a game to keep the school's athletes active and entertained during the winter. Naismith had peach buckets nailed to balcony railings at each end of the schools' gym, found a soccer ball, divided his class of 18 young men into two nine-player teams, and introduced them to the game of Basket Ball. The two teams competed by trying to toss the soccer ball into one of the crates (each team defending one of the crates, scoring in the other). The ball could only be advanced by passing, and players had to stop once they caught the ball.

At first any number of players could participate and a team scored a point only by making three consecutive field goals (baskets). Naismith soon limited teams to nine players on each side, awarded two points for a basket, introduced fouls (but only for particularly violent actions) and foul shots. The early game was rough and slow: since the peach baskets were closed at the bottom, someone had to climb on a ladder to retrieve the ball after each basket.

Improvements to the game came quickly over the next two decades as basketball spread in popularity. The peach basket was replaced by a metal rim with a net, and in 1906 the netting was opened to allow the ball to fall through. The ball was improved: basketballs were made from strips of leather stitched over an air-filled rubber bladder; a cloth lining was added for support and uniformity, then in the early 1940s a molded, factory-made basketball standardized the size and shape.

In Naismith's original 13 rules, the ball could be batted in any direction with one or both hands. Since players could not advance with the ball, dribbling was unnecessary. Ball handlers were allowed to move and dribble beginning around 1910, but a dribbler was not allowed to shoot the ball until 1916.

What are Naismith's **original 13 rules**?

Naismith's 13 "Basket Ball" rules were originally printed in the *Triangle*, a YMCA School for Christian Workers newspaper, on January 15, 1892. They read as follows:

1. The ball may be thrown in any direction with one or both hands.

2. The ball may be batted in any direction with one or both hands (never with the fist).

3. A player cannot run with the ball. The player must throw it from the spot on which he catches it; allowance to be made for a man who catches the ball when running at a good speed.

4. The ball must be held in or between the hands; the arms or body must not be used for holding it.

5. No shouldering, holding, pushing, tripping or striking, in any way the person of an opponent shall be allowed; the first infringement of this rule by any person shall count as a foul, the second shall disqualify him until the next goal is made; or, if there was evident intent to injure the person for the whole game, no substitute shall be allowed.

6. A foul is striking at the ball with the fist, violation of Rules Three, Four, and such as described in Rule Five.

How did professional basketball develop?

The first professional basketball association of teams was the National Basketball League (NBL), formed in 1898 principally as a way to organize competition against the Trenton Basketball Team, the finest organized team of the day in the YMCA League. The NBL didn't last long, but by 1920 there were at least 20 leagues in the east and midwest.

The American Basketball League (ABL) began play in 1925 and lasted into the 1930s, when college basketball became increasingly popular. The Basketball Association of America (BAA) was comprised of teams in eastern cities when it began in 1946. Meanwhile, another National Basketball League was founded with teams spreading into the midwest. The BAA and NBL teams competed for players and fans. In 1948, four NBL teams joined the BAA and six more joined the following year, banding with seven remaining BAA teams to form a 17-team league renamed the National Basketball Association (NBA).

7. If either side makes three consecutive fouls, it shall count a goal for the opponents. (Consecutive means without the opponents in the meantime making a foul.)

8. A goal shall be made when the ball is thrown or batted from the ground into the basket and stays there, providing those defending the goal do not touch or disturb the goal. If the ball rests on the edge and the opponent moves the basket, it shall count as a goal.

9. When the ball goes out of bounds, it shall be thrown into the field and played by the person first touching it. In case of a dispute, the umpire shall throw it straight into the field. The thrower-in is allowed five seconds. If he holds it longer, it shall go to the opponent. If any side persists in delaying the game, the umpire shall call a foul on them.

10. The umpire shall be the judge of the men and shall note the fouls and notify the referee when three consecutive fouls have been made. He shall have power to disqualify men according to Rule Five.

11. The referee shall be the judge of the ball and shall decide when the ball is in play, in bounds, to which side it belongs, and shall keep the time. He shall decide when a goal has been made, and keep account of the goals, with any other duties that are usually performed by a referee.

12. The time shall be two fifteen minute halves, with five minutes rest between.

13. The side making the most goals in that time shall be declared the winners. In case of a draw, the game may, by agreement of the captains, be continued until another goal is made.

How did **NBA teams** enter the league?

Three teams survive from the original BAA: the Boston Celtics, New York Knicks, and Golden State Warriors (known as the Philadelphia Warriors before moving to San Francisco in 1962).

Five franchises survive from the original NBL: the Detroit Pistons (moved from Fort Wayne, Indiana, in 1957); the Los Angeles Lakers (moved from Minneapolis in 1960); the Philadelphia 76ers (moved from Syracuse in 1963); the Atlanta Hawks (originally called the TriCity Hawks until 1951, relocated to Milwaukee from 1951–55, and to St. Louis from 1955–68); and the Sacramento Kings (originally the Rochester Royals before moving to Cincinnati in 1957; known as the Kansas City-Omaha Kings, 1972–75, and the Kansas City Kings from 1975–85).

The remaining teams came through expansion in the following years:

1961: Washington Wizards—Began as the Chicago Packers (1961), became the Baltimore Bullets (1963), the Capitol Bullets (1973) and then the Washington Bullets (1974); renamed the Wizards in 1997.

1966: Chicago Bulls.

1967: San Diego Rockets (moved to Houston in 1971) and Seattle Supersonics.

What was the American Basketball Association?

The ABA was a professional league that began play with 10 teams in 1967, featured a red-white-and-blue ball and introduced the three-point shot. The ABA lasted nine seasons before folding in 1976: four teams—the Denver Nuggets, Indiana Pacers, New York Nets, and San Antonio Spurs—joined the NBA. ABA innovations like the three-point shot and an All-Star break slam dunk contest were eventually adopted by the NBA. During its existence, the ABA competed with the NBA for professional and college players, leading to salary increases. Julius Erving of the Nets was the most famous ABA player. Rick Barry (who switched leagues), the flamboyant Connie Hawkins (who was exonerated from a college betting scandal that originally led the NBA to ban him), Spencer Haywood (who left college before finishing his eligibility), and Dan Issel (a highly sought-after graduate) were among the other stars to give the ABA credibility.

1968: Milwaukee Bucks and Phoenix Suns.

1970: Buffalo Braves (became the San Diego Clippers in 1978, became the Los Angeles Clippers in 1984), Cleveland Cavaliers, Portland Trailblazers.

1974: New Orleans Jazz (became the Utah Jazz in 1979).

1976: From the ABA merger into the NBA—Denver Nuggets, Indiana Pacers, New York Nets (became the New Jersey Nets in 1977), and San Antonio Spurs.

1980: Dallas Mavericks.

1988: Charlotte Hornets and Miami Heat.

1989: Minnesota Timberwolves and Orlando Magic.

1995: Toronto Raptors and Vancouver Grizzlies.

How did college basketball evolve?

The first intercollegiate game was held in 1897. In May 1901 several schools—Yale, Harvard, Trinity, Holy Cross, Amherst, and Williams—formed the New England Intercollegiate Basketball League. The development of collegiate leagues and conferences brought organization, scheduling, and rivalries. By 1905 more than 80 schools had organized teams. Colleges competed mostly in their regions until 1936, when a Stanford University team traveled to New York City to challenge top eastern squads. This tour helped bring variety to the game: eastern teams generally favored the two-hand, stationary shot, while western teams had turned to one-handed jump shots. The jump shot soon became popular in the east as well, and scores rose.

Was there a **color barrier** in basketball?

Yes. The NBA became integrated in the 1950s, but there were incidents where all-white college teams refused to play integrated or all-black teams as late as the 1960s.

An all-African American team—the New York Renaissance—was dominant in pro ball during the 1930s, when teams were not yet integrated. The Rens won 88 consecutive games during one stretch. In 1963 the Rens as a team were enshrined in the Basketball Hall of Fame, one of only four teams so honored.

The Harlem Globetrotters were founded in 1927 as a competitive team, but through the years they became better known for their displays of individual skills (ball-handling, trick shooting), acrobatics and humorous routines.

When did professional basketball **break the color barrier**?

Chuck Cooper and Earl Lloyd were drafted by the Celtics and Capitals, respectively, in 1950. The color barrier was broken when Lloyd became

Who was the first African-American All-American basketball player?

George Gregory of Columbia in 1931 was the first African-American named All-American. Don Barksdale of UCLA in 1948 became the first African-American Olympic basketball player, and he was also the first African-American NBA All-Star (1952).

the first African American to play in an NBA game. The Knicks obtained Sweetwater Clifton from the Harlem Globetrotters, and he also played during the 1950–51 season.

When did the **major tournaments** develop?

In 1937 the first national collegiate tournament was organized by the NAIA (National Association of Intercollegiate Athletics). The following year the Metropolitan Basketball Writer's Association, a group of New York City sportswriters, organized the National Invitational Tournament to conclude the 1937–38 season. The National Association of Basketball Coaches (NABC) founded the NCAA tournament the following year. Oregon defeated Ohio State 46–33 to win the first NCAA championship.

The NIT and NCAA tournaments were originally played at the same time: as a general rule, independent schools played in the NIT and conference-affiliated schools played in the NCAA. For the first 12 years, the NCAA tournament divided the country into eight districts, each with a regional selection committee sending a team to the eight-team tournament. As the tournament gained importance, the field gradually enlarged to 16, then 32 teams, and in 1985 to its present size of 64.

What is the **National Invitational Tournament**?

The NIT is a competition that commenced play in 1938 as a means of determining a national collegiate champion. In the first NIT final, Temple defeated Colorado 60–36. The next year, however, the NCAA decided to conduct its own tournament to determine a national champion. The NIT then began inviting teams that were out of the NCAA's competition. In 1950, however, City College of New York won both the NIT and NCAA tournaments. The NIT has always been held at Madison Square Garden in New York City. St. John's University has won five NIT tournaments and Bradley University has won four.

What's the history of **Olympic basketball**?

Men's Olympic basketball was introduced as a demonstration sport (with no medal awarded) at the 1904 games in St. Louis, and the first official Olympic basketball was played at the 1936 games in Berlin, Germany. The United States won the gold medal by defeating Canada 19–8 in the final round. The low score reflected the conditions of play: games were held outdoors on clay and sand tennis courts, which were wet from rain in the final, making running and dribbling another kind of Olympic challenge.

The United States dominated Olympic basketball, winning the first seven gold medals and running up a 62-game win streak. The Soviet team ended the streak in 1972, however, in a controversial game where the final seconds were replayed and a seemingly slim U.S. win turned into an agonizing last-second loss. The U.S. team won in 1976 and 1984 (the U.S. boycotted the 1980 games held in Moscow), Yugoslavia won in 1980 and finished second in 1976 and 1988, and the USSR team won in 1988.

Professional players were first allowed to compete in the 1992 Olympics. USA Basketball, the governing body of Olympic basketball in the United States, assembled a national group of NBA All-Stars called the Dream Team, which overwhelmed the other teams.

Women's Olympic basketball competition began at the 1976 games in Montreal, with the Soviet team winning. The U.S. team captured its first gold medal at the 1984 games in Los Angeles.

When did women's college tournaments begin?

In 1971 the Association for Intercollegiate Athletics for Women (AIAW) was founded and established a national tournament. In 1982 the NCAA held its first national championship for women. Louisiana Tech won the first championship, finished runner-up (to USC) in 1983, and finished third (USC repeated) in 1984. Through 1998, Louisiana Tech, USC, and Stanford have each won two championships, while Tennessee has won six championships and has made the final four 11 times.

WOMEN'S BASKETBALL

How did **women's basketball** develop?

One year after the 1891 invention of basketball, Senda Berenson Abbott, a Lithuanian-born physical education teacher, introduced the game to women at Smith College in Northampton, Massachusetts. Berenson Abbott introduced variations of rules for the women's game: the court was divided into three equal sections and players were required to stay in an assigned area; players were prohibited from stealing the ball from another player, from holding the ball for longer than three seconds, and from dribbling the ball more than three times.

Rules were refined through the years with major changes occurring during the 1960s, when unlimited dribbling became legal and the five-player, full-court game was played. Except for playing with a smaller basketball and using a 30-second shot clock, women's basketball is now played with the same rules, regulations, and styles as men's basketball.

What are the only three **undefeated NCAA women's basketball national championship teams**?

Tennessee joined the unbeaten ranks in 1998 when it finished a record 39-0. Texas went 34–0 in 1986 and Connecticut 35–0 in 1995.

65

Who was the **first woman to dunk** in an NCAA basketball game?

Georgeann Wells of West Virginia became the first on December 21, 1984 against Charleston.

What was the **highest scoring women's NCAA basketball game**?

Virginia defeated North Carolina 123–120 in a triple-overtime game.

How did **women's professional basketball** develop?

There was no professional women's basketball organization until the mid-1990s, when the American Basketball League (ABL) was formed. It began play with the 1996–97 season, and the Columbus Quest was the first league champion. In 1996 the NBA announced plans to help form a separate women's league, the WNBA, with play beginning in 1997. Houston won the first WNBA championship.

TECHNIQUES, RULES, AND EQUIPMENT

What are the **dimensions** of basketball courts and three-point lines?

NBA courts are 94 feet in length by 50 feet in width. A playing area of 84 ft by 50 ft is used in recreational and high school competition. The three-point line in high school and college games is 19 feet 9 inches from the basket, while in international play it is 21 feet 6 inches and in professional play it is 22 feet.

What are the five basketball **positions** and what types of skills do they require?

Guards: Two guards—the point guard (or 1-guard) and the shooting guard (or 2-guard) form the backcourt. The point guard is generally the

What five-medal Olympic track and field star was a four-year college basketball starter before becoming an Olympic champion?

Jackie Joyner-Kersey started for UCLA for four years, from 1980–81 through 1984–85. She went on to Olympic fame in the heptathlon and long jump

leader of the team on the court, doing most of the ball-handling and setting up plays through superb passing skills. The shooting guard is generally a good ball handler with excellent shooting skills.

Forwards: The small forward (3-player) is usually a strong scorer near and away from the basket. He is called on to rebound, handle the ball, and pass. Players like Larry Bird, Scottie Pippin, and Grant Hill combine these talents and have often served as a second point guard on the floor. The power forward (4-player) is big and strong, concentrating primarily on defense and rebounding. Though he is smaller than most power forwards, Dennis Rodman combines the defensive and rebounding skills of the ideal power forward.

The Center (5-player) is usually the tallest player on the team and serves as the cornerstone of most set plays. Centers use their height advantage to score over other players and rebound.

These are general characteristics, with some players specializing in a particular facet of the game and others transcending expectations of their position.

What are the different kinds of **passes**?

There are five types of passes: bounce—in which the ball is bounced on the ground from one teammate to another; chest—where the ball is passed from chest high; overhead—where the ball is thrown with both hands extended over the head; baseball-style—thrown like a baseball, usually featured in a long pass; and behind-the-back—when a player whips the ball around his back, waist high, sometimes for sheer showmanship, sometimes to avoid a defensive player who comes between onrushing teammates.

What are differences between **NBA and Olympic/International rules**?

Time: A 30-second time clock (rather than 24-second) is used in international competition. International games, like college games, have two 20-minute periods, and, similarly, each have five-minute overtimes in case of a tie. In international play, each team receives two one-minute timeouts per half and one time-out during an overtime period.

Fouling: The eighth team foul in each half, and all succeeding ones, result in two free throws for the other team in international play. The individual foul limit is five. No shots are awarded on offensive fouls.

Substitution: Substitution rules are somewhat different from the pro and college game. On a possession after a violation, the offense may substitute, and the defense may substitute only if the offense substi-

When did some of the basic techniques, such as the jump shot, come into practice?

Nat Holman, who played with the original Boston Celtics (1920) and coached City College of New York to both NIT and NCAA tournament championships in 1950, is generally credited with having invented the pivot play; Dutch Dehnert (elected to the Hall of Fame in 1968) helped introduce the give and go; and Joe Fulks (the NBA's first season scoring leader and a Hall of Fame member) popularized the jump shot.

tutes. After successful free throws, the shooter may be replaced if requested prior to the first free throw. The opponent is allowed one substitute if requested before the last free throw.

Lanes: The lanes on an international court flare out as opposed to the rectangular lanes in the NBA and NCAA; there are more three-second violations and driving lay-ups in international play.

Three-point play: The Olympic distance is roughly midway between those of the college and professional sports. The three-point distance in the international game is a little over 20.5 feet, or 6.25 meters, compared to 22 feet in the NBA, and the NCAA's 19 feet, nine inches.

What are the rules and organization of **international professional basketball**?

The shot clock is 30 seconds in international play, as opposed to the 24-second clock in American professional play and the 35-second clock in men's collegiate play; the three-point line is set at a distance between the collegiate and professional distances; and the "key" area is a wider, trapezoidal shape.

The Fédération International de Basketball Association (FIBA, Federation of International Basketball) governs international basketball and its more than 200 leagues. FIBA divides the world into five sections—Africa, Asia, the Americas, Europe, and Oceania—called zone commissions, and the zone commissions conduct regional championships. National federations are subdivided into leagues comprised of club teams. Most international leagues allow two foreign players on their rosters, and the game itself is similar to American basketball. International tournaments include the world championships, played every four years; the European championships, held annually; the championships at the Pan American Games, played every four years; and the Jones Cup, held annually.

PLAYERS

PRO

What players were among those voted the **top 50 NBA players**?

A league-approved panel of former players and coaches, current and former general managers, team executives, and media people voted on the 50 greatest players to coincide with the league's 50th anniversary in 1996. The players are listed here, with some career highlights:

Kareem Abdul-Jabbar: see question below.

Nate Archibald: 6-foot-1 "Tiny" Archibald was a fearless penetrator, an excellent passer, and had great range as a shooter. In 1972 he averaged 34 points and 11.4 assists per game for the Kansas City Kings, becoming the only player in NBA history to lead the league in those two categories in the same season. Archibald led the NBA in free throws made three times and the Boston Celtics to the 1981 NBA title and the NBA's best record from 1980 through 1982.

Paul Arizin: "Pitchin' Paul" Arizin was a Philly phenom of the '50s, beginning with his college days at Villanova, where he set a single-game scoring record of 85 points as a sophomore and led the nation in scoring (25.3 points per game) as a senior in 1950, when he was named College Player of the Year. Arizin played with the Philadelphia Warriors for 10 seasons (1950–52, 1954–62), interrupted by two seasons of military service. He was the NBA scoring champ twice and led the Warriors to the 1956 NBA championship over the Fort Wayne Pistons.

Charles Barkley: Called "Sir Charles" for his commanding court presence, Barkley is a great all-around player and fierce competitor. He was the league MVP during the 1992–93 season, when he led the Phoenix Suns to the championship finals before bowing to the Chicago Bulls.

Rick Barry: Barry was Rookie of the Year in 1966 and led the league in scoring (35.6 points per game) the following season. In 1975, Barry was named MVP of the NBA championship series, leading the San Francisco Warriors to a four-game sweep of the Washington Bullets. His 89.3 percent career foul-shooting, performed with an underhand technique, is second best in NBA/ABA history.

Elgin Baylor: In 1957–58, Baylor led Seattle University to the NCAA championship game and was the tournament MVP. He was the 1959 NBA Rookie of the Year (24.9 points per game) for the Minneapolis Lakers, who moved to Los Angeles in 1960. Baylor averaged 30 points or more three times during his career and became the first player in NBA history to score over 70 points in a game.

Dave Bing: Bing was the NBA's Rookie of the Year in 1967 for his playmaking and scoring. The following year he led the NBA in scoring with a 27.1 per game average for the Detroit Pistons. Bing was a smooth and skillful player who excelled in all aspects of the game.

Larry Bird: see question on page 85.

Wilt Chamberlain: see question below.

Bob Cousey: The "Houdini of the Hardwood," Cousey was the NBA's first great and flashy playmaker, spearheading the Celtic dynasty and winning six championships. Cousey led the NBA in assists eight consecutive years (1953–60). He coached the Cincinnati/Kansas City Royals from 1969–74 and played at age 41 during the 1969-70 season, making him the oldest player in NBA history.

Dave Cowens: During his rookie year Cowens averaged 17 points and 15 rebounds a game and shared the NBA Rookie of the Year Award with Portland's Geoff Petrie. Small for a center at 6-9, Cowens was a deft outside shooter and fearless player who could mix it up inside and hit long jumpers from the perimeter. Cowens was MVP of the 1972–73 season.

Billy Cunningham: The intense Cunningham teamed with fellow Hall of Famers Wilt Chamberlain and Hal Greer to win the NBA title for the Philadelphia 76ers in 1966–67, his second season. He was an athletic forward who could score on the run or from the outside. He later coached the 76ers to the 1983 NBA title.

Dave DeBusschere: DeBusschere was an all-around great player—a defensive specialist, floor leader, and potent offensive force inside and out. He played professional basketball for the Detroit Pistons and pitched for the Chicago White Sox in 1962 and 1963. At 24 he served as player/coach of the Pistons, making him the youngest NBA coach in history. He was traded to the Knicks after the 1967 season and helped them to championships in 1970 and 1973. DeBusschere served as vice-president and general manager of the New York Nets and as the ABA commissioner in its final season in 1976.

Clyde Drexler: "The Glide" is an agile master of the fast break and possessor of an excellent outside shot. After a great 11 years with Portland, in which he twice led the Blazers to the championship finals, the Glide returned to his native Houston, where he had starred as a forward on the University of Houston's "Phi Slamma Jamma" teams of the early 1980s. In 1991–92 with Portland he averaged 25 points per game and finished second to Michael Jordan in MVP balloting. A 1995 trade to Houston reunited him with college teammate Hakeem Olajuwon, and they propelled the Rockets to the their second straight NBA Championship.

Julius Erving: Dr. J became only the sixth player in NCAA history to average more than 20 points and 20 rebounds a game; he did it at the University of Massachusetts, where he also earned the nickname Dr. J. He redefined the forward position in pro basketball, becoming one of the first great jumpers to play the game above the rim with his long, loping slam dunks. He is one of only three players in pro basketball history to score over 30,000 career points, accumulating them over five years in the ABA and 11 in the NBA. He was the ABA's MVP in 1974 and 1976 and co-MVP in 1975 and led the ABA in scoring in 1973, 1974, and 1976. In 1981, Erving was named the NBA's MVP as he helped lead the 76ers to the NBA championship in 1983.

Patrick Ewing holds many of the New York Knicks' team records, has won two Olympic gold medals, and was a member of the national champion 1983–84 Georgetown team.

Patrick Ewing: Ewing led the Knicks resurgence in the 1980s and holds many franchise records, including games and minutes played, points, rebounds, steals, and blocked shots. He led the Knicks to the NBA Finals in 1994, played in 11 All-Star games, was the NBA Rookie of the Year in 1986 and played on gold-medal-winning Olympic basketball teams as a collegian (1984) and pro (1992). He played college ball at Georgetown, leading the Hoyas to the NCAA Championship Game three times and winning the 1983–84 championship, when he was named the Final Four Most Outstanding Player. He won the Naismith Award as a senior.

Walt Frazier: "Clyde" had style on and off the court as the smooth floor leader of great Knicks teams of the 1960s and 1970s, winning the NBA championship in 1970 and 1973. Along with being a great passer and inside/outside scorer, Clyde was named to the NBA's All-Defense First Team seven times (1969–75). Frazier averaged 20.7 points over 93 playoff games.

George Gervin: The "Iceman" could score and score and score with his smooth jump shot and finger rolls. He is one of three players in NBA history to win four or more league scoring titles (1978–80, 1982). He was an All-Star in 12 of 14 seasons (three ABA, nine NBA) and is second behind Oscar Robertson in scoring among guards. Gervin is one of seven players to score 2,000 points in six consecutive NBA seasons (1977–78 to 1982–83).

Hal Greer: Greer was an all-out and all-around performer, playing in more games—1,122—than anyone in NBA history until John Havlicek broke the record in the 1970s. He ranked among the top ten all-time in points scored (21,586), field goals attempted (18,811), field goals made (8,504), minutes played (39,788) and personal fouls (3,825). Greer teamed with Wilt Chamberlain and Billy Cunningham to lead the 76ers to the NBA championship in 1967, ending Boston's string of eight consecutive titles. As a collegian at Marshall University, Greer was the first African-American player for a major college team in West Virginia.

John Havlicek: "Hondo" was in perpetual motion on offense and defense, described by Celtics coach Red Auerbach as the "guts of the team." He started as a sixth man—in college at Ohio State, where he teamed with fellow Hall of Famers Jerry Lucas and Bobby Knight to lead the Buckeyes to the 1960 NCAA championship, and in helping Boston win four straight NBA titles from 1963 to 1966. Havlicek would win eight championships in Boston and he became the first player to score 1,000 points in 16 consecutive seasons. Havlicek was MVP of the 1974 NBA Finals and averaged 22 points in 172 career playoff games.

Elvin Hayes: The Big E was master of the turnaround jumper. He was a three-time All-America in college, leading Houston to an 81–12 record, two Final Four appearances, and starring in the historic January 20, 1968, game when his University of Houston Cougars ended UCLA's 47-game win streak in the "Game of the Century," the first-ever nationally televised college game, which was played before over 52,000 fans. Hayes averaged 28.4 points per game and led the NBA in scoring as a rookie. He teamed with Hall of Famer Wes Unseld to form a dominating front-court that led the Baltimore Bullets to three NBA Finals and the title over Seattle in 1978. Hayes played in 12 consecutive All-Star Games.

Magic Johnson: see question on page 85.

Sam Jones: One of the Celtics' "Jones Boys," Sam teamed with K.C. Jones in the Celtics' backcourt. He played on 10 NBA championship teams, was a five-time All-Star, and was known for his speed and graceful shooting. Jones led the Celtics in scoring three times, averaging a career-high 25.9 points in 1965.

Michael Jordan: see question on page 87.

Jerry Lucas: Lucas was a pure shooter with his over-the-shoulder style, including a league-leading 52.7 percent during his Rookie of the Year season in 1962. He was named to seven NBA All-Star teams and chosen MVP of the 1965 game. Lucas helped lead the New York Knicks to the 1973 NBA championship.

Karl Malone: One of the game's great power forwards, The Mailman was the NBA's Most Valuable Player for the 1996–97 season. He can run the floor and hit with deadly accuracy from the outside, averaging over 21 points and 9.5 rebounds in each season since his rookie year. Through the 1996–97 season he appeared in 980 of a possible 984 games over 12 seasons. He is in the top 10 all-time in scoring, field goals, and free throws.

Moses Malone: Malone became the first player to move from high school ball to a professional league, joining the Utah Stars of the ABA and immediately becoming a dominant force beneath the basket—scoring, rebounding, and drawing fouls. Teamed with Julius Erving, Maurice Cheeks, and Bobby Jones, Malone helped lead the Philadelphia 76ers to a 65–17 regular-season record and NBA championship in 1983, the year in which Malone won the regular season and playoff MVP awards. He was also the NBA MVP in 1979 and 1982.

Pete Maravich: "Pistol Pete" scored more points in college than any other player in history, averaging 44.2 points in 83 games and leading the NCAA in scoring three times. He led the NBA in scoring in 1977 with a 31.1 average and averaged 24.2 points per game during his career.

Kevin McHale: McHale was known for his low-post moves, including pump fakes, baby jump hooks, shovel shots, and fadeaways. As a sixth man he was a key contributor to the Celtics teams that won three championships (1981, 1984, 1986). He won the NBA Sixth Man Award in 1984 and 1985.

George Mikan: see question on page 80.

Earl Monroe: Earl "The Pearl" Monroe was a dazzling guard for the Baltimore Bullets and New York Knicks. In 1967 he was the NBA Rookie of the Year for the Bullets, teaming with Wes Unseld to form a spectacular fast-break offense. He was traded to New York in 1971 and teamed with Walt Frazier in a celebrated backcourt that helped the Knicks to the 1973 NBA championship.

Hakeem Olajuwon: Hakeem "the Dream" Olajuwon led the Houston Rockets to back-to-back NBA championships. In 1993–94 he became the first player to be named NBA MVP, NBA Defensive Player of the Year and NBA Finals MVP in the same season, and the following year he rallied the Rockets from a sixth seed in the playoffs to their second straight NBA crown. Olajuwon and Ralph Sampson—the Twin Towers—took the Rockets to the NBA Finals in 1986. He began playing basketball at age 15 in his native Nigeria, then enrolled at the University of Houston, playing three seasons for the "Phi Slamma Jamma" squad that reached the Final Four each year. In his rookie year, 1984–85, Olajuwon averaged 20.6 points and 11.9 rebounds while shooting .538 from the field, finishing second to Michael Jordan in Rookie of the Year balloting. With his height, agility, and creativeness, Olajuwon is virtually unstoppable around the basket. He won rebounding titles in 1989 and 1990, and in 1989 he became the first player to finish among the league's top 10 in scoring, rebounding, steals, and blocked shots for two straight seasons.

Shaquille O'Neal: The 7-1, 300-pound O'Neal has won a scoring title, led the expansion Orlando Magic into the NBA Finals, and revived the

Los Angeles Lakers—all during his first five years in the NBA. As a 20-year-old rookie, O'Neal won NBA Player of the Week honors for his first week in the league and was named 1993 NBA Rookie of the Year. His .599 field goal percentage led the NBA in 1993–94, and he won his first scoring title in 1994–95, averaging 29.3 points.

Robert Parrish: "The Chief"—named by fellow Celtic Cedric "Cornbread" Maxwell after Chief Bromden in *One Flew Over the Cookoo's Nest*—was a great rebounder, shot-blocker, and consistent scorer. A member of the 1981, 1984 and 1986 Boston Celtics NBA championship teams and the 1997 champion Chicago Bulls, he holds the career NBA playoff record for offensive rebounds (571) and averaged 15.3 points, 9.6 rebounds, and 1.7 blocked shots over 184 playoff games.

Bob Pettit: Like Michael Jordan, Pettit was cut from his high school basketball team and it only made him practice more and become more determined as he developed a never-quit attitude that became his trademark. He was NBA Rookie of the Year in 1954–55 for the Milwaukee Hawks. Pettit was the league's MVP in 1956 (25.7 points per game) and 1959 (29.2 points per game). He played in 11 straight All-Star Games and at the time of his retirement in 1965 he was the NBA's all time leading scorer (20,880) and second highest rebounder (12,849).

Scottie Pippen: A multiple threat on the floor, Pippen is an excellent passer, rebounder, shooter, and fast-break finisher. A key to the Chicago Bulls' five NBA championships of the 1990s, Pippen was selected to the NBA All-Defensive First Team six consecutive times. He averaged 21 points, 7.7 rebounds and 7.0 assists per game in 1991–92. Pippen had another great all'around season in 1995–96, helping Chicago set an NBA record with 72 victories and leading the team in assists.

Willis Reed: Reed became legendary for hobbling onto the floor for Game 7 of the 1970 championship series between the New York Knicks and Los Angeles Lakers and inspiring the Knicks to victory. He played 27 minutes in that game after being felled by a severe knee injury in Game 5. A second-round choice by the Knicks after having starred at Grambling, Reed was the NBA's Rookie of the Year for 1963–64 and an All-Star his first seven seasons. Reed is the only player named MVP of the All-Star Game, regular season and playoffs in the same year (1970). He won another championship with the Knicks in 1973.

Oscar Robertson: see question on page 108.

David Robinson: "The Admiral" has won a Rookie of the Year Award, a rebounding title, a scoring crown, a Most Valuable Player Award, and a Defensive Player of the Year Award, was selected an All-Star seven times, to the All-NBA First Team four times, and to the NBA All-Defensive First Team four times—all in his first seven seasons. A 1987 graduate with a mathematics degree from the U.S. Naval Academy, Robinson served two years in the Navy before joining the NBA. As a junior, he averaged 22.7 points per game, led the nation in rebounding (13.0 per game), and set an NCAA Division I record by averaging 5.91 blocks (including 14 in a single game and 207 for the season—both NCAA records). San Antonio had posted a 21–61 record in 1988–89, but in Robinson's rookie year the Spurs went 56-26 and captured the Midwest Division title. The 35-game improvement marked the greatest single-season turnaround in NBA history. Robinson scored 71 points against the Los Angeles Clippers on the last day of the 1993–94 season to win the NBA scoring title at 29.8 points per game. His career blocked shot average of 3.60 per game is the highest in NBA history among players with 400 or more games played.

Bill Russell: see question on page 82.

Dolph Schayes: Schayes was always there—scoring, rebounding, and playing in more NBA games than anyone at the time of his retirement in 1964, including a string of 706 consecutive games. He led the NBA in free throw shooting three times (1958, 1960, 1962) and shot 84 percent from the line in his career. He was the 1949 NBL Rookie of the Year, and after the merger of the NBL and BAA formed the NBA, Schayes led the league in rebounding in 1951. Schayes led his team into the playoffs 15 times, losing in the NBA championship finals in 1950 and 1954 to the George Mikan-led Minneapolis Lakers and winning it all in 1955. He played in 12 consecutive All-Star games.

Bill Sharman: Sharman teamed with Bob Cousey to form one of the NBA's greatest backcourt duos, winning four NBA championships (1957, 1959-61). He played in eight All-Star games. Sharman was also a renowned coach, leading the Los Angeles Lakers to their first NBA title in 1972, when they compiled a 69–13 regular season record that included 33 straight victories. He is the only basketball coach to win titles in three different leagues—the ABL (Cleveland Pipers, 1962), ABA (Utah Stars, 1971), and NBA (Los Angeles Lakers, 1972).

John Stockton: Stockton is the NBA's all-time career assist leader and holds assist average records for a season (14.5 per game) and career

(11.5 per game). Stockton has made the NBA All-Defensive Team three times, and through 1996–97 he missed only four games in 13 NBA seasons. Stockton and forward Karl Malone have led the Utah Jazz to the playoffs in each of the seasons they played together, and they shared MVP honors at the 1993 All-Star Game at Salt Lake City. From 1993 to 1996 he recorded the highest field goal percentage among guards.

Isiah Thomas: "Zeke" was one of the best small men in NBA history (defining "small" as 6-1 or less). He was a fearless guard, slashing inside to challenge the big men for lay-ups or to dish to the open man, shooting rainbows from outside, and running the show for the two-time champion Detroit Pistons. He made 12 All-Star appearances and won two All-Star Game MVP awards. Thomas averaged 19.2 points and 9.3 assists per game for his career and is one of only four players to amass more than 9,000 assists.

Nate Thurmond: A consummate team player, Thurmond was a smooth shooter, relentless rebounder, and tough shot-blocker. He played 14 seasons with San Francisco/Golden State, Chicago and Cleveland, and appeared in seven All-Star games. He once collected 18 rebounds in one quarter and was the first player to ever record a quadruple double—22 points, 14 rebounds, 13 assists and 12 blocked shots in one game.

Wes Unseld: Short for a center (6-7) but big and strong at 245 pounds, Unseld played a physical brand of basketball coupled with an intelligent court presence (he chose basketball over teaching coming out of college, but the teacher in him persisted on the court, as a coach, and as an executive). In 1969–70, Unseld became only the second NBA player after Wilt Chamberlain to be named Rookie of the Year and MVP in the same season. He finished his career as one of 20 players to score more than 10,000 points (10,624) and grab more than 10,000 rebounds. He was MVP of the NBA championship series in 1978, when his Bullets defeated Seattle for the crown. In 1975, Unseld received the NBA Walter Kennedy Citizenship Award for his community contributions.

Bill Walton: Walton was an excellent shooter, rebounder and outlet passer on the fast break. From the storied UCLA championship teams (he made 21 of 22 shots, scored 44 points, and collected 13 rebounds in the championship game to lead UCLA to the NCAA title in 1973, and the Bruins went 86–4 during his days there) to NBA championships with the Portland Trail Blazers (1977) and Boston Celtics (1987), Walton was a ferocious competi-

What was the Mikan Era?

The Mikan Era extended from 1949, the NBA's first season, to 1954: during this time the Minnesota Lakers were led by six-foot-ten-inch center George Mikan. The Lakers won five titles during that span, including three in a row from 1952 to 1954. Mikan was previously a star in the National Basketball League and quickly established himself as the NBA's dominant player. He sported a deadly hook shoot and was a tough rebounder and defender. Mikan led the league in scoring from 1949–51 and in rebounding in 1953. He retired after the Lakers won the 1954 title, became the Lakers general manager, coached briefly in 1957, and in 1967 he became the ABA's first commissioner.

tor and team leader. He was named league MVP in 1978 and won the Sixth Man Award during the Celtics championship season of 1986–87.

Jerry West: Always cool and calm, "Mr. Clutch" was one of the best pure shooters in NBA history. After an outstanding collegiate career at West Virginia (in his junior year, West led the Mountaineers to the 1959 NCAA Finals and won the tournament's Most Outstanding Player award) and playing for the fabled 1960 U.S. Olympic gold medal team, West played his entire career with the Lakers alongside Hall of Famers Elgin Baylor and Wilt Chamberlain. He retired third in scoring, second in free throws, and fifth in assists, was named to the NBA All-Defensive First Team four times, and played in 14 All-Star games. West was the NBA Finals MVP in 1969 and played on the 1972 Laker championship team.

Lenny Wilkens: see question on page 97.

James Worthy: Worthy was one of the finest small forwards, featuring one-handed swoop dunks and playing a speed game that made the Lakers a major team of the 1980s. Worthy was MVP of the 1988 NBA Finals, when his late heroics on offense and defense completed an incredible Game 7 performance in which he recorded 36 points, 16 rebounds and 10 assists. The Lakers also won championships in 1985 and 1987 with Worthy.

Wilt Chamberlain (right, shooting) and Bill Russell (left) battle in Game 2 of the 1964 NBA Championship.

Who was the NBA's next **big star**?

Bill Russell was the next big man in the Big Man era, leading the Celtic dynasty with his great defensive skills and court leadership. Russell led the league in rebounding four times and was a five-time MVP. In his 13-season career Russell averaged 15.1 points per game and 22.5 rebounds per game.

Who took over Bill Russell's title as the next **Big Man**?

In his rookie year of 1960, Wilt Chamberlain averaged 27 rebounds and 37.6 points a game. He had seven games with 50 or more points and won both Rookie of the Year and Most Valuable Player (MVP). Of the 25 highest point totals by an individual in a single game, Chamberlain holds 20 of them, including a 100-point performance in 1962. He also holds the record for rebounds in a game (55) and in a career.

What are some of **Kareem Abdul-Jabbar's** acheivements?

Some of the records Kareem holds include: Most Games Played, 1,560; Most Field Goals Made, 15,837; Most Field Goals Attempted, 28,307; Most Minutes Played, 57,446; Most Blocked Shots, 3,189; Most Personal Fouls, 4,657. Abdul-Jabbar, the NBA's all-time leading scorer, won three NCAA championships with UCLA, and six NBA championships, one with the Milwaukee Bucks and five with the Los Angeles Lakers. Bob Cousey, the first great passing guard who had played with Bill Russell during the Celtic glory years, said of Abdul-Jabbar, "he pretty much combines what Bill Russell and Wilt Chamberlain have individually specialized in."

What are some of the all-time NBA **individual game** performances?

Most Points Scored: 100, by Wilt Chamberlain (Philadelphia), March 2, 1962, versus New York Knicks in a regular-season game played in Hershey, Pennsylvania.

Most Rebounds: 55, by Wilt Chamberlain (Philadelphia), November 24, 1960, versus Boston Celtics.

Most Assists: 30, by Scott Skiles (Orlando), December 30, 1990, versus Denver Nuggets.

Who were some of the ABA's major stars?

The ABA had many great players, but the most important was probably Julius Erving, the gravity-defying forward who led the league in scoring on three occasions. Erving, like many other ABA stars, would prove equally formidable in the NBA. If three-time MVP Erving was the league's greatest player at the end, Connie Hawkins, masterful one-on-one attacker, was probably the ABA's strongest player in its debut year. Hawkins led the league with a 26.8 scoring average and was named MVP. Other dominating players in ABA history are Indiana center and two-time MVP Mel Daniels; masterful shooter Rick Barry, who later won an NBA title with Golden State; aggressive scorer George McGinnis; and such future NBA stars as Dan Issel and Artis Gilmore, two powerful centers. The league's last rookie-of-the-year was high-flying sensation David Thompson, who also starred in the NBA, once scoring 73 points in a game.

Most Steals: 11, by Larry Kenon (San Antonio), December 26, 1976 versus Kansas City Royals.

Most Blocked Shots: 17, Elmore Smith (Los Angeles), October 28, 1973 versus Portland Trail Blazers.

Most 3-point Field Goals: 11, Dennis Scott (Orlando), April 18, 1996, versus Atlanta.

Who ranks among the game's greatest **small players**?

Nate "Tiny" Archibald was a great player, but he was 6'1", despite the nickname. Tiny led the league in assists during the 1973-74 season and later starred with the champion Celtics. Calvin Murphy, a 5'9" guard with the Houston Rockets for thirteen seasons, must surely be considered the league's most proficient short player. Murphy scored nearly 18,000 points in his career. He twice led the league in free-throw percentage, and on eight other occasions he finished second. In 1981, he made 78 consecutive tosses from the foul line! He had his greatest

Julius Erving helped popularize one league (the ABA) and revitalize another (the NBA) with his fantastic above-the-rim style and slam-dunk prowess.

game in the 1981 playoffs when he scored 42 points and led the Rockets to a 105–100 victory in game seven of the Western Conference semifinal against the San Antonio Spurs.

What teammates are the **top tandems in winning percentage** in NBA history?

Through the 1996–97 season, Michael Jordan and Scottie Pippin have won 73.9% of all games in which they both played, followed by Magic Johnson/Kareem Abdul-Jabbar at 73.9% (Jordan/Pippin are higher factoring 1997–98), Larry Bird/Kevin McHale (73.5%), and Karl Malone/John Stockton at 63.8%.

What hoopster played the **most playoff games without getting a ring**?

Elgin Baylor with 134; coming up from behind through 1996–97 are John Stockton (127), Charles Oakley (119), and Karl Malone (117). Caldwell Jones (119) and Sam Perkins (118) are others who played long and hard but never won the last playoff game.

What effect did the **Magic Johnson-Larry Bird rivalry** have on the NBA?

They deserve their own individual chapters, but as contemporaries who met in the 1979 NCAA Final (Magic's Michigan State Spartans defeated Bird's Indiana State Sycamores, and Magic was the MVP), Earvin "Magic" Johnson and Larry Bird helped restore to glory the two most successful NBA franchises (Lakers and Celtics, respectively), and brought unprecedented national exposure to professional basketball.

As a rookie, Magic helped lead the Lakers to the 1980 NBA championship; in an amazing finale, he played center in the championship's final game when Kareem Abdul-Jabbar couldn't play because of a knee injury. Magic scored 42 points and was the playoff MVP, an award he won again in 1982 and 1987. He led the league in assists four times and

85

Michael Jordan has teamed with Scottie Pippen for the highest all-time winning percentage for teammates and five championships. He's also a pretty good player in his own right.

Michael Jordan has been called the greatest basketball player ever. What are some of his on-court accomplishments?

Michael Jordan was college basketball's Player of the Year in 1984, two years after having helped lead North Carolina to the NCAA championship as a freshman in 1982; he led the U.S. Olympic team in scoring in 1984 en route to their gold medal triumph (he later medaled gold as a pro); he is the only player to win the NBA's MVP and Defensive Player of the Year awards for a single season (1988); he led the league in scoring 9 times through the 1996–97 season, led in steals three times, and is the only player to ever lead the NBA in scoring and steals in a single season; he is the only player to have 200 steals and 100 blocked shots in a season, and he did it twice; he is the only player in any sport to win five MVPs and be on five Championship teams (Joe Montana is second with three).

held the career record until the 1996–97 season, when John Stockton surpassed it. He played on five championship teams for the Lakers.

Bird made an immediate and lasting impact, too. As Rookie of the Year during the 1979–80 season, he ignited the greatest season-to-season team turnaround at that time in NBA history: Boston was 29–53 the year before he was drafted by the Celtics, 61–21 during his first year. Bird led the Celtics to three championships (1981, 1984, 1986), was a two-time playoff MVP (1984, 1986), and was the league regular-season MVP three times, 1984–86.

Who is the only player to be named the **Most Valuable Player of both the ABA and the NBA**?

The Doctor, Julius Erving. The man who first made taking off from the free throw line to dunk famous is on the NBA's list of the 50 greatest

Larry Bird helps Magic Johnson off the floor during their epic battle in the 1979 NCAA final. Their rivalry would help revitalize the NBA in the 1980s.

players of all-time, and with good reason. In the ABA, he won three straight MVP awards for the New York Nets from 1974 to 1976. After he was traded to the Philadelphia 76ers and joining the NBA when the two leagues merged, Erving won the NBA's MVP award in 1981.

What player was involved with **more successful teams** than any other?

Bill Russell of Boston Celtics fame is widely recognized as one of the greatest players in NBA history. Beyond that, though, he is perhaps the winningest player in basketball history, experiencing unprecedented success at the college, Olympic, and professional level. In 1956, Russell led his University of San Francisco team to its second straight NCAA championship. Not only that, but the team won the last 56 games they played with Russell as its starting center. Shortly after the end of the tournament, he led the U.S. to an undefeated record and the Olympic gold medal in Melbourne, Australia. He then joined the Celtics in the middle of the team's season and finished off his spectacular year by helping the Celtics win the NBA championship. It was the fastest that anyone had ever pulled off the college-Olympic-NBA trifecta.

Russell went on to have an 13-year career with the Celtics, and in that time period, he led his team to the NBA title 11 times and to the championship finals one other time. In all, the Celtic teams that Russell was a part of had a regular-season winning percentage of .705 and playoff mark of .693.

Who are the only three NBA players to **average 20 rebounds and 20 points** per game for an entire season, and what was unique about one of them?

Two of the men who accomplished the feat are names that you would expect—giants Wilt Chamberlain and Bob Pettit, both of whom played center. Chamberlain pulled off the feat many times, while Pettit accomplished it once while playing for the old St. Louis Hawks.

The third man to pull off the feat might suprise some basketball fans. Jerry Lucas was generously listed as 6 feet, 8 inches in many media guides, but in reality he was just a shade over 6 feet, 7 inches. Lucas

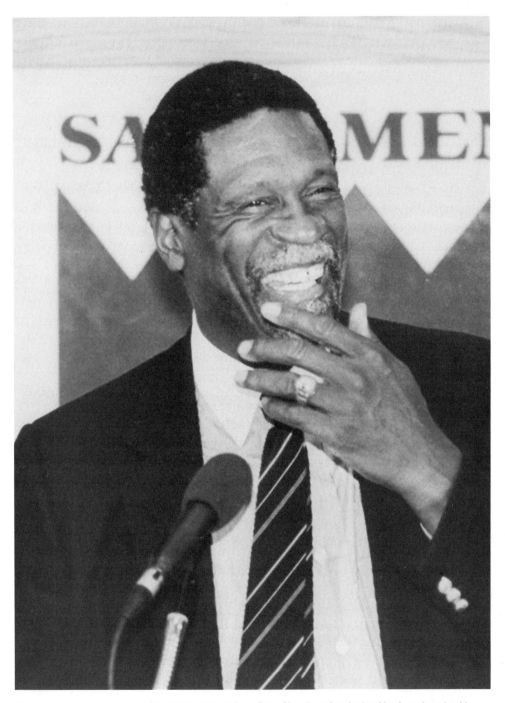

Bill Russell was a winner at every level, leading teams at the college, Olympic, and professional levels to championships.

made his living shooting from the outside, but he had the quickness and the hands to dart inside and pull down rebounds. During the 1965–66 season for the Cincinnati Royals, Lucas averaged 21.5 points and 21.1 rebounds per game during 79 regular season games, then also averaged 20–20 in the playoffs.

COLLEGE AND AMATEUR

What are some of the greatest scoring achievements by college players?

When it came to scoring, nobody matched Louisiana State University's gunning guard Pete Maravich, who nailed 1,381 points in 1970 for a game average of 44.5. Maravich owns the NCAA's top three season averages, all around 44 points, and three of the top five season point totals. Another phenomenal scorer was Notre Dame's Austin Carr, who averaged 34.6 points during his three school years. In 1970, Carr set an NCAA tournament record when he tallied 61 points against Ohio University. Still another great college player was Oscar Robertson, who joins Maravich as the only two players to lead the nation in scoring for three seasons. Robertson ended his college career with a 33.8 scoring average. His University of Cincinnati squad finished third in both the 1959 and 1960 NCAA championships.

Who is Bevo Francis, and why does he have a special place in college basketball history?

Clarence "Bevo" Francis is a true All-American story. Born in 1932, and an only child, Bevo was nicknamed after a popular softdrink at the time. He attended Wellsville High School in Wellsville, Ohio and averaged 31 points a game in leading his team to a 19–1 record—all pretty routine stuff to that point. He was recruited by more than 60 colleges, but he followed his high school coach down the road to tiny Rio Grande College (pronounced "Rye-o Grand"). With the school in danger of closing due to lack of money, Bevo and coach Newt Oliver teamed up to literally save the school. Playing against oher colleges, military bases, and any other takers, Bevo led Rio Grande to a 39–0 record in 1953. More amazingly, Francis became the first player to ever average more than 50 points per game for an entire season, highlighted by a 116-point performance against Ashland Junior College in Kentucky, which was also a record.

Newpaper and magazine reporters from around America took note of the Ohio scoring whiz and made him a national hero. That didn't set well with some of the big colleges that were used to getting all the attention, so the national coaches association voted to strip Bevo of most of his records, including his 116-point game, because they didn't occur against four-year colleges. Francis and Oliver were unfazed. With interest in Rio Grande at an all-time high, Oliver scheduled all 25 of the team's games in 1954 on the road, all against four-year colleges, and some against some of the best teams in the country. His efforts payed off. Rio Grande did lose a few games that year, but every game was in front of a packed house, including more than 13,000 at Madison Square Garden. Francis picked up right where he left off the previous season, scoring points in buckets. He failed to average 50 points per game, finishing at a still-record 46.5, but he did manage to break the 100-point plateau, hitting for 113 against four-year Hillsdale College of Michigan. Rio Grande won the game 134–91. His 113 points still stands as the college record for most points in a game, and he also still holds the mark for most field goals attempted in a game (71), most field goals made in a game (38), most free throws made and attempted in a game (37 and 45, respectively), most free throws attempted in a season (510), most 50-point games in a season (8), and most 50-point games in a career (14).

Who is the only **other man to score 100 points** in a college game, and has a **woman ever pulled off the feat**?

Just 11 days after Bevo Francis poured in 113 points against Hillsdale, another prolific scorer managed to break the century mark. Frank Selvy, who was averaging nearly 40 points per game for Furman University in Greenville, South Carolina, scored exactly 100 points against Newberry College, a small Lutheran school. His last two points came on a desperation heave from just inside the half-court line as time expired—the ball swished through the net for the last of his 41 field goals. Furman won the game 149–95.

Lisa Leslie poured in 101 points in one half of a high school basketball game. The score was 102–24 when the opposing coach took his team off the floor at halftime and didn't return.

No woman has managed to break the 100-point plateau at the major college level, but two very well-known stars of the women's game pulled off the feat in high school. Cheryl Miller, who went on to become one of the best female players of all time before switching into sportscasting, scored 105 for her Riverside, California high school in 1982. In 1990, current WNBA poster girl and model Lisa Leslie scored 101 points in a single *half* for Morningside High School in Inglewood, California in a game against South Torrance High. Leslie would have shattered the record if the South Torrance coach hadn't pulled his team off the court at halftime trailing 102–24, forfeiting the game because he felt Morningside was making a mockery of his team.

Who is the **oldest player to ever earn All-American honors** at the college level?

Thanks to six years in the United States Air Force and a later tour of duty during the Korean War, Doug Williams was in his late-20s by the time he finally got to go to college at St. Mary's University, which competed at the small-college level. Williams was 6 feet, 9 inches tall, and had always wanted to play college basketball. Not letting his age get in the way, Williams tried out for the St. Mary's team as a freshman and made the team, launching his four-year career there. He was a solid scorer who also played excellent defense and rebounded well. Balancing his school, basketball, a part-time job, and his home life with his wife and kids, Williams was rewarded for his efforts on the court his senior year when he was named a first-team selection on the National Association of Intercollegiate Athletics All-American team. Williams was 31 at the time.

Who are some of the stars of **NCAA women's** play?

Stars of six-time NCAA champion Tennessee include Tonya Edwards, named outstanding player of the 1987 competition, and Bridgette Gordon, leading player in the 1989 tournament. Gordon holds the record for most points, 388, in tournament play. Cheryl Miller led the University of Southern California to titles in 1983 and 1984 and was named player of the tournament on both occasions. She holds the record for most rebounds, 170, in tournament play. The all-time scorer for a season in women's play is Patricia Hoskins, who scored 3122 points for a 28.4 average during her four years at Mississippi State University. She also holds the highest single-season average with 33.6 in 1989. The greatest female rebounder is Wanda Ford, who tallied 1887 for a 16.1 per game average at Drake University.

Who is the **first woman to be named All-American in two sports** by the NCAA?

Natalie Williams, who played both basketball and volleyball at UCLA, earned All-American honors in both sports. She earned first-team volleyball honors four times and was once named national player of the year, and she was named first-team in basketball on one occasion.

TEAMS AND COACHES

What is the **longest winning streak** in basketball history?

While the Los Angeles Lakers' NBA winning streak of 33 straight games and UCLA's college winning streak of 88 straight wins are impressive, they fall far short of the amazing 159–game winning streak put together by Passaic High School in Passaic, New Jersey between December 1919 and February 1925. During the string of victories, it outscored opponents by an average of 59.5 to 20.2, topping 100 points on several occasions, including a 145–5 drubbing of a Stamford, Connecticut prep school. Those point totals don't sound like much, but scoring averages were very low in that era. The streak began with a 44–11 win over Newark Junior College and ended with a 39–35 defeat to nearby Hackensack High. During the 1922–23 season, a Passaic game was broadcast live over the radio, which was possibly the first basketball game at any level ever broadcast.

The record winning streak in women's basketball also belongs to a high school team. Beginning in 1947 and ending in 1953, Baskins High School in Louisiana won 218 straight games, winning by an average margin of 31 points. The streak ended when the girls lost 33–27 to Winnsboro High School.

What team has played in the most NBA finals?

The Lakers, originally based in Minneapolis, later in Los Angeles, have appeared in 24 finals, winning 11. The Celtics rank next with 19 appearances, of which they won 16. The Philadelphia 76ers have won three of eight finals, the New York Knicks two of seven, the Warriors (Philadelphia, San Francisco, Golden State) three of eight, and the Chicago Bulls five of five.

What was the **Celtic Dynasty**?

The Celtic Dynasty extended from 1957 to 1969, a thirteen-year period that coincided with Hall of Famer Bill Russell's career. During those 13 years the Celtics won an astounding 11 titles! Cigar-chomping mastermind Red Auerbach coached for nine of those titles, when the team featured a host of all-time greats. The 1957 team featured such stars as Bob Cousey and Bill Sharman, in addition to Russell, and succeeding teams would include such notables as Sam Jones, K.C. Jones, Tommy Heinsohn, Don Nelson, and prominent sixth-man John Havlicek. The team's greatest player, though, was center Bill Russell, a skillful defender and rebounder who assumed the dual role of player-coach after Auerbach withdrew to the front office. Russell led the Celtics to two more titles before retiring after winning the 1969 playoffs.

Who are the **Top 10 Greatest NBA coaches**, according to the 1996 50th anniversary voting in 1996?

The ten with their win and title totals through the 1996–97 season:

Red Auerbach (1037 wins, 9 titles)

Chuck Daly (638 wins, 2 titles)

Bill Fitch (982 wins, 1 title)

Red Holzman (754 wins, 2 titles)

Phil Jackson (579 wins, 5 titles)

John Kundla (485 wins, 5 titles)

Don Nelson (902 wins, 0 titles)

Jack Ramsay (908 wins, 1 title)

Pat Riley (1002 wins, 4 titles)

Lenny Wilkins (1138 wins, 1 title)

Where did **Red Auerbach** first establish his reputation?

Auerbach coached the Washington Capitols in the NBA's inaugural season, leading them to a league-best record, 49–11, that remained the highest winning percentage for many years. He won over 1,000 games and nine championships. The NBA's Coach of the Year trophy is named for him.

Who is the NBA's **all-time winningest coach**, was voted one of the Top 50 NBA Players of all-time, and was an All-Star Game and NIT MVP?

Lenny Wilkens won the NIT MVP in 1960 as a gaurd for Providence, ranks sixth all-time in assists in the NBA, coached Seattle to an NBA championship in 1979, and was named Coach of the Year in 1994 for his work with the Atlanta Hawks.

Who was the **first African-American head coach** in the NBA?

Bill Russell became the first African-American head coach in any major professional sport in 1966 and proceeded to lead the Celtics to two more championships.

Who is the only coach to **win the league championship** in the NBA, the ABA, and the ABL?

Bill Sharman, who had a great playing career with the Boston Celtics, was even better as a coach. In 1962, his first year as a professional coach, he led the Cleveland Pipers of the fledgling American Basketball League (ABL) to the league title—the only league title there would ever be, as it

97

Three times: John Wooden, appropriately, retired a champion in 1975; Al McGuire retired from Marquette after its 1977 win, and Larry Brown went to the NBA after winning it all with Kansas in 1988.

turned out, since the league folded after only one season. Moving on to the ABA, Sharman coached the Utah Stars for three seasons before leading that team to the league title in 1971. He was named ABA Coach of the Year for his efforts. The Los Angeles Lakers wasted no time in hiring Sharman as head coach for the 1971–72 season. It was a good move. The team ended up being one of the best in NBA history, winning a record 33 games in a row on its way to a then-record 69 wins in the regular season (since eclipsed by the Chicago Bulls). In the playoffs, the Lakers capped off a the record-setting season by winning the championship and earning Sharman yet another Coach of the Year honor.

Who is the **winningest coach** in basketball history?

John Wooden at UCLA and Red Auerbach of the Boston Celtics might be the most well-known coaches in basketball history, but not even they can match the feats of a man named Bob Douglas.

"Bob, who?" you ask. Douglas coached an all-African-American touring team from the 1920s until the 1940s. The team barnstormed around the country, taking on all-comers and playing up to 140 games a year. And they didn't face lousy competition either—they challenged all the top teams of the time period, defeating the original Boston Celtics on many occasions and winning six professional tournaments, at least one of which was considered to be the world championship. In his 26 years of coaching, Douglas compiled a record of 2,318 victories against only 381 defeats. That's more than twice as many victories as Auerbach posted. It is almost certainly a record that will stand forever.

Dean Smith passed Adolph Rupp in 1997 to become the all-time leader in wins by a college basketball coach.

What teams have won the **most NCAA championships**?

The University of California at Los Angeles dominated college basketball from 1963 to 1975. Coached by John Wooden, UCLA won 10 national championships during this time (1964, 1965, 1967–1973, 1975), including seven consecutively. From 1971 to 1974, UCLA also won 88 consecutive games, an NCAA record. UCLA has won 11 championships, Kentucky 7, Indiana 5, North Carolina 3.

How many teams have gone **undefeated in the regular season** en route to the NCAA title, and what was the last school to do it?

Seven, with Indiana being the most recent, in 1975–76. UCLA did it in 1963–64, 1966–67, 1973–74, and 1974–75; North Carolina did it in 1957 and San Francisco in 1956.

Who is the all-time **winningest college coach**?

Dean Smith of North Carolina retired in 1997 after compiling 879 victories, passing Adolph Rupp, who amassed 876 for Kentucky.

ODDS AND ENDS

Why are basketball players called "**cagers**?"

The Trenton Basketball Team, which originally competed in the YMCA league, introduced a fence, or cage, around the court to keep the ball in constant play. In addition, the fence protected fans from loose balls and charging players. Trenton players were thus called "cagers."

Why do professional basketball players have **low digits** on their jerseys?

So the referee can signal with his fingers the number of the player who committed a foul.

Who are the tallest and smallest players in NBA history?

Manute Bol and Gheorge Muresan at 7-7 are the tallest, followed by Shawn Bradley (7-6) and Mark Eaton, Priest Lauderdale, and Rik Smits at 7-4.

Muggsy Bogues at 5-3 is the smallest, followed by 5-7 players Greg Grant, Keith Jennings, Louis Klotz, and Spud Webb.

What is the name of the trophy given to the **NBA champion**?

The Larry O' Brien Trophy.

In any sport, the Most Valuable Player award in the playoffs almost always goes to a player on the winning team. Who is the only NBA player to be named **MVP of the finals despite losing**?

The current general manager of the Los Angeles Lakers, Jerry West. In the 1969 finals, West averaged 40 points per game against the Lakers' hated rivals, the Boston Celtics, but it wasn't enough—the Celtics still won the series and the league championship, four games to three.

What is the **longest shot ever made** in professional basketball?

A regulation basketball court is 94 feet in length, and the record-breaking shot made by Jerry Harkness of the Indiana Pacers was nearly that long. In an American Basketball Association game between the Pacers and the Dallas Chapparals on November 13, 1967, Harkness took an inbounds pass from teammate Oliver Darden with one second left on the clock and heaved the ball 92 feet and watched in amazement as it went in. Since the shot was beyond the ABA's 25-foot three-point line, the shot counted as a three and gave the Pacers an amazing 119–118 victo-

**Who is the only player to lead the
NCAA, NBA, and ABA in season scoring?**

Rick Barry: NCAA, 1965, Miami of Florida; NBA, 1967, San
Francisco; ABA, 1969, Oakland.

ry. Interestingly enough, Indiana coach Larry Staverman didn't even see
the winning shot drop in because he had already started for the Pacers'
locker room, convinced his team had lost the game.

Has anyone ever been **a member of NCAA, Olympic, and professional basketball championship teams**?

Clyde Lovelette
Kansas 1952
U.S. 1952
Minneapolis and Boston
(twice)

K. C. Jones
San Francisco 1955
U.S. 1956
Boston (8 times)

Bill Russell
San Francisco 1955 and 1956
U.S. 1956
Boston (11 times)

Jerry Lucas
Ohio State 1960
U.S. 1960
New York

Quinn Buckner
Indiana 1976
U.S. 1976
Boston 1984

Magic Johnson
Michigan State 1979
U.S. 1992
Los Angeles (5 times)

Michael Jordan
North Carolina 1982
U.S. 1984 and 1992
Chicago (5 times)

Sheryl Swoopes
Texas Tech 1973
U.S. 1996
Houston

Sheryl Swoopes in one of only eight basketball players (and the only woman) to win an Olympic gold medal, NCAA tournament, and a professional championship.

How are inductees
elected into basketball's Hall of Fame?

The Naismith Memorial Basketball Hall of Fame, located in Springfield, Massachusetts, was established in 1949 by the National Association of Basketball Coaches. Players and referees can be nominated five years after they retire, coaches must have coached for 25 years or have been retired for five, and contributors must have already completed their service. Nominees are voted on by a 24-member panel comprised of media professionals, Hall of Fame members, and trustees. If a nominee is not voted in after five years, he/she can be considered after another five year wait by the Veterans' Committee.

Who was the first rookie signed to a **million dollar** contract?

Ralph Sampson, Houston Rockets, 1983.

Why is it that a player who totals the **most points** during an NBA season won't necessarily win the scoring crown?

The scoring crown goes to the player with the highest points-per-game average. Say player A scores 2400 points and plays in all of his teams' 82 games: his scoring average is 29.2. Player B scores 2350 points but plays in only 80 games for a 29.3 average. Player B wins the title.

What are the famous "**Three Steals**" of Celtic lore?

1965 Division Final vs. Philadelphia:

In the seventh game of a rough series, Boston clung to a one-point lead with just seconds remaining in the contest. The problem: Philadelphia had the ball. Sixer Hal Greer prepared to inbound a pass to Chet Walker

Who makes up the NCAA's Selection Committee which determines the 64-team NCAA Men's Basketball Tournament field?

The Selection Committee is made up of NCAA officials, conference commissioners, and university athletic directors. Each year on the last weekend of the college basketball season, these orchestrators of "March Madness" gather together behind closed doors and determine which teams get a spot in the tournament (conference champions earn an automatic berth), how high each team will be seeded, and what region each team will play in.

with plenty of time for a two-point shot. Greer passed; John Havlicek reached out and stole the ball, preserving a Boston victory. Boston earned the right to meet the Los Angeles Lakers and went on to win championship number eight.

1984 Championship Finals versus Los Angeles:

Los Angeles had won the first game of the series and seemed poised to win the second as they led by two points with 20 seconds to go in the game. The Lakers had possession of the ball. Magic Johnson inbounded it to James Worthy, who tried to pass it to a fellow Laker but instead delivered it to Celtic Gerald Henderson, who singlehandedly converted a field goal to tie the game. Boston won in overtime, 124–121, and went on to take championship number fifteen.

1987 Eastern Conference Finals versus Detroit:

The series offered perhaps the quintessential grudge match between an aging Celtics team and a young, hungry group of Pistons. Detroit held a one-point lead in Game Five with just five seconds to go. Piston Isiah Thomas did not hear his coach's frantic calls for a time-out but instead inbounded the ball toward Bill Laimbeer. Larry Bird leaped in front of Laimbeer, grabbed the ball, and passed it to Dennis Johnson, who scored

105

What is the lowest-seeded team to ever win the NCAA tournament, and what team had the most losses—11—when it won the title?

Villanova was seeded eighth in the Southeast region in 1985 after finishing the regular season with a record of 19–10. That didn't stop the Wildcats. In the final, 'Nova defeated Big East conference rival Georgetown 64–63 in one of the biggest upsets in tournament history.

The University of Kansas did Villanova one better in the loss department in 1988, having lost 11 regular season games. Led by All-American Danny Manning however, the Jayhawks, or "Danny and the Miracles" as they became known, defeated Big Eight foe Oklahoma 83–79 to cap an amazing tournament run.

the go-ahead points at the buzzer. The Celtics went on to win the series in seven games.

What does it mean to be **on the bubble**?

As the end of the college basketball season nears, teams that have had good, but not great, seasons are said to be "on the bubble." That means that when the 64-team field is announced for the NCAA tournament, any team that has had a so-so season, say roughly a record of 19–11, is busy praying that it makes the field. Each year, several deserving teams are left out because there are more good teams than there are open slots in the tournament. Twenty wins used to almost guarantee that a team would get in, but no more. Parity has leveled the playing field and created more good teams from the smaller athletic conferences. To get off the bubble, teams need to either win their conference championship, thereby earning an automatic berth in the tournament, or win as many games as possible against highly ranked opponents.

What is the fewest amount
of free throws made by a team in a Final Four game?

University of Nevada, Las Vegas set a record for least free throws made in an NCAA Final Four against North Carolina in 1977. They made one in five attempts. UNLV lost the game 84–83.

What is the **RPI**?

RPI, or Ratings Percentage Index, is one of the factors the NCAA's Selection Committee uses to choose the field for the NCAA Tournament. RPI measures strength of schedule and how a team fared against that schedule. Unlike football, RPI does not take into account margin of victory, only wins and losses. Bubble teams are more likely to be affected by RPI than the perennial powers.

Who is the only player to play in the college national championship game for **two different teams?**

Bob Bender, currently the head coach of the University of Washington, pulled off the double in the late 1970s. In 1976, as a freshman at Indiana University, Bender was a guard on the Hoosier's legendary undefeated national championship squad. After transferring to Duke University, Bender returned to the title game in 1978 when the Blue Devils fell in the finals to the University of Kentucky. Bender has had NCAA success as a coach, also, leading Washington to the Sweet 16 of the tournament in 1998.

What teams have the **best records in NCAA Tournament competition,** having played at least 25 tournament games through 1997?

Duke	57–19	.750
UCLA	77–26	.748

Was there ever a player who averaged a triple-double for a whole season?

Incredibly, yes. Oscar Robertson scored 2,432 points, dished out 899 assists, and pulled down 985 rebounds in 79 games during the 1961–62 season, his second in the NBA. Robertson was a member of two high school championship teams in Indiana, led the nation in scoring three times for the University of Cincinnati, led the Olympic gold-medal-winning 1960 U.S. basketball team, and won an NBA championship with the Milwaukee Bucks.

UNLV	30–11	.732
Indiana	50–21	.704
North Carolina	72–31	.699
Michigan	40–18	.690
Kentucky	77–35	.688
Kansas	56–26	.683
Ohio State	31–17	.646

What is a "triple-double?"

The fairly rare triple-double refers to a player reaching double figures in points, assists, and rebounds in a single game. Blocked shots can take the place of rebounds or assists.

Who are the only three NBA players to total 20,000 points, 6,000 assists, and 6,000 rebounds during their careers?

Oscar Robertson, John Havlicek, and Clyde "the Glide" Drexler.

How many times has one team's final score doubled the loser's score in an NBA game?

Only once has that ignominious feat occurred, on February 27, 1998, when the Indiana Pacers defeated Portland 124–59. Needless to say, the Pacers were hot—making 64% of their shots—and the Trailblazers NOT—making 33% of theirs. Along with doubling the score, the Pacers made twice as many field goals, three-pointers, and free throws than the Blazers, and Pacers players passed around twice as many assists as well.

GAME TIME

What team scored the **fewest points (two) in a quarter** during an NBA game?

In an April 1996 game against the Lakers, the Dallas Mavericks reached an all-time low by scoring only two points in the third quarter—and those points came with just under two minutes left in the period. Derek Harper ended the agony with two free throws. Two other teams—the Sacramento Kings in 1987 and the Buffalo Braves in 1972—held the previous low at four points in a quarter.

What was the **biggest blowout** in NBA history?

The 1998 score-doubling drubbing of the Trailblazers by the Pacers, 124–59, is only the second largest margin of victory in NBA history: Cleveland's 148–80 scorching of the Miami Heat ranks as the worst.

What are the **highest and lowest total scores** in an NBA game?

1955 and 1996 were good years for bricks. The lowest scoring game ever occurred in 1955 when Boston defeated Milwaukee 62–57 (119 total), erasing the record set earlier that year when Ft. Wayne defeated Syracuse 69–66 (135 total). Miami defeated Philadelphia 66–57 (123 total) in February of 1996 for the second lowest total.

A triple overtime game between Detroit and Denver, which the Pistons won 186–184, on December 13, 1983, produced 370 points, and another three-OT game ranks second: San Antonio defeated Milwaukee 171–166 (337 total) in March of 1982. The most points in a game that ended in regulation time occurred in 1990, when Golden State beat Denver 162–158 (320 total), which eclipsed the previous record of 318 set in 1984 when Denver beat San Antonio, 163–155 (118).

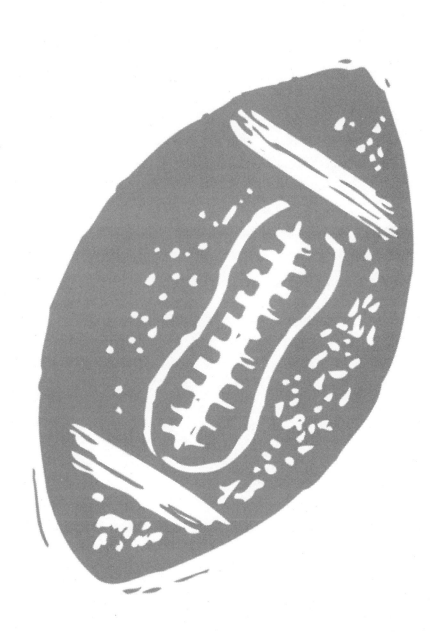

FOOTBALL

KICKOFF

THE ORIGINS OF FOOTBALL

When did **football begin**?

The ancient Greeks played a game in which the object was to move a ball across a goal line by throwing, kicking, or running with it. Several modern games derived from this, including English rugby and soccer, from which American football directly evolved. Soccer, of course, allows players to advance the ball only with their feet, but watch a game of rugby and you'll see what look like "downs" as well as laterals and scoring by carrying the ball over a goal line and by kicking it.

Football historians generally agree that the first game of American football was played on November 6, 1869, in New Brunswick, New Jersey, between teams from Rutgers and Princeton universities. They played on a field 120 yards long and 75 yards wide and used a round, soccer-style ball. Rutgers won the contest, 6–4; but in a rematch the next week, Princeton got revenge, 8–0. Other eastern schools, including Columbia, Yale, and Harvard, soon added the rough sport to their athletic programs. A set of rules was compiled in 1876, making the whole thing official.

At this point, however, the game still looked more like the English sports than the game we know as American football. But in the early

1880s, Yale player Walter Camp revised the rules. He limited teams to 11 players, established the scrimmage system for putting the ball into play, invented the concept of requiring a team to advance the ball a certain number of yards within a given number of "downs," and came up with the idea of marking off the field with yard lines, which led to the term "grid iron."

How did the **modern scoring system** evolve?

Scoring was fairly informal at first. One point was usually awarded for advancing the ball past the goal line, either by kicking or carrying it over. In 1883 the first real scoring system was put in place, with five points being awarded for field goals, two points for touchdowns, and four points for kicking the point-after through the uprights; obviously, the emphasis was still on kicking.

The next year, touchdowns were changed to four points, the point-after conversion to two points, while field goals remained five points. As the game moved farther away from its English roots, the rules reflected the new emphasis on carrying the ball, not kicking it. In 1898 the value of a touchdown was raised to five points and the point-after was reduced to one. The field goal stayed at five points until 1904 when it was lowered to four points; and in 1909 it was reduced again to its current three points. The touchdown was finally raised to its present value of six points in 1912.

When was the **forward pass** legalized?

As in rugby and similar games, advancing the ball by throwing it forward was illegal in the early days of American football. The emphasis on the running game (with minimal protective equipment) made it a very brutal sport, and, in fact, football was banned by some colleges (including Columbia) by 1905. As controversy brewed and football began to get a somewhat unsavory reputation, a number of changes were implemented to make it more of a finesse game than a show of brute strength. Among these was a 1906 rule allowing the forward pass.

Amid growing concern about the future of football, the organization that would eventually be known as the National Collegiate Athletic Asso-

An early football team *circa* 1915.

ciation (NCAA) was founded in 1910. This group embarked on a reform movement to keep the game both safe and interesting. Among other things, in 1910 and 1912 it further revised the passing rules to allow even more latitude in forward passes.

In 1912, Virginia Wesleyan College enjoyed its first undefeated season, becoming the first team to succeed while depending on the forward pass. The following year, Notre Dame, a very good but little-known team from Indiana, also went undefeated and brought national attention to the forward pass by staggering the mighty Army team 35–13 at West Point.

EQUIPMENT AND UNIFORMS

When did numbers get added to **uniforms**?

In the 1890s, officiating crews increased from one to three, but the officials were still having a hard time keeping the players straight and fans

When did players start wearing helmets?

In the 1890s many players began wearing leather helmets, which became common by World War I. But protective headgear—although widely worn—was not mandated by the NCAA until 1939. With advancements in plastics during World War II, plastic helmets came into use in the late 1940s. Face masks were actually illegal until 1951, and mouthpieces became mandatory in 1971.

were complaining that they found it difficult to keep an eye on their favorite grid iron heroes. Finally, in 1915, the rules were changed to allow the addition of numbers to the players' uniforms. But numbers were not required until 1937, when a rule was instituted mandating numerals on both the front and back of football jerseys.

In 1961 the University of Maryland became the first college team to add players' names to the back of their jerseys. In 1967, a numbering system was devised according to player position, with those offensive players ineligible to receive forward passes being assigned numbers in the 50–79 range.

PROFESSIONAL FOOTBALL

Who was the **first professional football player?**

American football began as an amateur sport, played primarily between college teams or athletic clubs. The inevitable move to professionalism took place in 1892, when Yale All-America guard William "Pudge" Heffelfinger received a $500 "performance bonus" from the Allegheny Athletic Association to join their team for a crucial game with the Pittsburgh Athletic Club. Heffelfinger proved to be worth every penny, as he

When did the first professional football game take place?

The game that is generally considered to be the first professional American football contest took place in 1895 in Latrobe, Pennsylvania, between the Latrobe YMCA and the Jeannetee (PA) Athletic Club. But, even in this game not all of the players were paid.

The first team to field an all-professional lineup was the Allegheny Athletic Club, for two games in 1896. The following year, for the first time, the Latrobe Athletic Association used paid personnel for its entire season.

returned a Pittsburgh fumble 35 yards for a touchdown to give the AAA a 4–0 win (touchdowns were worth four points at the time). Heffelfinger thus became the first professional football player on record.

Not to be outdone, the Pittsburgh Athletic Club hired triple-threat back Grant Dibert for the entire 1893 schedule. This was the first professional football contract. From that point, things began happening quickly, with other teams scrambling to buy players. Professional football was off and running.

What is the **early history of professional football leagues** in the United States?

In 1902, two Philadelphia baseball clubs, the Athletics and the Phillies, established pro football teams and joined the Pittsburgh Stars to form the National Football League, the first such professional league.

At the end of the first season, a World Series of Professional Football was conducted, featuring players from more than a dozen teams. The second, and last, football World Series took place in December of 1903. After that season, several Ohio teams were founded and recruited most

117

What coach named a team after himself?

The Cleveland Browns were named after legendary coach Paul Brown. Two previous Cleveland football franchises—the Indians (who folded) and the Rams (who moved to Los Angeles in 1945)—had gone, but Cleveland won a franchise in 1946 in a new league, the All-American Football Conference, and young Paul Brown was hired as coach. The Browns dominated the AAFC, going 52–4–3 from 1946–49. In 1950, the AAFC and the NFL merged, with the Browns, Baltimore Colts, and San Francisco 49ers joining the NFL.

of the top Pennsylvania players. By the 1904 season, seven of the game's top professional teams were located in Ohio.

In 1920, representatives of teams from a four-state area met in Canton, Ohio, to form a new, better organized league called the American Professional Football Association (APFA). A prime mover in this alliance was George Halas, manager and head coach of the Decatur (IL) Staleys. By 1921, the APFA was comprised of 22 clubs.

In 1922, the APFA changed its name to the National Football League (NFL), which is the league we know today. Halas renamed his team and moved them to a larger city: they became the Chicago Bears.

How did the NFL fare against the **college game?**

Despite the efforts of the NFL leadership, the professional game ran a poor second in popularity to the college version. On Saturdays, the major university stadiums were packed with cheering throngs, while the pros played before a relative handful of people on Sundays. Halas recognized the need to legitimize the NFL in the public's view or the league would not survive. Halas kept an eye out for a college star who might lend credibility to the professional game and to draw crowds on Sundays. He concentrated on a halfback from the University of Illinois named Harold "Red" Grange. The "Galloping Ghost" was a national sports hero: as soon as he could, Halas signed him to a pro contract. Using the services of an agent, C.C. ("Cash and Carry") Pyle, Grange leveraged Halas for a share of the gate receipts.

Grange made his pro debut at Wrigley Field on Thanksgiving Day, 1925, in front of 36,000 Bears fans, the largest crowd ever assembled for a professional football game at that time. At the end of the day, Grange was $12,500 richer. When the Bears went on the road, fans around the country flocked to see Grange work his magic. At New York's Polo Grounds, a record 73,000 spectators watched the Galloping Ghost lead the Bears to a 14–7 win over the Giants. The National Football League had arrived.

When was the AFL formed?

The first American Football League was founded in 1926. Red Grange, the highest-paid player in professional football (he earned almost $100,000 in his three months with the Chicago Bears in 1925), quit the Bears in a salary dispute. The new AFL was hastily concocted by his agent, C.C. Pyle. This league folded after the 1926 season, but Grange's team, the New York Yankees, was absorbed into the NFL for 1927.

Then there was the All-America Football Conference (AAFC), which was formed in 1945 and fielded eight teams, including the Yankees, the Brooklyn Tigers, the Cleveland Browns, and the Buffalo Bills. This league folded in 1949, and three of its teams were taken into the NFL: the Browns, the San Francisco 49ers, and the Baltimore club. The Browns made an immediate impact, playing in the NFL Championship game its first six years, winning the league title in 1950, 1954, and 1955, losing in 1951 through 1953.

The modern American Football League (AFL) was founded by Lamar Hunt of Dallas and a consortium of other monied sportsman, who put together eight teams to begin play in the fall of 1960. On January 26, 1960, Hunt was named the new commissioner of the AFL, and on that same day Pete Rozelle became commissioner of the NFL. Thus began a battle—for players, for television contracts, and for status—that continued throughout the 1960s.

What is the history of crowning professional football's champion?

From 1920 to 1931 the league champion was the team with the best regular season record. That period covers the American Professional Football Association (1920–21), which changed its name to the National Football League in 1922, and the early NFL. In 1932, the NFL held its first postseason game to break a tie between the Chicago Bears and the Portsmouth (Ohio) Spartans, each of whom won six games. Beginning in 1933, the NFL created two divisions and held a championship games between the division winners. Following the 1966 season, the NFL champion played the American Football League champion (which held championship games from its inception in 1960) in what has become known as the Super Bowl. When the NFL and AFL merged in 1970, the Super Bowl began pitting the National Football Conference and American Football Conference Champions.

When and how did the **NFL and the AFL merge?**

During the spring of 1966, a series of secret meetings between the NFL and AFL led to a merger of the two leagues. The decision was made to maintain separate schedules through 1969, with a World Championship game (the Super Bowl) between the two leagues' champions set to begin in 1967, along with a common college draft. Then, the leagues would come together officially in 1970. Congress approved the merger, exempting it from antitrust legislation.

When was the **first NFL Championship to be played indoors?**

Surprisingly, it was in 1932, in Chicago—the first NFL Championship game. The Bears finished the season 6–1–6, having beaten the three-time champion Green Bay Packers in the last game of the season to finish tied in wins with the Portsmouth Spartans, who had a record of

6–1–4. Up until then the league champion was simply the team with the best season record. No one wanted the 1932 season to end in a tie, so they came up with the idea of a playoff game.

The NFL Championship game was scheduled to be played at Wrigley Field on December 18, 1932. But as the date approached, Chicago was snowed in, and there was no way to make the field playable. A couple of years earlier, an indoor exhibition football game had taken place at Chicago Stadium, home of the Blackhawks hockey team. Bears owner George Halas proposed moving the 1932 playoff game there.

The field was only 80 yards long, it was 15 feet narrower than normal, the end zones were not regulation size, and the stadium had a cement floor. On the plus side, a circus had just left town, so there was already a layer of dirt in place (further cushioning being provided by leftover elephant droppings), and the stadium looked a lot better to the players than the outside sub-zero temperature and driving snowstorm.

A few special rules were needed for the unusual circumstances: there were no field goals (the field was too short) and all kickoffs were spotted at the ten-yard line. Each time a team crossed the mid-field point, it was automatically penalized 20 yards, thus making the field 100 yards long. And inbounds lines—or hashmarks— were created: when the ball went out of bounds it could be spotted on one of those lines, rather than being placed next to a wall.

The Bears won the game, 9–0. More importantly, the concept of an NFL Championship game was born. The fans loved it, and the owners saw the potential for generating extra income. The next year, the NFL was split in half, with the two division winners playing a final championship game.

What game could be called **the original "Ice Bowl"**?

While many football games, both college and professional, have been played under brutally frigid conditions, one that stands out is an NFL championship game that took place on December 16, 1945, between the Cleveland Rams and the Washington Redskins. An hour before game time, the temperature on the field in Cleveland stood at three degrees below zero, Fahrenheit. By kickoff, the needle barely nudged six above.

A week earlier, the groundskeepers had covered the turf with hay to keep the ground from freezing, but even this measure, requiring the help of 275 men to spread 9,000 bales of hay into a four-foot thick blanket of insulation, had failed to keep the field in playable shape: the hay was cleared, but the ground was frozen solid.

Snow began sticking to the field, and the wind whipping off Lake Erie further added to the players' misery. Both veteran Washington quarterback Sammy Baugh and Cleveland rookie Bob Waterfield had trouble gripping the ball and reported that passing it felt like throwing rocks—which didn't matter much, since the receivers could barely hold on to it, anyway.

Late in the third quarter, a water main broke at the south end of the stands. The concrete steps were first a waterfall, then a solid sheet of ice. The stands were like a walk-in freezer, and the field was as hard as a concrete parking lot. When the game ended, with Cleveland on top 15–14, players and spectators alike fled the stadium for warmer environs.

A month later, the entire Cleveland team headed for a warmer climate, as owner Daniel F. Reeves announced that they were moving west to become the Los Angeles Rams.

What game is **best known as the "Ice Bowl"?**

On December 31, 1967, Vince Lombardi's Green Bay Packers won their fifth NFL title in seven years, defeating the Dallas Cowboys 21–17 on what NFL Films has immortalized as "the frozen tundra of Lambeau Field." At game time the temperature was 13 below. But Lambeau Field sported a new heating system that was supposed to keep the top six inches of ground from freezing. It might be cold, but at least the field would be playable. Unfortunately, the heating system worked only as long as a tarp covered the field. Once it was removed, the ground froze solid in minutes, leaving the turf slick on the coldest New Year's Eve in Green Bay history.

With 16 seconds left to play, and Dallas ahead by three points, Lombardi conferred on the sidelines with his quarterback, Bart Starr, during the Packers' last time out. The ball rested two feet outside the Dallas end zone. A field goal would send the game into overtime, but Lombardi

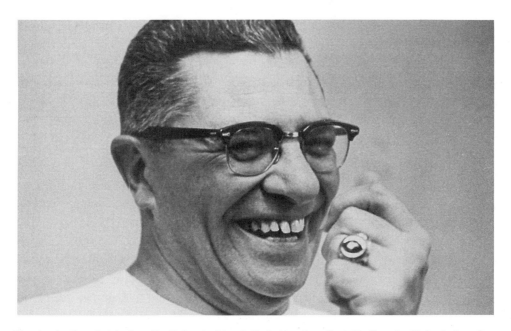

Vince Lombardi coached the Green Bay Packers to victory in the first two Super Bowls. The Championship trophy (as well as an award for college linemen) is named for him.

worried that, at this point, the kicker might not be able to feel his foot. And on their last two running plays, Green Bay's Donny Anderson had slipped on the icy ground, barely avoiding fumbling. "I can sneak it in," Starr told his coach. Lombardi replied, "Then do it, and let's get the hell out of here."

Following an outstanding block by guard Jerry Kramer, Starr sneaked the final yard for the game-winning touchdown. Asked later about his decision to go for the TD rather than a field goal, Lombardi said, "I wanted the touchdown so everyone could go home and get warm." Two weeks later, in considerably warmer conditions at Miami, Green Bay defeated the AFL champion Oakland Raiders in Super Bowl II. And two weeks after that, Lombardi resigned as head coach of the Packers.

When was the **first Super Bowl?**

On January 15, 1967. The Green Bay Packers of the NFL defeated the AFL's Kansas City Chiefs, 35–10, at Los Angeles Memorial Coliseum. The Packers were favored by 13 points, but head coach Vince Lombardi was careful not to allow his team to become complacent in the California sun. Kansas City was not to be taken lightly, in his opinion. Chiefs quarterback Len Dawson was a seasoned veteran with NFL experience. Wide receiver Otis Taylor was capable of breaking a game wide open. The KC defense featured huge linemen and an outstanding linebacker in Bobby Bell. And, finally, they were coached by the experienced and innovative Hank Stram.

Two networks, CBS and NBC, televised Super Bowl I, and each paid an unprecedented $1 million for the privilege. With daily televised interviews and insults flying back and forth between the two teams, the pregame hoopla rose to a fever pitch. Kansas City cornerback Fred "The Hammer" Williamson told reporters, "I have broken thirty helmets with my forearm . . . I can't wait to add to my total against the Packers." Meanwhile, Lombardi professed in an interview to being so blase about the upstart league that he had never even seen one AFL game, live or on television.

To everyone's surprise, the Packers struggled on their opening series, but they established their running game on their second possession. Still, Kansas City refused to roll over. At halftime, the score was 14–10, Green Bay.

The Packers defense came on strong on the first series of the second half. Willie Wood intercepted a Dawson pass and ran the ball to the KC five-yard line. Running back Elijah Pitts carried it in on the next play and Green Bay increased their lead to 21–10. Kansas City would not score in the second half: in fact, they never got inside the Green Bay 40, as the Packers went on to score two more touchdowns. In the fourth quarter, the Packers ran a sweep to Williamson's side of the field. Following a huge collision with Donny Anderson, "The Hammer" failed to get up. He was carried off the field with a broken arm. After the game, Lombardi summed up the game: "The Chiefs are a good team. But they don't compare with the top teams of the NFL."

Which Super Bowl made the game truly Super and ensured that it would become one of America's premier sporting events?

In 1969, Super Bowl III was assumed to be a done deal: The mighty Baltimore Colts were favored by 18 points over the New York Jets, the upstart team from the Mickey Mouse league with the quarterback who wore fur coats and white shoes. CBS personnel had already marked out camera positions in the Colts' locker room for the postgame celebration.

But, absurdly, the Jets' "Broadway" Joe Namath had guaranteed a victory to the press. Moreover, Namath told reporters there were at least four quarterbacks in the AFL who were better than league MVP Earl Morrall of the NFL champion Colts—including Namath! And it wasn't all talk. The Jets had spent hours poring over Baltimore game films, and they spotted a few holes. They felt the Colts had no big running threat and there were some weaknesses in the secondary that Namath could exploit. Baltimore had a great team, but they weren't unbeatable.

New York was forced to punt on its first series of the game, and Baltimore immediately drove to the Jets' 19-yard line. But on the next play, wide receiver Willie Richardson fumbled on his way into the end zone. Then Morrall overthrew an open receiver on second down and was tackled at the line of scrimmage on third down. Lou Michaels' 27-yard field goal attempt went wide. Namath came back with a long pass, proving that Baltimore could be beaten deep. The Colts continued their series of miscues by failing to score on a fumble. But, with 9:03 left in the first half, Randy Beverly of the Jets intercepted a pass by Morrall, spawning a 12-play, 80-yard touchdown drive.

Behind by seven at the half, Baltimore coach Don Shula wondered if he should replace Morrall with Johnny Unitas, who had been out with an elbow injury. He stuck with Morrall, but the Colts fumbled on the first play of the second half, and the Jets recovered and drove for a field goal, putting them up 10–0. When the Jets kicked another field goal, Shula turned to Unitas. But the great Unitas, too, looked flat, and the Colts failed to move the ball. Namath, on two nice pass plays, led the Jets to the Baltimore 10-yard line, and another field goal made it 16–0.

But suddenly Unitas kicked into gear. Within seconds the Colts were at the 25 of the Jets, and the crowd of 75,000 began to roar. Unfortunately, Unitas threw short to a receiver in the end zone, and the pass was intercepted. Later, Baltimore was able to take advantage of three Jets penalties and score from the New York 1-yard line. They recovered an on-side kick and got to the Jets' 19 but failed in their touchdown attempt. Final score: 16–7, Jets.

Joe Namath (throwing) played in two of the most famous games in football history—winning Super Bowl III, and losing the "Heidi" game.

The closing moments of television coverage on the field saw Namath jogging out of the Orange Bowl with his index finger extended, indicating his team's status in the world of football. It was the first championship for the AFL and remains the biggest upset in Super Bowl history. The game legitimized the AFL, which was about to become the American Football Conference under the merger and cemented the importance of the Super Bowl.

What was **the *Heidi* game?**

It was November 17, 1968, and the New York Jets were playing their perennial rivals, the Oakland Raiders. Recent meetings of the two AFL teams were pockmarked with brawls and trash talk by colorful personalities on both sides, and this game had the makings of great television. NBC was broadcasting the game, and the network's executives expected both an exciting match and high ratings from the national audience.

The game turned out to be even better than anticipated. On the opening kickoff, the Jets were penalized for a personal foul; and after that it

Which are the only
two wild-card teams to have won Super Bowls?

Along with divisional champions, teams with outstanding records can also qualify for the playoffs as wild card teams. Only two nondivision winners have won Super Bowls, though, Oakland in 1981 and Denver in 1998.

seemed that every play resulted in players getting angrier and angrier. They went after each other, verbally and physically, and yellow flags filled the air.

In between penalties, the teams played an incredible football game. Both Jets quarterback Joe Namath and the Raiders' Daryle Lamonica ran exciting offenses, and the lead bounced back and forth repeatedly. With 1:05 remaining in the game, and the score tied at 29, Namath had taken the Jets down the field and the team prepared for a 26-yard field goal.

By this point—undoubtedly due to the unusual number of penalties—the game had used up the three-hour time slot NBC allotted for it. Someone at the network dutifully threw a switch, and the national broadcast switched over to the next scheduled program: the children's movie *Heidi*. As the national audience stared at a little Swiss girl on their screens, Lamonica connected for two quick passes following the Jets' field goal. On the second one, rookie Charlie Smith ran 43 yards for a touchdown, putting the Raiders ahead 36–32, with 42 seconds to play. The Raiders' kickoff was fielded by the Jets' Earl Christy at the 15-yard line, but Christy was hit by several Raiders and fumbled the ball. It was picked up at the two by fullback Preston Ridlehuber of the Raiders and carried in for Oakland's second touchdown in nine seconds. Final score: Raiders 43, Jets 32.

Needless to say, NBC received tens of thousands of complaints. The next day, network president Julian Goodman issued a public apology. The damage was done, and the *Heidi* Game was in the record books, but—in light of the national furor caused by enraged sports fans—it's unlikely

127

that any television network will ever make that mistake again, which is why "60 Minutes" used to come on late (7:15 or 7:30) on Sunday nights in the fall, even while it was the highest-rated show on television.

What was the **NFL's longest game** ever?

A grueling playoff game between the Miami Dolphins and the Kansas City Chiefs, on Christmas day, 1971, lasted an incredible 82 minutes and 40 seconds (a regulation game is 60 minutes). Heavily favored Kansas City had won Super Bowl IV the previous year and, according to Miami coach Don Shula, still had the best personnel in the AFL. Miami had never beaten the Chiefs.

The Dolphins had a well-rounded offense, with quarterback Bob Griese's passing ability balanced by a running attack that featured the great Larry Csonka, Jim Kiick, and a speedy array of linemen. But Kansas City coach Hank Stram had an outstanding bunch of linebackers ready to control the Miami offense, while the Chiefs' potent offense was led by quarterback Len Dawson.

The teams turned out to be well matched. The score was tied at 10 at the half. Kansas City marched 75 yards for a touchdown in the third quarter, then Miami came right back to tie it again. The Chiefs scored in the fourth following an interception, making it 24–17, but the Dolphins tied the game once more on an outstanding series of passes by Griese. KC's Ed Podolak ran the kickoff back to the Miami 22-yard line and, with 35 seconds remaining in the game, kicker Jan Stenerud trotted confidently onto the field for the chip-shot field goal. But, amazingly, the reliable Stenerud missed by inches, and the game went into overtime.

Miami placekicker Garo Yepremian had the chance to end it in the first overtime with a 52-yard field goal, but his effort sailed wide to the left. The game went into double-overtime. Miami's running game had been thwarted all day by the Kansas City linebackers, but Griese and Csonka were confident they could come up with a play that would surprise the Chiefs. Finally, on a roll-right, trap-left play, Csonka found some running room. At 7:40 into the second overtime he ran 29 yards to the Kansas City 36. A couple of plays later, Yepremian kicked a 37-yard field goal to end the game, 27–24, Miami.

What was the **Immaculate Reception?**

It was December 23, 1972, at Three Rivers Stadium in Pittsburgh. The Steelers, after years of failing to make the playoffs (since 1947), had finally put together a respectable team, going 11–3 in the regular season and taking the AFC Central Division championship under the leadership of quarterback Terry Bradshaw. Now they had to get past coach John Madden's Oakland Raiders to keep their season alive.

The game was a defensive battle, which Pittsburgh led most of the way on the strength of two field goals by Roy Gerela. Then, with 1:13 to go, Oakland backup quarterback Ken Stabler (playing for Daryle Lamonica, out with the flu) ran 30 yards for a touchdown. After the kickoff, the Steelers, down 7–6, were on their own 40-yard line with 22 seconds left in the game. Three straight Bradshaw passes had gone incomplete; only one play left.

Bradshaw took the snap and dropped back seven steps. He was flushed out of the pocket and was scrambling to his right when he saw running back John "Frenchy" Fuqua burst into the open 20 yards downfield, followed closely by Oakland's All-Pro safety Jack Tatum. With a crash, the ball and Tatum arrived at the same time.

The next few seconds have been analyzed thousands of times—with little assistance from video replays that gives different stories from different angles. Bradshaw's pass was deflected backwards 15 yards, having hit either Tatum or Fuqua, and it was grabbed at shoe level by Steelers rookie running back Franco Harris, who ran it all the way into the end zone.

Madden accosted the nearest official screaming, "No good. No good." At the time, an NFL rule stated that a pass deflected by one offensive player to another was not legal—it was an incomplete pass and a dead ball. But who touched the ball last, Fuqua or Tatum? The officials weren't immediately sure; no touchdown had been signaled. After conferring with other officials and calling the league's supervisor of officials from the field telephone, referee Fred Swearingen finally raised his arms: Touchdown.

The entire Oakland bench went berserk, screaming at the call. Tatum was incensed. He grabbed Fuqua, shouting, "Tell them you touched it." But Fuqua, a joker who was always willing to stir up controversy, merely erupted with laughter. Ever since, he has reportedly refused to tell even his teammates what happened, at one point even alleging that the Immaculate Reception was a planned play that he and Harris had cooked up. Unlikely, but proof once again that in football anything can happen.

What game featured **"The Catch"?**

It was January 10, 1982, at Candlestick Park in San Francisco. The 49ers were playing the Dallas Cowboys for the NFC Conference championship. San Francisco had scored first in the game when Freddie Solomon caught an eight-yard touchdown pass from quarterback Joe Montana. Dallas replied with a 44-yard Rafael Septien field goal and a touchdown pass from Danny White. Each team scored again, making the halftime score 17–14, Dallas.

Johnny Davis put San Francisco ahead 21–17 with a two-yard run in the third quarter. Then, following a field goal and a touchdown after a fumble recovery, Dallas went ahead in the fourth quarter, 27–21. That's where the score stood with a minute to play in the game, Niners' ball at the Cowboy 6, third down and three.

Montana took the snap and rolled right. Almost immediately his blocking coverage broke down, and he was forced to scramble with Dallas's Ed "Too Tall" Jones and Larry Bethea bearing down on him. He was close to the sidelines: he could step out and try again on fourth down. With a split second to make a decision, Montana couldn't even see his receivers, just Too Tall Jones. He jumped as high as he could and heaved the ball to an area where he knew receiver Dwight Clark should be.

Clark was not the primary receiver on the play. He expected to be serving mainly as a decoy so that Solomon, the primary target, could get open. Montana's blind pass had been thrown high, and Clark was not particularly known for his jumping ability. But on this play he leapt into the air and came down with the ball, his feet just inches from the back line of the end-zone. Touchdown!

With 51 seconds left in the game, Dallas came close to scoring again, but the San Francisco defense held. Final score: 28–27. Looking at tape

Joe Montana led the San Francisco 49ers to their first Super Bowl with the help of Dwight Clark's miraculous leaping catch in the end zone. The play came to be known simply as "The Catch."

of The Catch later, Montana said: "Dwight must have jumped three feet to get that. I don't know how he got it. He can't jump that high!"

What game featured **"The Drive"**?

First down and 98 yards to go. The Denver Broncos had botched a kick-off from the Browns on January 11, 1987, in the NFC Championship game at Municipal Stadium in Cleveland. The Broncos were down, 20–13, with five minutes left in the game, maybe the season.

Denver quarterback John Elway called a short pass to running back Sammy Winder, who took it for a five-yard gain. Winder's next run was almost stopped by Browns defensive end Reggie Camp, but he still squeezed out three yards. With two yards to go, Winder got the ball again and just barely made the first down.

Winder again, for three more. Then, on second down, Elway called a pass play but couldn't find an open receiver. With the Browns closing in, he was forced to scramble, still looking for someone to throw to. Finally, he tucked the ball in and ran for 11 yards, sliding safely to the 26-yard line.

The next play was a 22-yard pass to Steve Sewell, one of the fastest Denver receivers, taking the Broncos to their own 48. Elway next passed to Steve Watson: another 12 yards and a first down, with 1:59 to play. After the two-minute warning, Elway was caught behind the line of scrimmage and was forced to throw the ball away. It was almost intercepted by Cleveland safety Ray Ellis, but Ellis just barely failed to hold on. Then, on the next play, Elway was sacked by nose tackle Dave Puzzuoli. With his already sprained left ankle re-injured on the play, Elway called time out. The Cleveland fans were rejuvenated. They began dancing in the stands as Elway conferred with Coach Dan Reeves.

Ball at the Cleveland 48, third down and 18, 1:47 to go in the game. Denver lined up in the shotgun formation. On the snap, the ball grazed Watson, who was in motion, and bounced off the ground. Elway grabbed it and passed to Mark Johnson for 20 yards. On the next play, Elway was forced to throw the ball away when no receivers could get open. Next, a screen pass to Sewell went for 14 yards, then a pass to Watson near the goal line was ruled out of bounds. Second down at the

John Elway engineered one of the most thrilling (and heartbreaking, if you're a Browns fan) comebacks in history on January 11, 1987.

Which NFL team has never won a post-season game?

Oddly enough, it's not one of the four most recent franchises to enter the NFL—Tampa Bay, Seattle, Jacksonville, and Carolina all have won at least one playoff game. The Ain'ts of New Orleans ain't never won a post season game since entering the league in 1967. They've made the playoff four times during those years. The City of New Orleans has hosted five Super Bowls, though, and could qualify as a permanent neutral field site.

14-yard line. Reeves called a quarterback draw play: when the hole failed to develop, Elway ran to the outside and made it to the five. Third and one, with 39 seconds left. The blitz was on, and Elway had to throw the ball while he was still backpedalling. It was a classic Elway pass, something like a smoking fastball, but Mark Jackson hung on for the touchdown. The extra point was good.

Cleveland received the kickoff in overtime, but the Broncos defense, charged up by The Drive, did its job. Elway immediately connected on two passes for 50 yards. Winder drove up the middle three times, and kicker Rich Karlis won the game for Denver with a 33-yard field goal. Final score: 23–20.

Has there ever been a perfect season in the NFL?

One. It was put together by the Miami Dolphins in 1972. Miami coach Don Shula had been hired away from Baltimore, where his Colts had gone 73–26–4 between 1963 and 1969. In 1970 he took the Dolphins to second place in the AFC East, and, following an outstanding 1971 season, the team made it to the Super Bowl, where they were humbled by the Dallas Cowboys, 24–3.

The Dolphins of 1972 featured such standouts as quarterback Bob Griese; running backs Larry Csonka, Jim Kiick, and Mercury Morris; and receivers Paul Warfield and Howard Twilley—not to mention the legendary No-Name

> ## What two coaches coached in the Super Bowl and the Canadian Football League's Grey Cup championship game?
>
> **B**ud Grant (Minnesota and Winnipeg) and Marv Levy (Buffalo and Montreal). Bud Grant was 4–1 in Grey Cups, Levy was 2–1. They share another distinction: both were 0–4 in Super Bowls.

Defense, a group of players little-known at the beginning of the season but famous by its conclusion: Nick Buoniconti, Mike Kolen, Doug Swift, Manny Fernandez, Bill Stanfill, Bob Heinz, Dick Anderson, and Jake Scott.

Miami shut out the Baltimore Colts 16–0 in the last game on their schedule, making them the only team in NFL history to have a 14–0–0 regular season. The No-Namers had allowed the fewest points in the league, and backs Csonka and Morris had each rushed for 1,000 yards or more, the first time one team ever had two 1,000-yard rushers.

The Dolphins defeated the Cincinnati Bengals 34–16 in the AFC Conference playoff game and went on to a 27–17 victory over the Pittsburgh Steelers for the AFC title. They lined up against the Washington Redskins on January 14, 1973, in the Super Bowl at Los Angeles. Surprisingly, Washington was favored. The word was that Miami had enjoyed an easy schedule; they had been lucky in several games; Griese was coming back from a broken ankle; and Washington had a veteran defense, strong at stopping the run, Miami's major strength.

The Dolphins dominated early, leading 14–0 throughout most of the contest. Late in the game, Washington scored on a botched Miami field-goal attempt. The kick was blocked and little Garo Yepremian, the Miami placekicker, picked up the ball, ran, and then tried to throw it. The ball slipped from his hands, he batted it, and a Redskins' defensive back caught it and ran in for a touchdown. Miami held the 14–7 lead, and the Dolphins emerged as the first team in NFL history to go undefeated through the regular season and all the playoffs.

What is the highest scoring game in NFL history?

The Washington Redskins and New York Giants kept the scoreboard operators hopping on November 27, 1966 when the Giants blitzed the 'Skins 72–41, a total of 113 points. Only one other game topped 100 points, when the Oakland Raiders defeated Houston 52–49 in an AFL game on December 22, 1963.

What was the **worst defeat** in professional football?

On December 8, 1940, the Chicago Bears beat the Washington Redskins, 73–0, in the NFL Championship game at Griffith Stadium. Several weeks earlier, in the regular season, the Redskins had beaten the Bears, 7–3, on a close call by the officials. After that game, Washington owner George Marshall called the Bears "cry babies" for protesting the call and referred to them as "quitters." Before the rematch in the championship game, Chicago coach George Halas read Marshall's remarks to his team for inspiration. The enraged Bears scored 21 points in the first 13 minutes of the game, and the score at halftime stood at 28–0. And they didn't let up in the second half, scoring another 45 points. In all, the Bears gained 501 total yards and intercepted Washington eight times, with three returned for touchdowns.

When the Bears scored their tenth touchdown, officials asked Halas if he could please not kick for the extra point; so many balls had been kicked into the stands and kept by fans that they were down to their last football. So, with a 66-point lead, Halas had his team pass for the two-point conversion. At the final gun, a reporter in the press box remarked, "Marshall just shot himself."

When was the **first televised football game?**

On October 22, 1939, New York fans huddled around the City's 1,000 television sets to see the Philadelphia Eagles play the Brooklyn Dodgers at Ebbets Field. For the first time, they would be able see the action as it

What are the longest plays in NFL history?

There have been eight touchdown passes of 99 yards. In 1983, Tony Dorsett ran 99 yards from scrimmage against the Minnesota Vikings. Robert Bailey of the Rams returned a punt 104 yards in a 1994 game against New Orleans, and three players have returned kickoffs for 106 yards. James Willis of Philadelphia intercepted a pass four yards deep in the endzone, ran out to the ten, and lateralled to Troy Vincent, who took it the remaining 90 yards to complete the longest interception return—104 yards—in NFL history in 1994.

was described by the announcer. The broadcast wasn't exactly a rousing success, however. TV cameras then weren't what they are now: they needed a lot of light. Every time a cloud passed over the field, the television picture grew dark, and as the day got cloudier, fans were reduced to listening without pictures, just as they had with radio.

What are the longest **field goals?**

Tom Dempsey's 63-yard game winning field goal against Detroit in 1967 in the closing seconds still stands as the longest of all time. Tulane Stadium went wild. Alex Karras, the great Lions defensive tackle, later joked that players were so sure Dempsey wouldn't make it that they battled on the line of scrimmage for the best view of watching the ball fall back to Earth. Steve Cox kicked a 60-yarder in 1984 for Cleveland, and Morten Andersen booted a 60-yarder in 1991 for New Orleans.

Eleven teams have **never played in the Super Bowl.** Who are they?

Arizona Cardinals, Atlanta Falcons, Baltimore Ravens, Carolina Panthers, Cleveland Browns, Detroit Lions, Jacksonville Jaguars, New Orleans Saints, Seattle Seahawks, Tampa Bay Buccaneers, and Tennessee Oilers.

137

Jim Brown dominated his era, leading the league in rushing eight times in a nine-year career.

Which famous running back (a movie was made based on a book he wrote) is the all-time leader in kickoff return yardage (based on at least 75 returns)?

Gale Sayers returned 91 kicks for 2,781 yards—an astounding 30.6 yard average—and six touchdowns. Sayers also shares the record with four others for longest run from scrimmage in a college football game—99 yards—which he ran in a 1963 game for Kansas against Nebraska.

What is the **largest stadium** in the NFL? The smallest?

The Detroit Lions have the distinction of owning the largest stadium in the league, the Pontiac Silverdome, which seats 80,365. The Silverdome also has the distinction of being the only cold-weather stadium to host the Super Bowl. The smallest stadium is an outdoor multipurpose park—Three Rivers Stadium, home to the Pittsburgh Steelers, seats 59,600.

PLAYERS

Who won the NFL rushing title in 1940 and later went on to become a U.S. Supreme Court justice?

Byron "Whizzer" White was an outstanding athlete who excelled on the football field and in the classroom. As a running back for the University of Colorado in 1938, White finished second in the Heisman Trophy voting and then moved on to the NFL. He only played for three years before quitting to begin his law career and was appointed to the Supreme Court in 1962 by John F. Kennedy.

Who is the only player to **rush for more than 200 yards in the Super Bowl**?

Timmie Smith was hardly a household name at the start of Super Bowl XXII, but he was by the end of the game. After rushing for only 126 yards during the entire regular season for the Washington Redskins, Smith broke loose for 204 yards in the 'Skins 42–10 rout of the Denver Broncos. Unfortunately for Smith, his success didn't last. He played only two more seasons in the NFL and ran for only 612 more yards in his entire career.

Who is the only running back to **win the league rushing title five years in a row?**

Jim Brown led the league in rushing eight times during his nine-year career, from 1957–61 and 1963–65. Brown is also the only back in the top 10 in career rushing to average more than five yards per carry. Barry Sanders is next at 4.9 through 1997.

Who are the only three backs to **rush for 2,000 yards** in a season?

Eric Dickerson, 2,105 yards in 1984; Barry Sanders, 2,053 in 1997; and O. J. Simpson, 2,003 in 1973.

Barry Sanders has a 2,000-yard and four straight 1,500-yard rushing seasons under his belt.

Who is the only back to **rush for 1,500 yards or more for four straight seasons?**

Barry Sanders, 1994–97.

What's the record for **most yards rushing in a single game?**

Walter Payton ran for 275 yards in a 1977 game against Minnesota. O. J. Simpson had the next two best games, 273 yards against Detroit in 1976, and 259 yards against New England in 1973.

What legendary quarterback threw the **most career interceptions?**

George Blanda threw 277 career interceptions. Rounding out the top five are John Hadl (268), Fran Tarkenton (266), and Norm Snead and Johnny Unitas with 253 each. Blanda—who is also the oldest player (48) to ever appear in a professional football game—was the AFL MVP in 1970 and still holds the record for regular season and playoff scoring

141

among place kickers. He was 43 during that legendary MVP season, in which he was also named AP Male Athlete of the Year. During one amazing five-week stretch in 1970, Blanda replaced injured starting QB Darryl Lamonica and led a comeback by throwing three touchdown passes in a 31–14 victory; he kicked a 48-yard field goal with three seconds left the next week to tie the game (which ended 17–17); he came into the next game with his team down late and threw a tying touchdown with 1:14 left, then won the game with a 52-yard field goal with three seconds left; the next week he came in with four minutes left and Oakland down 19–17, led the Raiders on an 80-yard drive and tossed a game-winning TD; and the fifth week he booted a 16-yard field goal with four seconds left for a 20–17 victory.

What is the record for **longest punt** in an NFL game?

Steve O'Neal of the New York Jets got a great roll when he booted a 98-yarder against the Denver Broncos on September 21, 1969.

What number is the **most popular retired jersey number** in the NFL?

The number 14, which was worn by five players whose teams have retired their jerseys: Dan Fouts of the San Diego Chargers, Otto Graham of the Cleveland Browns, Steve Grogan of the New England Patriots, Don Hutson of the Green Bay Packers, and Y.A. Tittle of the New York Giants. Three other numbers—7, 12, and 40—have been retired by four teams each.

Where is the **Pro Football Hall of Fame,** and how is one elected to it?

The Pro Football Hall of Fame was established in 1963 in Canton, Ohio. To be eligible, players must be retired for five years, coaches must be retired, and other contributors to the game can still be active. Voting on entry is done by a 36-member panel, composed of 30 media representatives (one from each NFL city), one representative from the Hall of Fame, and five electors-at-large.

The Heisman Trophy has often been the kiss of death for college players when they moved on to the NFL. In fact, only six winners of college football's top award have made it to the Pro Football Hall of Fame. Who are they?

Doak Walker, half back; Paul Hornung, running back; Roger Staubach, quarterback; O.J. Simpson, running back; Tony Dorsett, running back; and Earl Campbell, running back. Campbell and Dorsett pulled off a bit of a trifecta by also being named NFL Rookie of the Year, Dorsett in 1977 and Campbell in 1978.

COLLEGE FOOTBALL

What colleges have won the **most national championships?**

National championships officially began with Associated Press polling in 1936. In AP polling, Notre Dame has won nine times, Alabama seven, Ohio State and Oklahoma six each, and the University of Southern California, five.

What were the results when **the No. 1 and No. 2 teams met** in bowl games?

Here are the results of the 11 times that has happened:

In 1963, No. 1 USC defeated No. 2 Wisconsin 42–37 in the Rose Bowl.

In 1964, No. 1 Texas defeated No. 2 Navy 28–6 in the Cotton Bowl.

In 1969, No. 1 Ohio State defeated No. 2 USC 27–16 in the Rose Bowl.

In 1972, No. 1 Nebraska defeated No. 2 Alabama 38–6 in the Orange Bowl.

In 1979, No. 2 Alabama defeated No. 1 Penn State 14–7 in the Sugar Bowl.

How many times has the No. 1 team in the AP poll played the No. 2 team?

Thirty-one times, 11 of which were bowl games. No. 1 holds an 18–11–2 advantage, but No. 2 is 10–6 since 1979, including No. 2 Florida State's 24–21 victory over No. 1 Florida in 1996.

In 1983, No. 2 Penn State defeated No. 1 Georgia 27–23 in the Sugar Bowl.

In 1987, No. 2 Penn State defeated No. 1 Miami 14–10 in the Fiesta Bowl.

In 1988, No. 2 Miami defeated No. 1 Oklahoma 20–14 in the Orange Bowl.

In 1993, No. 2 Alabama defeated No. 1 Miami 34–13 in the Sugar Bowl.

In 1994, No. 1 Florida State defeated No. 2 Nebraska 18–16 in the Orange Bowl.

In 1996, No. 1 Nebraska defeated No. 2 Florida State 62–24 in the Fiesta Bowl.

When have **unbeaten teams met in bowl games?**

Unbeaten teams have met 15 times in bowl games. In addition to the 1972, 1987, 1988, 1993, and 1996 games listed in the answer above concerning No. 1 versus No. 2, the other 10 are:

1921 Rose Bowl, when California defeated Ohio State 28–0.
1922 Rose Bowl, when California tied Washington & Jefferson 0–0.
1927 Rose Bowl when Stanford tied Alabama 7–7.
1931 Rose Bowl when Alabama defeated Washington State 24–0.
1939 Orange Bowl when Tennessee defeated Oklahoma 17–0.
1941 Sugar Bowl when Boston College defeated Tennessee 19–13.
1952 Sugar Bowl when Maryland defeated Tennessee 28–13.
1956 Orange Bowl when Oklahoma defeated Maryland 20–6.
1973 Sugar Bowl when Notre Dame beat Alabama 24–23.
1989 Fiesta Bowl when Notre Dame beat West Virginia 34–21.

Will the Bowl Alliance
promise more of these match-ups?

After the 1998 season, all major conferences are included in an alliance in which a designated bowl will host a showdown between the nation's No. 1 and No. 2 teams. This should guarantee a national title game. In the past, some conferences were locked into certain bowls—the Big Ten and Pac Ten with the Rose Bowl, for example.

However, some questions still persist. What if there are three or more undefeated teams at season's end, or only one undefeated team and several teams with only one defeat? Which poll is going to be used—the AP, ESPN/*USA Today*, or another? At press time, such questions were still unanswered.

Which 10 teams have **finished in the AP Top 10 the most?**

The top 10 of the top 10 (with No. 1 rankings in parentheses) are:

Notre Dame	34 (8)
Michigan	33 (2)
Alabama	30 (6)
Oklahoma	29 (6)
Nebraska	27 (4)
Ohio State	24 (3)
Penn State	21 (2)
USC	20 (3)
Tennessee	20 (1)
Texas	19 (2)

Which colleges have **won the most bowl games?**

1. Alabama   28–17–3

2. USC	25–13	
3. Tennessee	21–17	
4. Penn State	21–11–2	

Who was the legendary **Knute Rockne?**

Rockne, head coach of the Notre Dame Fighting Irish from 1918 to 1930, is still considered by many to be the greatest college coach in history. Rockne's record of 105–12–5, a winning percentage of .881—still the best of all-time—certainly bears this out. "The Rock" was not particularly known as an innovator, but he was a master at studying the work of coaches who preceded him and implementing the best of their ideas. For instance, his masterful use of the new forward pass was instrumental in gaining national attention—and a winning record—for his early teams. His one major innovation was the Notre Dame Shift, a finesse move intended to allow his smaller, faster players to outmaneuver bigger, clumsier opponents.

But, above all, Rockne had a magnetic personality, and he is still widely known as the best motivator in football history. He knew when to stroke players' egos and when to berate them for sloppy performance, and his halftime pep talks are the stuff of legend. His most famous halftime talk came in a game against Army in 1928, when his team entered the locker room with a 0–0 tie. Rockne told his players about the time in 1920

Who are the five winningest coaches in college football history?

Eddie Robinson of Grambling closed out a 55-year career in 1997 with 411 victories; Bear Bryant had 323 victories, Pop Warner 319, and Amos Alonzo Stagg 314; Joe Paterno at Penn State has 298 and is the leader among active coaches.

when George Gipp, the Notre Dame All American, had looked up from his deathbed and related his last request: "Some day . . . when the odds are against us, ask a Notre Dame team to win a game for me—for the Gipper." Said Rockne, "This is the day, and you are the team." Whether the Gipper story was true or not, the pumped-up team went out and upset Army 12–6.

What famous college football players were known as "Mr. Inside" and "Mr. Outside?"

The two star running backs from the powerhouse Army teams of the 1940s—Doc Blanchard and Glenn Davis—earned those nicknames while winning back-to-back Heisman Trophies. Blanchard won in 1945 and Davis turned the trick in 1946. The pair combined for 97 touchdowns in their college days at West Point.

Who were the Four Horsemen?

The most famous football backfield of all time, the Four Horsemen played for Notre Dame under head coach Knute Rockne from 1922 to 1924. The group consisted of quarterback Harry Stuhldreher, halfbacks Don Miller and Jim Crowley, and fullback Elmer Layden. They were named by sports writer Grantland Rice in a *New York Times* story on October 18, 1924. Rice wrote: "In dramatic lore [the Four Horsemen] are known as famine, pestilence, destruction, and death. These are only aliases. Their real names are: Stuhldreher, Miller, Crowley, and Layden."

A week after the story appeared, a Notre Dame student publicity aide posed the players on four horses from the school's farm. The photo was published nationwide, and by the mid-point of their senior-year schedule the Four Horsemen had become legends.

They began playing together in their sophomore year, and during the three years they played on the varsity team, Notre Dame compiled a record of 26–2–1. In their senior year, the team went 9–0 in the regular season and went on to a victory over Stanford in the Rose Bowl to claim Notre Dame's first national championship.

Who is the **career rushing leader** in college football?

Tony Dorsett amassed 6,082 yards from 1973 to 1976 for Pittsburgh.

Who was the first college player to **catch more than 100 passes in a season?**

Howard Twilley of Tulsa caught 134 passes for 16 touchdowns in 1965.

What about **700 yards passing?**

David Klingler tossed for 716 yards for Houston in a 1990 game against Arizona State. His own Houston team was lit up for 690 yards passing

> ## Has a college player
> ## ever rushed for 400 yards in a game?
>
> No, but Tony Sands of Kansas managed 396 in a 1991 game against Missouri. That same year, Marshall Faulk ran for 386 yards for San Diego State in a game against Pacific. Troy Davis reached 378 yards for Iowa State in a 1996 game against Missouri.

that year by Matt Vogler of TCU. They both topped the 631 yard mark set by Scott Mitchell of Utah against Air Force in 1988.

Who kicked the **longest field goals** in a college game?

In 1977, Steve Little of Arkansas kicked a 67-yarder against Texas; not to be outdone, Texas's Russell Erxleben kicked a 67-yarder that year against Rice; Joe Williams of Wichita State tied them with a 67-yarder against Southern Illinois in 1978.

Has anyone ever **won the Heisman Trophy twice?**

Archie Griffin of Ohio State is the only multiple winner of the Heisman, taking it in 1974 and 1975. He finished college in 1975 as the nation's all-time leading rusher with 5,179 yards. He still ranks fourth, behind Tony Dorsett (6,082), Charles White (5,598) and Herschel Walker (5,259), who won their Heismans in 1976, 1979, and 1982, respectively. Billy Sims of the University of Oklahoma came close to winning the award twice, winning it in 1978 as a junior and then finishing second to White in 1979.

What are the other **major college awards?**

The Maxwell Award: Beginning in 1937, the Maxwell Memorial Football Club of Philadelphia presented its award to the outstanding football

149

Who are some of the defensive players (besides 1997 winner Charles Woodson) to have garnered significant Heisman voting?

Don Whitmire, a tackle for Navy, finished 4th in 1944; Alex Karras, a tackle for Iowa, finished 2nd in 1957, and another tackle, Lou Michaels of Kentucky, finished 4th that year; Bobby Bell, a tackle from Minnesota, finished 2nd in 1962; Rich Glover, a middle guard from Nebraska, finished 3rd in 1972; Hugh Green, a defensive end from Pittsburgh, finished second in 1980; Brian Bosworth, a linebacker from Oklahoma, finished 4th in 1986; Gordie Lockbaum, a two-way player (receiver/defensive back) from Holy Cross finished third in 1987; Steve Emtman, a defensive tackle from Washington, finished 4th in 1991; and Marvin Jones, a linebacker from Florida State, finished 4th in 1992.

player in the nation. The award is named after Robert (Tiny) Maxwell, who was a great lineman for the University of Chicago at the turn of the century. The Maxwell and the Heisman are similar awards and have gone to the same player in the same season 32 times. The Maxwell voters have shown more variety than the Heisman voters, who have chosen either a quarterback, running back, or receiver every year except one (1997, Charles Woodson, defensive back, Michigan; the Maxwell for 1997 went to Peyton Manning, quarterback, Tennessee). A center (Chuck Bednarik, Penn State, 1948), a tackle (Bob Reifsnyder, Navy, 1957), two linebackers (Tommy Nobis, Texas, 1965; Jim Lynch, Notre Dame, 1966), a defensvie tackle (Mike Reid, Penn State, 1969), and two defensive ends (Ross Browner, Notre Dame, 1977; Hugh Green, Pittsburgh, 1980) have won the Maxwell.

O'Brien Quarterback Award: The O'Brien Memorial Trophy was first presented in 1977 to the outstanding player in the Southwest Conference; in 1981 it was renamed the O'Brien Quarterback Award and has since been given to the nation's outstanding quarterback. The award is

How many times has the player who won the Heisman Trophy played on a team that won the national championship the same year?

Eleven times, the most recent occurring in 1997 when Charles Woodson of Michigan became the first defensive player to win the trophy, leading his team to a 12–0 record and a share of the national championship. Other players to pull off the double play include Danny Wuerffel, quarterback, University of Florida, 1996; Charlie Ward, quarterback, Florida State, 1993; Tony Dorsett, running back, University of Pittsburgh, 1976; John Huarte, quarterback, Notre Dame, 1964; Leon Hart, end, Notre Dame, 1949; Johnny Lujack, quarterback, Notre Dame, 1947; Doc Blanchard, fullback, Army, 1945; Angelo Bertelli, quarterback, Notre Dame, 1943; Bruce Smith, quarterback, Minnesota, 1941; and Davey O'Brien, quarterback, Texas Christian, 1938.

bestowed by the Davey O'Brien Educational and Charitable Trust of Fort Worth, Texas and is named after 1938 Heisman-winning quarterback Davey O'Brien of Texas Christian University.

The Outland Trophy: Presented by the Football Writers Association of America since 1946 to the nation's outstanding lineman. The award is named for its benefactor, Dr. John H. Outland (graduate of Kansas, 1898). Center Dave Rimington of Nebraska is the only two-time winner (1981–82), and he, Ross Browner (defensive end, Notre Dame, 1976), Steve Emtman (defensive tackle, Washington, 1991), and Orlando Pace (offensive tackle, Ohio State, 1996) are the only juniors to win the award.

Lombardi Award: Presented since 1970 by the Rotary Club of Houston to the best lineman. Named after Vince Lombardi, coach of the Green Bay Packers and a college football player (he was one of the famed "seven blocks of granite" linemen at Fordham during the 1930s). The Outland

151

and Lombardi both honor linemen, and a player has won both awards in the same year 10 times.

Butkus Award: Presented since 1985 by the Downtown Athletic Club of Orlando, Florida, to honor the nation's outstanding linebacker. The award is named for Dick Butkus, two-time All-American linebacker at Illinois.

Thorpe Award: Presented since 1986 by the Jim Thorpe Athletic Club of Oklahoma City to the nation's outstanding defensive back. Named after Olympic champion and football great Jim Thorpe.

Payton Award: Presented since 1987 by the Sports Network and Division I-AA Sports Information Directors to honor the nation's outstanding Division I-AA player. Named after Walter Payton, an All-American at Jackson State and the NFL's all-time leading rusher.

Hill Trophy: Presented since 1986 by the Harlon Hill Awards Committee of Florence, Alabama, to the nation's outstanding Division II player. Named after Northern Alabama and NFL star Harlon Hill.

Why were there 14 years between the **first Rose Bowl and the second?**

The first Rose Bowl was played on January 1, 1902, as an adjunct to the town of Pasadena's annual Rose Festival. That inaugural game pitted Stanford against Michigan, which had gone 11–0 in the regular season and scored 555 points while shutting out every opponent. It was only a postseason exhibition game, but many people thought Stanford didn't belong on the same field as the Michigan team. As it turns out, they were right. The Wolverines knocked most of the Stanford starters out of the game, then went to work on the second- and third-stringers. With the score 49–0 and eight minutes left in the game Stanford surrendered and walked off the field. The Tournament of Roses committee was humiliated. They dropped football from the Rose Festival until the West Coast was able to put together a stronger team.

Walter Payton, the NFL's all-time leader in career and single-game yardage, is the namesake of the award given to the outstanding Division I-AA player.

What player returned a fumble the wrong way in a Rose Bowl?

During the second quarter of the 1929 Rose Bowl between California and Georgia Tech, Golden Bear running back Stumpy Thompson coughed up the ball on Tech's 36 yard line. Roy Riegel, the California center, caught the ball in the air and headed toward the end zone, but in trying to elude tacklers he got turned around and headed toward open field—toward the opposite end zone. Georgia Tech players ran along for the show, but Riegel's teammates took up the chase; quarterback Benny Lom caught him inside the 10 yard line, but Riegel shook him off, alledgedly yelling, "Get away from me, this is my touchdown!" But Riegel realized something was wrong and stopped short of the goal line. Georgia Tech players hoping to congratulate him tackled Riegel instead on the one-yard line—resulting in a 64 yard loss for Cal. The Golden Bears punted on the next play, but it was blocked and resulted in a safety. "Wrong Way" Riegel became a Rose Bowl legend.

What is the **longest winning streak** in college football history?

From early 1953 until 1957, the University of Oklahoma went, 47–0. The Sooners actually went 48 games without a loss, having tied Pittsburgh 7–7 in 1953 before winning the next 47.

The streak came to an end on November 16, 1957, when Dick Lynch of Notre Dame scored with four minutes left in the game to give the Irish a 7–0 win. The loss also brought an end to an Oklahoma scoring streak of 123 consecutive games.

What about **unbeaten streaks?**

Washington, from 1907–17, sported a 63-game unbeaten streak (59–0–4) before losing to California. From 1908 through 1914 they had a 39-game winning streak—second longest to Oklahoma's 47—before being tied 0–0 by Oregon. Michigan had a 56-game streak from 1901–05, going 55–0–1. They had won 29 in a row before being tied by Minnesota, 6–6, in 1903, then went on another 26 game winning streak until losing to Chicago, 2–0, in 1905.

What was the **worst team** in college football?

Depending on how you count, there are a couple of choices. The Macalester College Scots lost 50 games in a row, from 1974 through 1980, setting an NCAA record for consecutive losses. Macalester, a small liberal arts college in St. Paul Minnesota, best known for its academic excellence, lost big during that streak. In 1977, they lost all eight of their games by a combined score of 532–39; in one game that year they were defeated 97–6. The torture finally ended on September 6, 1980, when Macalester defeated Mount Scenario College of Ladysmith, Wisconsin, 17–14.

The Northwestern Wildcats of 1976–82 went 3–65–1 and set a major-college record of 34 losses in a row. The Wildcats' worst year was 1981, when they were outscored a total of 505–82 (average game score: 46–7). Northwestern has since fielded some fine football teams, but on November 7, 1981, the Wildcats broke the existing major-college record of 29 straight losses—and the excited fans mobbed the field, tore down the goalposts, and carried them through the streets of Evansville chanting, "We are the worst. We are the worst."

As for losing streaks, Prairie View A&M lost 68 in a row between 1989 and 1996, breaking Columbia's streak of futility of having lost 44 straight between 1983 and 1988.

What is the **worst football defeat** on record?

On October 7, 1916, Tennessee's Cumberland College lost to Georgia Tech, 222–0. Cumberland had a pickup team coached by a law student. Georgia Tech, coached by John Heisman (for whom the Heisman Trophy is named), was coming off an unbeaten season. The suggestion was made that the game be called off before it started, but Cumberland stood

The Big 10. In 1895 the presidents of seven Midwestern universities gathered in Chicago to discuss ways to maintain better control of intercollegiate athletics. This led to the formation, in February 1896, of the Intercollegiate Conference of Faculty Representatives, known informally as the Western Conference and later the Big 10.

The charter members of the Big 10 included Illinois, Chicago, Michigan, Minnesota, Purdue, Northwestern, and Wisconsin. Indiana and Iowa were added in 1899. Michigan left the conference in 1907, then returned in 1917. Ohio State entered in 1912. Chicago dropped football in 1939 and left the conference in 1946. Michigan State was admitted in 1949. Membership remained stable until 1990, when Penn State joined, taking membership in the Big 10 to 11 schools.

to forfeit $3,000 in good-faith money if it withdrew, so officials decided to give it a try.

On the first play of the game, the Cumberland quarterback was knocked unconscious and carried off the field. Things went downhill from there. Georgia Tech scored on every one of its possessions, racking up 32 touchdowns—13 on interceptions, fumbles, kickoff returns, and punts. Cumberland failed to make a single first down, rushed for minus 45 yards, connected on two of 11 passes, threw four interceptions, and fumbled nine times.

At halftime, with a 63–0 lead, Heisman told his players to keep up the pressure in the second half: "You never know what those Cumberland players have up their sleeves." It's not that he was a sadist. Sportswriters at the time rated teams solely on the total points they scored, a system Heisman disagreed with. So he wanted to run up the score as much as possible to demonstrate how meaningless it was to humiliate a weaker team.

Many schools play for a trophy or prize when they face off against one of their heated rivals. What are some of the **unique trophies** that are a part of college football?

The oldest of the well-known rivalry trophies is the Little Brown Jug, which goes to the winner of the Michigan-Minnesota game. The jug was first contested in 1909. Other popular trophies include the Axe (California vs. Stanford); the Beer Barrel (Tennessee vs. Kentucky); the Commander-in-Chief Trophy, which goes to the head-to-head winner of the games between the Army, Navy, and Air Force Academy; the Floyd of Rosendale trophy (Minnesota vs. Iowa); the Golden Egg (Mississippi vs. Mississippi State); the Old Oaken Bucket (Indiana vs. Purdue); the Paul Bunyan Axe (Minnesota vs. Wisconsin); the Tomahawk (Illinois vs. Wisconsin); and the Victory Bell (Southern Cal vs. UCLA).

What **college stadium** known as "The Big House" is the largest in college athletics?

Michigan Stadium, home to the Michigan Wolverines, currently seats 102,501 people and is undergoing a renovation in 1998 that will raise the capacity to 107,701. The Stadium, which was built in 1927 at a cost of $950,000 originally held 72,000 fans. The stadium holds the NCAA record for highest single-game and season attendance and has led college football in attendance for 23 consecutive seasons. The last crowd of less than 100,000 to watch a game there was on October 25, 1975 when the Wolverines defeated Indiana University 55–7.

Where is the **College Football Hall of Fame,** and how does one get elected to it?

The College Football Hall of Fame was established in 1955 by the National Football Foundation and is located in South Bend, Indiana. Player nominees must be out of college for 10 years and must have been a first team All-American; coaches must be retired for three years. Voting is done by a 12-member panel of athletic directors, conference and bowl officials, and media representatives.

ODDS AND ENDS

Who were the **"Steagles"**?

During the mid-1940s. NFL players were in short supply since so many were off fighting in World War II. A few teams, such as the Cleveland Rams, suspended operations altogether, while others came up with more unique solutions. The Pittsburgh Steelers and Philadelphia Eagles decided to merge and share a roster, playing home games in both cities—hence, the "Steagles" were born. The experiment lasted for only the 1943 season—in 1944 the Eagles resumed as a separate team, while the Steelers merged with the Chicago Cardinals for the 1944 season.

What are the various **field officials responsible for** beside positioning themselves to enforce rules?

The referee supervises the other officials. He decides matters not under the other officials' specific jurisdiction, he enforces penalties, and he identifies them (through hand signals and over a loud speaker) to teams and fans. The referee indicates when the ball is out of play and when it can be put into play again. The umpire makes decisions on questions concerning the players' equipment, their conduct, and their positioning. The head linesman marks the position of the ball at the end of each play and has assistants who mark the spot of the ball on the sideline and who man the yard markers. The linesman also watches for violations of the rule requiring players to remain in certain positions before the ball is put into play. The field judge times the game with a stopwatch to coincide with a stadium's scoreboard clock.

What quarterback engineered the **largest comebacks** ever in NCAA and NFL football?

Frank Reich. In the 1992 AFC playoffs, Reich replaced Bills all-time great quarterback Jim Kelly in the second half in a game against Hous-

An aerial view of Michigan Stadium. The "Big House" will expand to over 107,000 seats in 1998.

ton, with the Bills trailing 35–3. By the final gun, the score was tied 38–38, then Buffalo won in overtime. It was an incomparable turn-around: just the week before, in the final regular season game, Houston had beaten Buffalo 27–3. Buffalo made the second-half playoff comeback without quarterback Jim Kelly, running back Thurman Thomas, and linebacker Cornelius Bennett—all All-Pros that year.

In college at Maryland, Reich completed 62.9 percent of his passes for 2,097 yards and ranked among the top passers in the country as a senior. He rallied the Terrapins to a comeback 42–40 victory after being down 31 points to the Miami Hurricanes. While at Maryland, Reich roomed with another great college and pro quarterback, Boomer Esiason: they later went into business together, owning and operating a boot store.

Why did the referee **award Dick Moegle a touchdown** in the 1954 Cotton Bowl even though Tommy Lewis had tackled him?

Lewis had jumped off the bench to make the tackle.

What two coaches **coached national champions** in college and also **coached in the Super Bowl?**

Barry Switzer coached the 1975 and 1985 national champion Oklahoma teams and won the 1996 Super Bowl with Dallas, while Jimmy Johnson coached the 1986 University of Miami national champions as well as the 1993 and 1994 Dallas Cowboys championship teams. Johnson's Miami Hurricanes defeated Switzer's Sooners in the 1987 Orange Bowl for Miami's national championship.

Bobby Ross, on the other hand, was twice a bridesmaid. Ross's 1990 Georgia Tech team (11–0–1) was UPI champ but was outpolled in the AP by Colorado (11–1–1), and Ross's San Diego Chargers lost Super Bowl XXIX (1995) to San Francisco.

What **author once played quarterback** for the Detroit Lions?

Famous for his first-person looks at the world of professional sports, George Plimpton worked out with the Lions at their training camp in 1966 and played quarterback during an exhibition game. The story of his dering-do was told in the book *Paper Lion*. Plimpton also once played goaltender for the Boston Bruins.

Who was the only person to be enshrined in the **college football, pro football, and baseball halls of fame**?

Cal Hubbard was a star at Centenary College in Louisiana before going on to become a four-time All-Pro in the NFL. After his football career was over, Hubbard switched sports and was a professional baseball umpire for 16 seasons.

What was the **worst halftime show** ever put on during a football game?

Tough call, but there are a couple good contenders. On October 28, 1967, the Columbia Marching Band engaged in some sociological analysis on a major development of the era: the birth control pill. They formed a giant calendar and played "I Got Rhythm" (dedicating the song

Where did the term "taxi squad" originate?

The taxi squad referred to players under contract to an NFL team, but who didn't suit up for games because of 40-man roster limit. At one time, the Cleveland Browns couldn't put all their players on the roster, so they employed some as part-time taxicab drivers.

to the Vatican), then reformed into a shotgun to the tune of "Get Me to the Church on Time."

But then on September 14, 1985, the Stanford University band (known for some outrageous halftime antics) did a "Tribute to Presidential Diseases." They began with a commemoration of the removal of a cyst from President Ronald Reagan's nose by forming a large nose with a bump on it. Then other band members formed gigantic pincers that squeezed the bump until it burst. They followed this with an even more unbelievable homage to the removal of part of Reagan's colon, spelling out the word "benign" to the tune of the song "Kick It Out."

GOLF

GENERAL

ORIGINS AND HISTORY

What are the **origins of golf**?

Golf, as we know it by today's rules, equipment, and even the 18-hole course layout, evolved over several centuries in Scotland. It has been played there since the early 1400s, and it was in Scotland where rules were first codified: the *Rules of Golf* was published in 1754 by the St. Andrews Golfers, later called the Royal & Ancient Golf Club.

Previous to the 1400s, variations of golf and field hockey had been played in many different societies. Romans, for example, had turned their penchant for hitting things with sticks into a game called *Paganica* that involved knocking a stone toward a target. Variations on the game of field hockey (without the running) were played in the 1300s in several western European countries, including Holland, where they played a game called *kolf* with balls and clubs, and France, where they played a stick and ball game called *chole*. As trade increased between western European nations, such games spread fairly quickly.

The first recorded reference to *chole* in Flanders (Belgium) occurred in 1353, and around 1420 *chole* was introduced to a Scottish regiment aiding the French against the English at the Siege of Bauge. Hugh

When and why was golf banned?

In 1457, golf (referred to as "golfe" and "the gouf") and football were banned by the Parliament of King James II of Scotland because the games were interfering with military training for the wars against England. The ban was not seriously enforced, and in 1502, with the signing of the Treaty of Glasgow between England and Scotland, the ban on golf was lifted altogether.

The banning of golf from the streets of Albany, New York, in 1659 is the first known reference to golf in America.

Kennedy, Robert Stewart and John Smale, three of the players, are credited with introducing the game of *chole* back in Scotland.

What was the **first club of golfers**?

The Honourable Company of Edinburgh Golfers was formed and began playing at Leith links in 1744.

Where was the **first club of golfers** in the **United States**?

The South Carolina Golf Club was formed in Charleston in 1786. As early as 1743 a shipment of 96 clubs and 432 balls arrived in Charleston from the Port of Leith in Scotland.

What is the **oldest surviving golf hole** in the United States?

The first hole at The Homestead, White Sulphur Springs, West Virginia, survives from the original Oakhurst Golf Club, founded in 1884, and is, thus, the oldest golf hole in the United States.

When was golf first played at St. Andrews, and why is it referred to as The Royal and Ancient Golf Club of St. Andrews?

The first recorded evidence of golf being played at St. Andrews in Scotland is 1552. A license was granted by John Hamilton, Archbishop of Sanctandros, to the city's people allowing them "inter alia to play at golf, futball, schuting at all gamis with all uther manner of pastime." Since this act was a matter for record and reference is made to "the common Links where golf was played," golf was obviously played there before that date, perhaps as early as 1413, when the University of St. Andrews was founded.

In 1754, the Gentlemen of Fife invited the Gentlemen of Leith to join them in forming the St. Andrews Society, which eventually became the Royal & Ancient that developed as the governing body for the rules of golf. The Royal and Ancient Golf Club of St. Andrews was so named in 1834 with the permission of King William IV. Golf had long been called "a royal and ancient game."

When did **stroke play** originate?

The earliest reference to stroke play is 1759, occurring at St. Andrews. Previously, all golf was match play. In match play, players or teams compete on a hole-by-hole basis rather than going by their total scores for eighteen holes. The winner in match play is determined by who has the lowest score on the most holes. In stroke play, golfers compete on the basis of who has the lowest individual score for 18 holes, or some multiple of 18 (72 holes for tournaments).

What was the first **18 hole golf course**?

The number of holes on a golf course wasn't settled as 18 until 1764. Previous to that, most courses had seven holes, and as late as 1851 Prest-

Was golf ever an Olympic competition?

Golf was played during the second modern Olympiad, held in 1900 in Paris. Margaret Abbott won the competition by shooting a 47 in the nine-hole event, becoming the first American athlete ever to win an Olympic medal.

wick, which hosted the first 12 British Opens, was formed with only 12 holes. The Opens at Prestwick consisted of three rounds of 12 holes.

St. Andrews originally had 12 holes, then one of the original holes was abandoned. Because the land of the course was so narrow, golfers played rounds of 22 holes—11 holes going out, away from the clubhouse, then turning around and playing the same 11 in reverse order coming in. In 1764, the first four holes were combined into two, leaving nine holes and reducing the round from 22 holes to 18. St. Andrews thus became the first 18-hole golf course and set the standard for future courses.

The greens on six of the nine holes were later expanded to accommodate two holes, creating the famous two-hole greens (2 and 16, 3 and 15, 4 and 14, 5 and 13, 6 and 12, 7 and 11, 8 and 10) in the 18-hole layout of 1842, still in place today.

When was the **Ryder Cup** competition established?

In 1926, an unofficial match between a group of professionals from the United States and a team made up of golfers from England and Ireland was played in Wentworth, England. British seed merchant Samuel Ryder, an avid golfer, was so impressed with the competition that he donated the Ryder Cup to be awarded to the winning side in the biennial Ryder Cup competition. The first official Ryder Cup match was played at the Worcester Country Club in Massachusetts and was won by the host U.S. team.

In 1979, the competition changed to a United States *vs.* European team format. The competition had been dominated by the U.S., but the European team won four and tied another competition while only losing twice from 1979 to 1997.

Where was the first **miniature golf course**?

The first miniature golf course opened in 1916 in Pinehurst, North Carolina.

TOURNAMENTS

When did the **British Open** begin?

After the first British Amateur Championship was held in 1859 (and won by George Condie of Perth), The Prestwick Club hosted a Professionals Championship played at Prestwick in 1860. Contenders played for a trophy—a belt of red Morrocan leather with silver inlays, including one depicting four golfers on a green—presented by the Earl of Eglington. The first Championship Belt was won by Willie Park. In 1861 The Professionals Championship was opened to amateurs, thus becoming the first true British Open.

When was the first **U.S. Open** played?

The first U.S. Open Championship was held in 1895 on the Rocky Farm Course at the Newport (Rhode Island) Golf Club, which was founded by Theodore Havermeyer. He was President of the United States Golf Association and reportedly covered all expenses to ensure that the best golfers would compete. The first Open was scheduled for early September but was moved back to October so it wouldn't be overshadowed by the America's Cup yacht races being held out in a huge water hazard near the course.

An Open competition for professionals was held at St. Andrews Golf Club in Yonkers, New York, in 1894, and both Saint Andrews and Newport Golf Club held Amateur Open competitions that year as well. The United States Golf Association was formed late in 1894 by representatives from those two clubs as well as The Country Club (Brookline, Massachusetts),

What is the Grand Slam of Golf?

Four tournaments, collectively referred to as the Majors, form the Grand Slam of Golf: the British Open, begun in 1860 and usually held during the end of the third week of July; the U.S. Open, begun in 1895 and usually held during the end of the second week of June; the PGA Championship, begun in 1916 and usually held during the end of the second week in August; and the Masters, begun in 1934 and usually held during the end of the second week of April.

Shinnecock Hills (Southampton, New York), and the Chicago Golf Club to conduct national golf championships in the United States. The first U.S. Open was won by Horace Rawlins, who shot a 173 for the tournament, which was played in four, nine-hole rounds during one day.

What are the tournaments that make up the **Grand Slam of Women's Golf**?

The first Women's Open was organized by the Women's Professional Golf Association, which began with efforts immediately after World War II to organize a professional women's golfing tour. The first Open was played in 1946 and consisted of qualifying rounds leading to match play competitions. Patty Berg defeated Betty Jameson, 5 and 4, to become the first Open champion. The Open switched to stroke play in 1947.

The LPGA Championship began in 1955 with a match play format: Beverly Hanson won in the final over Louise Suggs, 4 and 3. The format turned to stroke play in 1956 and delivered immediate drama, as 22-year old Marlene Hagge topped Patty Berg in a sudden death playoff.

The Colgate Dinah Shore Tournament began play in 1972 and became a major in 1983. The Peter Jackson Classic, played in Canada, was designated as a Major in 1979; it was originally called La Canadienne (1973), then the Jackson from 1974 to 1982, and became the du Maurier Ltd. Classic in 1983.

170

The Titleholders Tournament, which ran from 1937 to 1966, was considered a Major on the LPGA Tour. Patty Berg won the event seven times, Louis Suggs was a four-time winner, and Babe Zaharias was a three-time champion. The Western Open ran from 1937 to 1967 and was also considered a Major. Multiple winners include Patty Berg (7), Louise Suggs and Babe Zaharias (4 each), Mickey Wright (3) and Betsy Rawls (2). Considering the Titleholders and the Western Open as Majors, Babe Zaharias completed a Slam (or The Triple) in 1950, winning those two tournaments plus the Open—all the women's Majors that year.

GOLF TERMS

How did the term **caddie** originate?

Mary, Queen of Scots, generally credited as being the first woman golfer, is also credited as having been the source of the word caddie. She was raised in France and returned to Scotland at age 19. Her royal assistants, called pages in English, retained their French title—cadets. Among other duties, the Cadets (pronounced ka-day in French) lugged her golf clubs.

What is the **Slope Rating** on a golf card?

The Slope Rating is one way to measure a course's difficulty. The Slope Rating is calculated by dividing the average score of "bogey golfers" by the average score of scratch players (a scratch player has a zero handicap—meaning he/she usually shoots par) over 27 holes from the back and front tees. The lowest Slope Rating is 55, and the highest is 155; a course of standard playing difficulty would have a USGA Slope Rating of 113. Examples of slope ratings on famous courses: Pinehurst #2—131/135; Pebble Beach—142/130.

What does the phrase **"up and down"** mean in golf?

"Up and down" is most commonly used to describe reaching the green and holing out, with one approach shot (up) and one putt (down). A

Mary, Queen of Scots is said to have been the first woman golfer, and is also credited with the origin of the term "caddie."

confident golfer (often deluded) might step into a greenside bunker and say, "I can get up and down from here," meaning he thinks he can place the ball close enough to the hole to putt it in.

Why is the word **"Fore!"** used as a warning call?

Use of the word "Fore!" to warn golfers that a ball is heading their way probably derives from a phrase yelled in the British military. Artillery men called out "Beware before!" to warn the infantry ahead that a volley of cannonballs were about to be discharged at the enemy.

What is the Vardon grip?

Also called the overlapping grip, the Vardon grip is a way of holding the golf club so that the little finger of the right hand overlaps the space between the forefinger and middle finger on the left hand for a right-handed golfer. Six-time British Open winner Harry Vardon developed the grip around the end of the nineteenth century, when slimmer shafted clubs became widely used. The Vardon grip remains the most widely-used method for gripping golf clubs. Vardon promoted and demonstrated the grip in his book, *The Complete Golfer*, published in 1905.

What are the odds of getting a **hole-in-one**?

For an amateur, the odds are generally given at about 12,600 to 1; the chances of a touring professional hitting a hole-in-one are about 3,708 to one. A hole in one is also called an ace.

The only golfer to record consecutive holes-in-one was Bob Hudson, who aced the 11th and 12th holes at the Martini International at Norwich, England, in 1971. He probably ended up buying quite a few double martinis that afternoon: tradition has it that a player who makes a hole in one should buy a round of drinks for everyone in the clubhouse when he concludes his round of golf.

What was golf's **"Shot heard 'round the world?"**

After the fanfare of the opening of Augusta National and the playing of the first Masters Tournament in 1934, the tournament still needed to be established as a major event. Less than two dozen people were in the gallery when Gene Sarazen reached the 15th hole of the final round of the 1935 Masters. Sarazen was trailing leader Craig Wood, who was already in the clubhouse. Sarazen conferred with his caddie, Stovepipe, and the two figured that Sarazen would need a birdie four on 15, birdie two on 16, then a birdie three on either 17 or 18 for a tie. Sarazen

What is an albatross, and what are the odds of getting one?

An albatross describes a hole completed in three strokes under par—shooting a two on a par five, for example. The more common term is a double eagle (an eagle being two under par for a hole). The odds of making an albatross have been put at 1 in 5.85 million. An amateur named John Cook did it on the 14th hole (475-yard par 5) at the Ocean Course on Hilton Head Island using a 3 Wood and an 8 Iron. That was in the morning; in the afternoon he did it again on the same hole, using a 3 Wood and a Wedge. Only one player ever scored an albatross in a U.S. Open: T. C. Chen achieved it in the opening round of the 1985 championship at Oakland Hills in Michigan. Chen had a more unfortunate rarity later in that tournament: he hit the same ball twice on one swing—a double hit, and both count—on the 5th hole of the final round, taking an 8 for the hole and losing his four-stroke lead; he finished tied for second.

One of the most famous golf strokes ever—called "the shot heard 'round the world"—was an albatross.

thought he had a decent chance, until he saw his lie in the rough after his drive on 15. It was, as he says in his book, *Thirty Years of Championship Golf*, "None too good." He and his caddie huddled, again, and he decided on hitting a 4-wood, the rough lie eliminating his 3-wood from consideration. What occurred next has been called the "Shot Heard Round the World" and is considered by some as the most spectacular shot in the history of golf.

With the flag 220 yards away, Sarazen was concerned about the possible loss of yardage with the 4-wood and toed the club in to decrease loft and seek the extra distance. He tore into the shot with everything he had and the ball rose no more than 30 feet off the ground, heading straight for the flag. Sarazen began running to watch the flight and saw the ball

What is a bogey in golf and how did the term originate?

To bogey a hole means to play it in one over par. The term bogey comes from the Great Yarmouth Golf Club in England, where Major Charles Wellman referred to failure to achieve par as "getting caught by the bogey man." Club members created an imaginary Colonel Bogey, who would always play each hole in one over par.

hit the green on a perfect line. When he heard the tiny crowd explode in cheers, he knew he'd scored an albatross.

That shot wiped out the 3-stroke deficit and Sarazen played the final three holes in par to force a playoff, then took the 36-hole playoff by five strokes.

EQUIPMENT AND THE FIELD OF PLAY

GOLF BALLS

How have **golf balls** evolved?

The first golf balls were probably small stones, later small wooden balls. Some 15th century Dutch paintings show golf being played with wooden balls, probably made of beech. Leather balls stuffed with wool or feathers were most common from the early 1600s through the mid-1800s. The leather was cut in strips and then soaked in a solution of alum. The strips were then sewn together and turned inside out, leaving a small hole through which feathers were stuffed with an awl. The feathers, usually from goose and chickens, were boiled first to soften them. After the hole was sewn up, the ball was left to dry, during which the feathers expanded and the leather shrunk, creating a hard ball.

175

When did dimples first appear on a golf ball?

In 1880, molds were used to dimple the gutta-percha ball. Golfers had long noticed that the guttie flew much better after it had been hit several times and scuffed up. The first dimple pattern for golf balls was patented by William Taylor in England.

Around 1848 the gutta-percha ball was introduced. Gutta-percha is Malaysian for "tree sap," and the balls were formed from the sap, an early form of rubber. William Montgomerie, a surgeon employed by the East India Company, had traveled to Malaya and brought back samples of gutta-percha to the Western world, and gutta-percha was soon applied to golf balls. The gutta-percha ball was cheaper than the featherie and lasted longer, but it didn't fly as well until after being scratched up. This led a St. Andrews ballmaker, Robert Forgan, to hammer in regular patterns on the ball's surface.

Two improvements occurred around 1870: golf balls were being made by machine and became more uniform, and the introduction of cork, leather, and metal fillings ground together with gutta-percha formed a more lively ball called the gutty. Many other improvements and experimentations took place through the end of the century, but the Haskell Ball of 1898 was the next major improvement. Developed in Akron, Ohio, by Coburn Haskell, a bicycle manufacturer, and Bertram Work, a rubber worker, the Haskell ball consisted of a small rubber core wound over with elastic thread and covered with gutta percha. Since then, the insides of the ball have remained the same while manufacturers have experimented with the outer covering, developing such rubber-based products as balata and Surlyn.

What is the **standard size and weight** of a golf ball?

The maximum weight is 1.62 ounces and the minimum diameter is 1.68 inches. The United States Golf Association sets the requirements for

When did the size and depth of a golf hole become standardized?

The games that evolved into golf usually involved hitting a round object—a stone, wooden ball, or a stuffed leather ball—toward a target, usually a post. Playing the game in fields required continual trimming of grass around the pole so that the ball could be maneuvered toward it, thus you have the first greens. Holes replaced poles, and knives or other cutting implements were used to form the hole, usually by tracing around the bottom of a flowerpot. A turf cutting tool developed in the eighteenth century was designed to cut a hole $4\frac{1}{4}$ inches wide, and the Royal and Ancient decreed in 1894 that $4\frac{1}{4}$ inches shall be the uniform size of the hole, with a depth of not more than four inches.

maximum weight, minimum size, spherical symmetry, initial velocity, and overall distance. Historically, American golf balls have tended to be somewhat larger that those used internationally.

CLUBS AND HOLES

Why do golf club heads have **grooves**?

The grooves help prevent the ball from sliding up and over the face of the club on impact. The grooves hold the ball on club, helping to propel the ball forward. However, the grooves hold on only long enough to prevent slipping and sliding: a golf ball stays on the face of a driver for only .0036 seconds.

When were **wooden tees** first used, and what preceded them?

Wooden tees came into use in 1922. Previously, golfers used sand or dirt to build a small mound from which they hit their first drive. Sandboxes were common at tee areas until the tee came into use.

COURSES

What are some of the different **layouts of golf courses**?

The layout, or routing, of a golf course is dictated by the course architect. The greatest course architects are almost always masters at routing the course to attain the best natural locations for holes on a piece of property. Golf courses set beside the sea and exhibiting terrain with sandy soil and odd dune shapes are called Links.

Some of the strategies for routing used by famous architects include the Heroic style, the Penal style, and the Strategic style.

What is the **Penal style of design**?

Penal designs force golfers to hit over hazards instead of giving them options of whether to risk hitting over a hazard or playing around it. Courses designed by Pete Dye and C. B. Macdonald best exemplify this style of design.

Where can the largest green be found?

The largest single green on any golf course is on the fifth hole of the International Golf Club in Bolton, Massachusetts. It has an area of more than 28,000 square feet, big enough for three average suburban houses and yards.

What is the **Strategic style of design**?

Augusta National and the Old Course at St. Andrews showcase the Strategic style of design, which provides players with various options and routes, with different rewards depending on the shot that is carried out. Miss-hit shots usually aren't as severely penalized by the Strategic style as they are by the Heroic style.

What is the **Philadelphia School of Design**?

Five influential golf architects were raised in the Philadelphia area between 1870 and 1930: A. W. Tillinghast, George Crump, Hugh Wilson, William Flynn, and George Thomas. Crump's work at the Pine Valley course in New Jersey and Wilson's at Merion, near Philadelphia, united the architects and provided a general style they followed in their individual work.

What famous course was developed on land that had been a nursery?

You know it's spring when the magnolias, azaleas, and dogwoods are in bloom during the annual Masters tournament in April. Augusta National was built on 365 acres of land that had been developed by a Belgian-born horticulturalist. Golfing great Bobby Jones designed the course with noted golf architect Alister Mackenzie.

Mackenzie died in 1934, not long after Augusta National was completed. His ashes were spread over the Pasatiempo course in Santa Cruz, California, another of his brilliantly designed courses.

179

How is par for a hole determined?

Par is the number of strokes a good golfer can expect to make on a particular hole. Guidelines for par are based on distance:

Par 3: holes up to 250 yards for men, 210 for women.

Par 4: holes from 250 to 470 yards for men, 210 to 400 for women.

Par 5: holes over 470 for men, over 400 for women.

Instead of reporting their scores in raw numbers, golfers may say they shot so many stokes over or under par, or they shot even par. Par didn't become part of golf parlance until the early 1900s. Until then, playing the equivalent of bogey golf was considered good. An informal system for rating holes was in effect at least as early as 1870 when a newspaper reported that Young Tom Morris' opening round in the British Open that year was achieved two strokes "in excess of absolutely faultless play." His 149 total in the three rounds of 12 holes format was the lowest score ever achieved with the gutty ball.

RULES

When were the **rules of golf first codified**?

The Society of St. Andrews Golfers spelled out their "Thirteen Basic Rules of Golf" in 1754:

1. You must tee your ball within a club length of the hole.

2. Your tee must be on the ground.

3. You are not to change the ball which you strike off the tee.

4. You are not to remove stones, bones, or any break-club for the sake of playing your ball, except upon the fair green, and that only within a club length of your ball.

5. If your ball come among water or any watery filth, you are at liberty to take out your ball and throw it behind the hazard six yards at least; you may play it with any club, and allow your adversary a stroke for so getting out your ball.

6. If your balls be found anywhere touching one another, you are to lift the first ball until you play the last.

7. At holing you are to play your ball honestly for the hole, and not to play upon your adversary's ball, not lying in your way to the hole.

8. If you should lose your ball by its being taken up or any other way, you are to go back to the spot where you struck last and drop another ball and allow your adversary a stroke for the misfortune.

9. No man at holing his ball is to be allowed to mark his way to the hole with his club or anything else.

10. If a ball is stopped by any person, horse, dog or anything else, the ball so stopped must be played where it lies.

11. If you draw your club in order to strike and proceed so far with your stroke as to be bringing down your club, if then your club should break in any way, it is to be counted a stroke.

12. He whose ball lies farthest from the hole is obliged to play first.

13. Neither trench, ditch, nor dike made for the preservation of the links, nor the Scholar's Holes, nor the Soldier's Line shall be counted a hazard, but the ball is to be taken out, teed, and played with an iron club.

How are **handicaps** established?

A handicap is a golfer's average score over 18 holes, expressed as strokes over par (a 3 handicap golfer will usually shoot in the mid-70s, an 18 handicap golfer will shoot around 90). Handicaps allow golfers with different abilities to compete, as scores are adjusted based on a player's established handicap. A "Course Handicap" is the number of handicap strokes a player receives from a specific set of tees at the course being played.

In order to obtain a handicap, golfers must join a golf club and post their adjusted scores, which are subject to peer review; an authorized golf association may simply be a group of people who play golf together on a regular basis. They must establish a Golf Committee and follow all the requirements of the USGA Handicap System. After at least five scores have been posted, the club will issue a USGA Handicap Index to the golfer.

The formula used for determining a USGA handicap:

1. Take the best 10 of your last twenty scores.

2. Subtract the USGA Course Rating from the sum total of your 10 best scores; multiply the difference by 113 (the Slope Rating of a course of standard difficulty); then divide the resulting number by the USGA Slope Rating for the course. Round to the nearest tenth.

3. Average the differentials.

4. Multiply the average by .96.

5. Delete all numbers after the tenths digit, but do not round to the nearest tenth. This will give you your Handicap Index, but unless you establish it through the United States Golf Association procedures no one will take it seriously.

For more information, call the USGA (908)234-2300 and/or visit their web site: http://www.usga.org

What is the regulation concerning the **number of clubs a golfer may carry** in his bag?

A player is allowed to carry a maximum of 14 clubs in his bag. He can replace a damaged club during a round. The player selects among three types of clubs: Woods—broad-headed clubs used for longer shots and numbering 1 to 9; irons, numbered 1-9, have metal clubheads with faces of increasingly severe angles as the numbers increase, plus various wedges for pitching and sand play; and putters.

FAMOUS GOLFERS

Who was the **first woman golfer**?

Mary, Queen of Scots (1542–1587), is generally credited as being the first female golfer. She was reportedly seen playing golf, in fact, shortly after the death of her husband, Lord Darnley, who had been found strangled in a house blown up by gunpowder in 1567. Mary didn't have much time for golf after that: she was involved in various intrigues, eventually imprisoned, and was beheaded (but that has nothing to do with the fact that golfers are often told to keep their head down).

However, another woman golfer may have preceded her. Catherine of Aragon (1485–1536), the first wife of Henry VIII, wrote in one of her many correspondences with Thomas Cardinal Wolsey, the Archbishop of York, that the king's subjects would be happy that she would be busy with golf, "for my heart is very good to it."

Who was the **first amateur to win the U.S. Open**, and why was it so memorable?

Even though the U.S. Amateur Open was considered more prestigious than the U.S. Open Championship during the early years of the twentieth century, an amateur didn't win the U.S. Open until 1913. That win, called the "Ouimet Miracle," was accomplished by little-known Francis Ouimet, who outdueled the two greatest golfers of the day, Harry Vardon and Ted Ray, in a playoff. The win began a trend that changed golf dominance from Great Britain to the United States. When the U.S. and British Opens resumed after being canceled during World War I, Americans won 11 of the next 13 British Opens.

Ouimet grew up in Brookline, Massachusetts, just across the street from The Country Club where the 1913 U.S. Open was held. He learned golf as a young boy, frequently sneaking onto the course at The Country Club to play and also caddying there. He also played at the Franklin Park public course, but getting there involved a mile-and-a-half walk with his golf clubs, three street car changes, and another walk of a mile

183

to the course. Only 13 at the time, he would play 54 holes there and then come home.

Ouimet won the 1909 Boston Interscholastic championship when he was 16. He failed to qualify for the U.S. Amateur for three years before finally making it in 1913, just prior to the U.S. Open. He gave eventual winner Jerry Travers a good match in the second round but finally lost, 2–3. His play was observed by Robert Watson, president of the USGA, who asked Ouimet to enter the U.S. Open at The Country Club in Brookline. Ouimet was reluctant to enter because he had already taken time off work to play in the U.S. Amateur. Enter he did, though, and his understanding boss gave him the necessary time off.

Ouimet followed up his surprise victory in the U.S. Open with a win in the 1914 U.S. Amateur. His career was disrupted when the USGA revoked his amateur status because of a business association with a sporting goods concern. The outcry over Ouimet's banishment caused the USGA to rescind the ban in 1918, and Ouimet returned to amateur competition. He reached the finals of the U.S. Amateur in 1920 and took his second victory in the 1931 U.S. Amateur. Ouimet was a member of the Walker Cup team in 1922 and played on eight Walker Cup teams between 1922 and 1934. He also served as non-playing captain of the Walker Cup team five times between 1936 and 1949. He was subsequently elected captain of the Royal & Ancient in 1951, the first American to hold the post.

Who was the first golfer to amass **$1 million in lifetime earnings**?

Arnold Palmer, who had 61 Tour victories, became in 1968 the first golfer to amass $1 million in career earnings.

Who was the **first woman golfer to amass $1 million in lifetime earnings**? Who was the first to do it in a **single year**?

Kathy Whitworth was a dominant force on the LPGA Tour from 1962, when she won her first tournament, to 1981, when she became the first woman golfer to surpass $1 million in career earnings. She won the

Who was the first player to amass $1 million in earnings in a single year?

Curtis Strange. He did it in 1988, winning $1,147,644 after almost accomplishing it the year before, when he pocketed $925,000. Strange was the PGA's leading money winner three times—1985, 1987, and 1988—and won back-to-back U.S. Opens (1988–89).

most LPGA tournaments from 1965–68, taking 35 during that span and never fewer than eight in a season.

In 1996, Karrie Webb became the first woman to win $1 million is a single year, reflecting her great talent as a 22 year old rookie and also the tremendous growth in purses on the LPGA Tour. Webb won three tournaments and finished second in five others.

Who holds the record for **most PGA tournament wins in a year**?

Byron Nelson won 19 tournaments, including an astounding eleven in a row, during the 1945 Tour. At one point he carded 19 consecutive sub-70 stroke rounds and he had a stroke average of 68.33 per round for the season.

How many **majors** has **Greg Norman** won, and how many times has he been the runner up?

The Shark has won two British Opens: in the 1986 Open he won by a whopping 5 strokes, helped by a record-tying 63 in the second round, and in 1993 his British Open victory came in record-setting fashion with an all-time tournament total score of 267, including a closing-round 64.

185

Arnold Palmer thrilled fans with his rousing comeback in the 1960 U.S. Open.

Norman's second place finishes have been dramatic. One of his three second-place Masters finishes was the 1987 tournament when Larry Mize chipped in a 140-foot shot on the second playoff hole. Norman had a playoff loss in the U.S. Open in 1984 and finished second again in 1985. His 64 final round in the 1989 British Open was enough to force a playoff, but Mark Calcavecchia completed a round of amazing shots in a four-hole playoff to win. In the 1986 PGA Championship, Norman lost on the final hole when Bob Tway holed a shot from a bunker, and in 1993 he lost a sudden death playoff to Paul Azinger. That's 10 Top-2 finishes for Norman in Majors, with two wins.

Has anyone achieved the Grand Slam?

Previous to the inception of the Masters in 1934, golf's four most prestigious tournaments were the British and U.S. Opens and the British and U.S. Amateur Opens. Bobby Jones won all four events in 1930. His other legendary season was 1926, when he won the British and U.S. Opens, finished second in the U.S. Amateur, and made it to the fifth round of the British Amateur match play competition. Two men have won three majors in a given year: Lee Trevino won the PGA, British Open, and U.S. Open in 1974, and Ben Hogan took the Masters, U.S. Open, and British Open in 1953.

What Hall of Fame golfer had the **greatest final round comeback in U.S. Open** history?

During the first three rounds of the 1960 Open, Arnold Palmer had turned in a respectable, but not spectacular performance, 72–71–72, which left him seven strokes behind the tournament leader, Mike Souchak. Palmer started out the fourth round by driving the green on the 346-yard, Par-4 first hole; he missed the eagle putt but left himself a tap-in for birdie. On the 410-yard second, he hit another long drive, just missed the green with his pitch, but chipped in for another birdie. Palmer smashed his tee shot again on the next hole, a 348-yard dogleg left, and put a wedge shot a foot from the pin: birdie. His fourth consecutive birdie came on the 426-yard fourth hole when he sank an 18-foot putt. He settled for a par on the Par-5 fifth but came back with another birdie after a 25-foot putt on the Par-3 sixth. On the 411-yard, Par-4 seventh hole, Palmer stopped a wedge shot six feet from the stick and holed out for his sixth birdie in seven holes. Parring the eighth and ninth, he turned in a 30 for the front nine and solidified his reputation for final-round charges, with "Arnie's Army" vigorously cheering him on. Arnie's Army was a term coined by sportswriter Johnny Hendrix to describe the swarm of fans cheering Arnold Palmer on to victory at the 1958 Masters.

Even after this spectacular front nine performance in the 1960 Open, Palmer's win was far from a done deal. At this point in the tournament, Souchak was tied for the lead and several other players had a chance to win the Open, including young Jack Nicklaus (still in college) and the legendary Ben Hogan, who were playing together two groups ahead of Palmer. Arnie arrived at the seventeenth needing pars on the last two holes to win. He played the Par-5 seventeenth conservatively, laying up short of the water with his second shot and ensuring the par. Then, although he missed the green with his second shot on the Par-4 eighteenth, his neat little chip and four-foot putt won the Open for him. Palmer's final-round 65 (30 for the front and 35 on the back) was the lowest ever score by an Open winner on the last round of the tournament.

Who won the **most LPGA tournaments in a single year**?

Mickey Wright won 13 tournaments in 1963. Wright also won 10 events in 1962 and eleven in 1964 among her 82 tournament victories that also included four U.S. Women's Open triumphs.

Who has won the **most majors**?

Jack Nicklaus, "The Golden Bear," has the most impressive professional resume in golf history. Named "Golfer of the Century" by *Sports Illustrated*, Nicklaus has recorded 70 wins on the PGA Tour, including an astounding 18 Major wins (six Masters, four U.S. Opens, three British Opens, and five PGA Championships). Just as amazing are the 18 times he finished as runner up or tied for second in Majors (three Masters, four U.S. Opens, seven British Opens, and four PGA Championships).

What track and field gold medalist, college basketball All-American, and professional baseball player also won 32 professional golf tournaments?

Babe Didrikson Zaharias won gold medals in the javelin, high jump, and 80-meter hurdles during the 1932 Summer Olympics at Los Angeles.

Lee Trevino won the PGA, British Open, and U.S. Open in 1974.

Mickey Wright took 34 of her 82 career tournament victories in a three-year span (1962–1964).

She also played pro baseball in a woman's league and toured with an exhibition team of male players and was a basketball All-American in 1930 and 1932.

Babe didn't take golf seriously until she was in her twenties, winning the Texas Amateur in 1935. It was said she could drive the ball over 250 yards and sometimes as far as 300. She lost her amateur status in 1935 because of her professional activities in other sports and would not regain it until 1943. By then she had married wrestler George Zaharias and had tried and given up tennis. In 1946 and 1947 she is said to have won 17 consecutive golf tournaments. She took both the 1946 U.S. Amateur and the British Amateur.

Zaharias and Patty Berg reorganized the struggling Women's Professional Tour and set up eight events in 1948, three of which Zaharias won, including the U.S. Women's Open by 8 strokes. She was the leading money winner from 1948 to 1951 and was the biggest draw on the Tour. In 1953 Zaharias underwent a major operation for cancer. She made an astounding comeback in 1954, winning five events. She won her tenth and final major with her third U.S. Women's Open championship (by 12 strokes). Her cancer reappeared in 1955 and limited her schedule to eight events. She won her final two golf tournaments that year, then died of cancer in 1956 while still in the top rank of female American golfers.

In the film *Tin Cup*, Roy McAvoy loses his chance at winning the U.S. Open by repeatedly hitting his ball into the water on the final hole. What pro golfer hit **five consecutive tee shots** into Rae's Creek at the par-3 12th hole of Augusta National during the 1980 Masters Tournament?

Tom Weiskopf couldn't keep his tee shot on the 12th green, which slopes dramatically toward the creek, during the 1980 Masters. A fiery competitor, Weiskopf tried again, and again his shot took a dive and bath. After three more dumps, Weiskopf finally kept it on the green and putted out for a 13. It was on that same hole, usually put in around 155 yards from the tee and placed between tough bunkers in front and behind the hole, that Greg Norman found the water during the final

Jack Nicklaus, *Sports Illustrated*'s "Golfer of the Century," has won 18 Majors in his illustrious career.

Who is recognized as the first golf architect?

Old Tom Morris (1821-1908), a four-time British Open champion, ball and club manufacturer, and groundskeeper is recognized as the first golf course architect. He created the basic routings and designs of Muirfield, Prestwick, and Dornach, and he redesigned the Old Course at St. Andrews, Carnoustie, and Machirihanish—all landmarks in Scotland. Several renowned architects were mentored by Old Tom, including Donald Ross, C. B. Macdonald, Aleister Mackenzie and A. W. Tillinghast.

round of the 1996 Masters, completing a swoon that saw him go from a six stroke lead over Nick Faldo at the beginning of the round to two strokes behind Faldo after the 12th hole.

At the 1998 Bay Hill Invitational tournament, John Daly hit six consecutive shots into the water on the sixth hole (par 5, 543 yards) of the final round. Daly had managed to carry the corner of a lake that runs along the left side of the nearly L-shaped fairway in the practice rounds, but couldn't do it in the final round. Daly used a driver on his tee shot, then moved up 30 yards after that shot found the water, then hit water five more times with a 3-wood. His sixth 3-wood shot barely cleared the water but was buried in an adjacent hazard. He took the penalty drop for stroke number 14, hit his next shot into the bunker, blasted out to the green, then two-putted for 18.

Who are the only golfers to win the same event four years in a row?

Only two men have pulled off the feat and one woman. The most recent is Laura Davies, who won the Standard Register Ping tournament in Phoenix, Arizona four straight years between 1994 and 1997. Prior to her quad, the only men to do the same were the legendary Walter Hagen and Gene Sarazen. Hagen's wins are even more impressive because they came in one of the four major championships when he won the PGA

Championship four straight times beginning in 1924, when the PGA was a match-play tournament. Davies and Hagen both lost in their bids to win the same tournament five straight years, but Sarazen never got a chance to go for five. He won the Miami Open four straight times in the late 1920s; after his last win, the tournament was dropped from the PGA schedule.

Who is the **youngest golfer to score a hole in one**?

The youngest acer on record was four-year-old Scott Statler, who had a hole in one on a par-three course in Greensburg, Pennsylvania, in 1962.

Who is the **oldest golfer to score a hole in one**?

99 and ¾ year-old Otto Bucher scored a hole in one at La Manga Golf Course in Spain in January of 1985. The Swiss native was on vacation at the time.

Who was the **oldest golfer** ever to **score an ace during a Major**?

Gene Sarazen capped a brilliant career by acing the famous Postage Stamp green (the 126-yard 8th hole) at Troon during the 1973 British Open. He was 71 at the time.

What are some of the records **Tiger Woods** holds?

In 1997, Tiger Woods became the first golfer to earn $2 million in a season and at age 20 the youngest golfer to win the Masters Tournament. In 1996, after having won an unprecedented three straight U.S. Amateur Championships, he won two of eight PGA Tour events and became the youngest golfer ever to earn $1 million.

In 1995, Tiger won the NCAA individual title, and in 1993 he became the first three-time U.S. Junior National Champion (having been the youngest ever Junior National Champion in 1991). There will be plenty more to come.

Tiger Woods took the PGA by storm in his rookie year of 1996, winning two tour events and bringing younger fans to the game.

What club works best on the moon?

In 1971, Alan Shepard, an astronaut on the Apollo 14 moon mission, chose a six iron to launch a drive from the dusty surface. He claimed it went for miles and miles, but it likely landed in the Sea of Tranquility, which may or may not have led to a penalty stroke.

In technical terms, what makes **Tiger Woods** such a great golfer?

A comprehensive study of Woods and his golf-swing properties by Titleist at a testing site near New Bedford, Massachusetts, concluded that Woods generated more golf-ball speed at one of the lowest rates of golf-ball spin ever recorded—an optimum combination that reflects a near-perfect launch angle at impact. That helps explain why a man of 6 foot 2, 155 pounds, can hit a tee shot 350 yards, or reach a 500 yard green (such as the par 5 15th at Augusta), with a drive and a wedge shot.

Along with efficient method of striking the ball for long distances from the tee and the fairway, Woods is also deadly accurate with his wedges, which often follow his booming and accurate drives. Woods also has a great putting touch and superb concentration—a rare, complete package of golf skill and attention.

HOCKEY

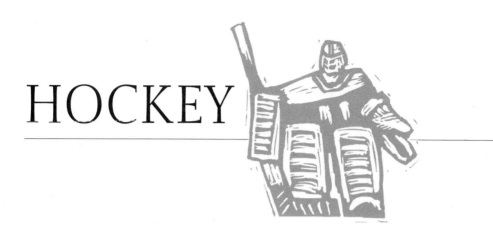

FACE OFF

ORIGINS AND HISTORY

What are the **origins of hockey**?

Hockey has its roots in several ball and stick field sports played in the British Isles, including: shinny, an English game; hurley, an Irish game; and shinty, a Scottish game. Ice hockey's first appearance on the North American mainland is speculated to have happened in the 1870s. There is no doubt that Canada was the birthplace of hockey, although the cities of Kingston, Ontario, and Halifax, Nova Scotia, both claim to be the sites of this historic occurrence. The first organized game—replete with rules—is thought to have been coordinated in December of 1879 by J.G.A. Creighton in Montreal, Quebec, for students of McGill University. Several amateur clubs and leagues were established in Canada by the late 1880s.

How has hockey developed **outside of North America**?

Seven European countries—Sweden, Belgium, Switzerland, Czechoslovakia, France, Russia, and Slovakia—took part in the first Olympic hockey tournament, which was held during the summer games in 1920 at Antwerp, Belgium.

From where does the word hockey derive?

It is generally held that the word hockey was adapted by the British in the 18th century from the French word *hoquet* (shepherd's crook) to describe a kind of stick used in shinty. The word was applied to the ice sport in 19th century Canada.

In Russia, the sport of hockey had its origins in a game called bandy, which was reminiscent of field hockey on ice. There were eleven players on each team, and no substitutions were permitted. The first public game of hockey took place in 1946 in an outdoor stadium in Moscow. Although the Russians wanted to compete and challenge in international tournaments, they had few resources in terms of coaches, players, and playing sites. They centralized their training system, bringing the best people associated with the sport to Moscow. This mindset was the genesis of the 16-team Soviet league. The Red Army Club, or CSKA, is recognized as the best, having won the national championship 31 times in 43 years. Other top teams are Dynamo, Spartak, and the Soviet Wings. By 1954, the Soviets were ready to take part in the World Championships, where they stunned Canada 7-2 in the final.

What are the origins of **hockey in the United States**?

The first professional hockey team found a home in the United States, taking shape in 1903 in the city of Houghton, Michigan. Frank and Lester Patrick later brought professional franchises to the Pacific Northwest, including Portland, Oregon (the Rosebuds, 1914-15), and Seattle, Washington (the Metropolitans, 1915-16). The Seattle Metropolitans of the Pacific Coast Hockey Association (PCHA) defeated the Montreal Canadiens of the National Hockey Association (NHA) in 1917 to claim the Stanley Cup. The first U.S.-based NHL club still in existence is the Boston Bruins, founded in 1924. Three other U.S. clubs, the Detroit Cougars (later the Red Wings), Chicago Black Hawks, and New York Rangers, began play in 1926-27.

When did the National Hockey League begin?

On November 22, 1917, the NHL was organized, and on November 26th, its five member clubs received charters. Those teams were the Montreal Canadiens, the Montreal Wanderers, the Ottawa Senators, the Quebec Bulldogs, and the Toronto Arenas. According to legend, the NHL was formed by the leaders of four former NHA clubs in a calculated attempt to oust Toronto Blueshirts' owner Eddie Livingstone from professional hockey. There had been such animosity between Livingstone—who was angry, in part, because the league would not allow him to run two clubs—and the other NHA owners that in 1916-17 the league had cancelled Toronto's games and reassigned its players to other clubs. Although Livingstone took legal action against the new league, he lost his court case.

When did **professional hockey** begin, and what leagues predate the NHL?

The first professional team took shape in 1903 in the city of Houghton, in Michigan's Upper Peninsula. Called the Portage Lakers, the team was run by Americans, but its roster was purely Canadian. The following year saw the formation of the International Pro Hockey League (IPHL). The first Canadian-based professional team, the Sault. Ste. Marie Soos, was a member club of the IPHL. Four years later, Canada could boast of its first professional league, the Ontario Professional Hockey League (OPHL). In 1909 the Canadian Hockey Association (CHA) joined the professional ranks, housing five teams that each paid a fee of $30 to join the association. In 1910, the five-team National Hockey Association (NHA) had its genesis. One club from the National Hockey Association remains to this day: the Montreal Canadiens. It was the NHA that introduced the six-player team (previously, seven players were allowed on the ice for one team at the same time) in the 1911-1912 season. In 1911, the legendary Patrick brothers—Lester and Frank—organized the Pacific Coast Hockey Association (PCHA). To

These two innovations became necessary for the sake of
hockey's television audience. Starting in the 1949–50 season
the ice surface was painted white for contrast, so that television
viewers—watching on black and white television—could better
follow the (black) puck. The center-ice red line was checkered to
distinguish it from the blue lines that border the neutral zone.

attract fans, the Patricks lured big-name players away from eastern
Canadian clubs.

Where were the early hockey **rinks**?

The first rinks were outdoors and their dimensions were much smaller
than today's NHL standard of 200 by 85 feet. The ice surface was surrounded by low boards and the goals consisted of a set of stakes without
netting to join them.

When did hockey move **indoors**?

Canada's Pacific Coast province of British Columbia boasted the first two
indoor rinks in 1911. Built under the supervision of Frank and Lester
Patrick, the arenas were located in the cities of Vancouver and Victoria.
Indoor rinks were not common, however, until the 1920s.

What was the **Gondola**?

The term "gondola" referred to the custom-built broadcast booth at
Toronto's Maple Leaf Gardens that was 56 feet above ice level. It was
reachable only via a catwalk with no railing. Canadian broadcasting legend and Hall of Famer Foster Hewitt announced from this spot. The

When were the first hockey games broadcast on radio and television?

Starting on January 1, 1933, the games of the Toronto Maple Leafs were broadcast across Canada via radio. On March 21, 1951, the Canadian Broadcasting Company (CBC) produced the first television broadcast of a game; the contest was the Leafs versus the Montreal Canadiens. As it was a test run, only six people—those in the Maple Leafs Gardens' radio-control room— actually saw the game. Regular television coverage began during the 1951-52 season. At that time it was necessary for teams to wear contrasting white or dark uniforms when they faced off against each other for the benefit of the home viewer.

most storied announcer for Canada's Saturday night tradition of *Hockey Night in Canada*, Hewitt served as the hockey announcer for 50 years. When the gondola was demolished to make room for luxury boxes in 1979, Hewitt is reported to have broken down in tears.

Who first uttered the famous line, "He shoots! He scores!"

Tha same man who made his living in the Gondola—Foster Hewitt. With a voice that was known across Canada, Hewitt first used his now-signature line during the 1933 playoffs. The Toronto Maple Leafs were facing the Boston Bruins in the Stanley Cup semifinals. The five-game series was tied 2–2 at the end of three periods. Overtime dragged on and on—five of them—with no score. Finally, in the sixth overtime, Hewitt made the call to end what was the longest game ever at that point:

"There's Eddie Shore going for the puck, in the corner beside the Boston net. Andy Blair is on for the Leafs now. He hasn't played as much as the others and seems a little fresher than some. He's moving in on Shore, in the corner.

203

"Shore is clearing the puck. Blair intercepts! Blair has the puck! Ken Doraty is dashing for the front of the net! Blair passes! Doraty takes it! He shoots! He scores!"

After 104 minutes and 46 seconds of overtime play, Toronto had finally won the marathon game. Unfortunately for Toronto fans, the Maple Leafs went on to lose to the New York Rangers in the Stanley Cup finals.

What was the **World Hockey Association**?

The WHA was a rival professional league to the NHL from 1972–79. Four teams—the Edmonton Oilers, Hartford Whalers (later moved to Carolina), Quebec Nordiques (later moved to Colorado), and Winnipeg Jets (later moved to Phoenix)—merged with the NHL after the WHA folded. Bobby Hull was the first great player to change leagues. Gordie Howe played in the league for six seasons, including stints with his sons, Marty and Mark. Wayne Gretzky and Mark Messier are among the NHL greats whose careers started in the WHA.

The Stanley Cup is well known as the NHL's championship trophy. What was the name of the **trophy awarded to the WHA's championship team** and who was the first team to win the trophy?

The Avco Cup, sponsored by Avco Financial Services was won by the New England Whalers in the WHA's inaugural season (1972–73).

PLAYERS AND AWARDS

What are the different **NHL awards** and for whom are they named?

Unless otherwise noted, the award is voted on by hockey writers and broadcasters.

Hart Memorial Trophy: Awarded to the player "most valuable to his team." The award has been presented by the NHL since 1960 after the original Hart Trophy (donated in 1923 by Dr. David A. Hart, father of Cecil Hart, former manager-coach of the Montreal Canadiens) was retired to the Hockey Hall of Fame.

Art Ross Trophy: Awarded to the player who compiles the highest number of scoring points during the regular season. If players are tied for the lead, the trophy is awarded to the one with the most goals. If still tied, it is given to the player with the fewer number of games played. If these do not break the deadlock, the trophy is presented to the player who scored his first goal of the season at the earliest date. The trophy was presented by Art Ross, the former manager-coach of the Boston Bruins, to the NHL in 1947.

Vezina Trophy: Awarded to the goalie voted most valuable by the hockey writers and broadcasters. Until the 1981–82 season, the trophy was awarded to the goalie or goalies for the team that gave up the fewest goals during the regular season. The trophy was presented to the NHL in 1926–27 by the owners of the Montreal Canadiens in memory of Georges Vezina, former Canadien goalie.

Frank J. Selke Trophy: Awarded to the forward "who best excels in the defensive aspects of the game." The trophy was presented to the NHL in 1977 in honor of Frank J. Selke, who spent more than 60 years in the game as coach, manager and front-office executive.

James Norris Memorial Trophy: Awarded to the league's best defenseman. Presented in 1953 by the four children of the late James Norris, Sr., in memory of the former owner-president of the Detroit Red Wings.

Calder Memorial Trophy: Awarded to the league's outstanding rookie. To be eligible for the trophy, a player cannot have participated in more than 20 games in any preceding season or in six or more games in each of any two preceding seasons. From 1932–33 to 1936–37 the top rookies were named but no trophy was presented. The Calder Trophy was originated in 1937 by Frank Calder, first president of the NHL. After his death in 1943, the league presented the Calder Memorial Trophy in his memory.

Conn Smythe Trophy: Awarded to the Most Valuable Player in the Stanley Cup playoffs. Selected by vote of the NHL Governors. The trophy was presented by Maple Leaf Gardens Ltd. in 1964 to honor the former coach, manager, president and owner of the Toronto Maple Leafs.

Lady Byng Trophy: Awarded to the player combining the highest type of sportsmanship and gentlemanly conduct plus a high standard of playing ability. Lady Byng, the wife of the Governor-General of Canada in 1925, presented the trophy to the NHL during that year.

Bill Masterton Trophy: Awarded by the Professional Hockey Writers' Association to "the NHL player who exemplifies the qualities of perseverance, sportsmanship and dedication to hockey." Named for the late Minnesota North Star player.

Jack Adams Award: Awarded by the National Hockey League Broadcasters' Association to the "NHL coach adjudged to have contributed the most to his team's success." Presented in memory of the late Jack Adams, longtime coach and general manager of the Detroit Red Wings.

King Clancy Memorial Trophy: Awarded the player who best exemplifies leadership qualities on and off the ice and has made a noteworthy humanitarian contribution to his community. Awarded in honor of the Hall of Fame defenseman, referee, and coach.

Lester Patrick Trophy: Awarded for outstanding service to hockey in the United States. Eligible recipients are players, officials, coaches, executives and referees. Selected by a six-man committee consisting of the President of the NHL, an NHL Governor, a hockey writer for a U.S. national news service, a nationally syndicated sports columnist, an ex-player in the Hockey Hall of Fame and a sports director of a U.S. national radio-television network. Presented by the New York Rangers in 1966 to honor the memory of the long-time general manager and coach of the New York Rangers.

Lester B. Pearson Award: Presented to the NHL's outstanding player as selected by members of the NHL Players' Association. Lester B. Pearson was Prime Minister of Canada.

Bobby Orr, who revolutionized the defense position with his speed and scoring ability, was rated number two in the *Hockey News*' 50 Greatest Players of All Time.

Who was voted to the *Hockey News*' list of the **Top 50 Hockey Players of All Time**?

As part of the *Hockey News*' 50th anniversary celebration in 1997, the periodical commissioned a panel of 50 voters—including coaches, management officials, broadcasters, former players, hockey writers, and league historians—to assemble the league's top players into an ordered list. What follows is that numerical listing and a brief description of the player's accomplishments.

1. **Wayne Gretzky:** The NHL's all-time scoring leader holds 62 NHL records. He has been a part of four Stanley Cup-winning teams, won the Conn Smythe Trophy twice, and has appeared in 17 All-Star games through the 1997–98 season. Several of his most notable records include scoring 50 goals in only 39 games, scoring 92 goals in a season, scoring 215 points in a season, and compiling a 51-game scoring streak.

2. **Bobby Orr:** Credited with reshaping the game from his defense position, Orr won the Norris Trophy eight consecutive seasons and was the first defenseman to win the Art Ross Trophy as the league's high-

est scorer—a feat he accomplished twice. Orr's record of 139 points for a defenseman in a season still stands.

3. **Gordie Howe:** Played an unmatched 33 seasons of professional hockey, including a 25-year stint with the Detroit Red Wings. Howe held the NHL record for career points (1,850) until that mark was eclipsed by Wayne Gretzky. Howe was a six-time winner of both the Hart and Art Ross trophies, and he finished in the top five in league scoring for 20 consecutive years.

4. **Mario Lemieux:** Scored on his first shift in his first NHL game, a sign of prodigious scoring to come. Lemieux won the Art Ross Trophy six times, the Hart Trophy three times, and the Conn Smythe Trophy twice in leading the Penguins to two Stanley Cups. During his 12 NHL seasons he returned from both back surgery and Hodgkin's disease. Lemieux retired following the 1996-97 season and was inducted into Hockey's Hall of Fame without the usual waiting period.

5. **Maurice Richard:** Played 18 years for the Montreal Canadiens, earning 17 NHL records before he retired. An intense competitor, he was a part of eight Stanley Cup-winning teams. Richard was the first player to score 50 goals in 50 games, a feat he accomplished in the 1944–45 season.

6. **Doug Harvey:** Known as a highly skilled passer, Harvey was an integral component of the Montreal Canadiens' power play. He led the league's defensemen in scoring three times, won the Norris Trophy seven times, and the Stanley Cup six times.

7. **Jean Beliveau:** Captain of the Montreal Canadiens for ten seasons, Beliveau also was a part of ten Stanley Cup-winning teams. He was the first-ever recipient of the Conn Smythe Trophy as playoff MVP. In addition to his athletic accomplishments, Beliveau was known as one of the classiest players in NHL history.

8. **Bobby Hull:** Known for blazing speed and a high-speed shot that intimidated goaltenders, Hull lead the league in goal scoring seven times. A charismatic figure, Hull helped legitimize the World Hockey Association (WHA) when he signed an unprecedented, multimillion-dollar contract with the Winnipeg Jets in 1972.

9. **Terry Sawchuk:** Holds the career record for victories by a goalie with 447. Sawchuck backstopped his teams to four Stanley Cups and earned 103 shutouts in 971 career games.

10. **Eddie Shore:** Distinguished both by his feistiness and his scoring prowess, Shore was considered the best offensive defenseman of his day. Shore was designated the league's most valuable player four times, something no other defenseman has accomplished.

11. **Guy Lafleur:** Part of the Montreal Canadiens team that won four consecutive Stanley Cups, Lafleur led the league in scoring three times. He was defined by his speed and grace on the ice and the fact that he was an equally talented goal scorer or playmaker.

12. **Mark Messier:** Deemed one of the greatest leaders in sports, Messier has captained two clubs to Stanley Cup championships and was a part of four other championship teams. He has appeared in more playoff games than any other NHL player.

13. **Jacques Plante:** The goalie who popularized the facemask, Plante won the Vezina Trophy seven times. His career record of 434 wins ranks second in NHL history.

14. **Ray Bourque:** Considered one of the most well-rounded defenseman of his era, Borque has spent his entire career with the Boston Bruins.

15. **Howie Morenz:** Despite having won three Stanley Cups, three Hart Trophies, and two scoring titles, Morenz has been immortalized by the circumstances surrounding his death. A month after breaking his leg in a game, Morenz died in the hospital; 40,000 people passed through the Montreal Forum to view his casket in a service on the Forum ice.

16. **Glenn Hall:** Hall is credited with originating the butterfly style of goaltending. A three-time winner of the Vezina, Hall battled nerves before every NHL start, yet still managed to play in 502 consecutive regular-season games.

17. **Stan Mikita:** Played 21 seasons with the Chicago Black Hawks, retiring as the team's record-holder for games played, assists, and points.

18. **Phil Esposito:** Won the Art Ross Trophy five times as the league's leading scorer. As of 1997, Espo stood as the fourth leading goal scorer of all time. In 1970–71, he scored 76 goals in 78 games.

19. **Denis Potvin:** In nine seasons, Potvin scored 20 or more goals and ranks second among defensemen in career scoring.

20. **Mike Bossy:** One of only three players to score 50 goals in 50 games and the lone player to record nine consecutive 50-goal seasons.

21. **Ted Lindsay:** When he retired, "Terrible" Ted held the NHL record for career penalty minutes. He was also an eight-time all-star who was part of Detroit's famed Production Line (with Gordie Howe and Sid Abel). Lindsay spearheaded the attempt to create the first players' union.

22. **Red Kelly:** The first winner of the Norris Trophy, Kelly led the NHL in goals by a defenseman eight times.

23. **Bobby Clarke:** Captain of Philadelphia's Broad Street Bullies, Clarke led the expansion team to two Stanley Cup championships.

24. **Larry Robinson:** In every year of his 20-year career, Robinson and his team qualified for the playoffs. This streak is an NHL record. This high-scoring defenseman was the winner of six Stanley Cups.

25. **Ken Dryden:** Goalie Dryden won the Vezina Trophy five times and was part of six Stanley Cup-winning teams in Montreal.

26. **Frank Mahovlich:** A nine-time all-star who won the Cup four times with the Maple Leafs; since he was traded away, Toronto has not yet recaptured the Cup. The "Big M" was part of two more championship teams in Montreal during the twilight of his career.

27. **Milt Schmidt:** Won two Stanley Cups, the Art Ross Trophy in 1940, and was part of Boston's famed "Kraut" Line. During World War II, he left the NHL to serve for three years in Canada's Royal Canadian Air Force.

28. **Paul Coffey:** A three-time Norris Trophy winner, the smooth-skating Coffey is the NHL's top-scoring defenseman of all time.

29. **Henri Richard:** Part of eleven Cup-winning teams, Richard was a great all-around player who was a steady, but not flashy or prolific, scorer.

30. **Bryan Trottier:** In his 15 years with the New York Islanders, Trottier won four Cups and emerged as the club's all-time leading scorer. He came back from retirement to win two more Cups with Pittsburgh.

31. **Dickie Moore:** With the grit of a utility player, Moore fit in effortlessly with the Canadiens' offensive stars of the 1950s and 1960s and

once turned in a 96-point season. Considered by his teammates as a great team player, Moored helped the Habs to six Stanley Cup championships.

32. **Newsy Lalonde:** During an NHL career that spanned the first decade of the league's existence, Lalonde led the league in scoring five times.

33. **Syl Apps:** In a ten-year career interrupted by service in World War II, Apps captained the Maple Leafs for six years and became a nationwide star with exposure from the newfound medium of radio broadcasts.

34. **Bill Durnan:** Won the Vezina Trophy six times in a seven-year career. He was also distinguished by his ambidexterity and the fact that he was the last goaltender to serve as captain of his team.

35. **Patrick Roy:** In both the AHL and NHL, Roy led his clubs to championships in his rookie season. A four-time Vezina winner and two-time playoff MVP, Roy hold the NHL record for postseason wins by a goaltender.

36. **Charlie Conacher:** Part of the famed "Kid" Line, Conacher played for the Maple Leafs for twelve years, earning two scoring championships and one Stanley Cup.

37. **Jaromir Jagr:** The youngest player on the top-50 list, Jagr (born in 1972) has already scored more than 650 career points, won two Stanley Cups, earned an Olympic gold medal, and set an NHL record for season assists by a right winger.

38. **Marcel Dionne:** The third-leading scorer in NHL history, Dionne racked up impressive offensive statistics—including six 50-goal seasons—but never had the chance to play with a championship team.

39. **Joe Malone:** Played during the first seven years of the NHL's existence, and in one season averaged an unmatched 2.20 goals per game. He scored what remains an NHL record of seven goals in one game; this occurred at an outdoor rink in Quebec when the temperature was minus 20.

40. **Chris Chelios:** A three-time Norris winner who is considered on of the league's feistiest players and most intense competitors, Chelios has tallied at least 60 points in seven of his 14 NHL seasons.

What are some of the Great One's records?

Gretzky has re-written just about every page of the NHL record book. Here's a record of his records: most career goals, assists, points, scoring titles, and hat tricks; most points in a season (the top four totals and the only 200 + point seasons by an individual), most assists in a season (the top eight totals and eleven of the top 12), and most goals in a season (the top two totals).

41. **Dit Clapper:** The first NHLer to play 20 seasons, the Bruins' Clapper served eleven years as a forward and nine as a defenseman. He was named an all-star at both positions.

42. **Bernie Geoffrion:** Credited with introducing the slap shot, "Boom Boom" Geoffrion was overshadowed by other star players on the Montreal Canadiens, yet was a prolific goal scorer and six-time Stanley Cup winner.

43. **Tim Horton:** In 22 NHL seasons, Horton averaged slightly more than one penalty minute per game. A dominating defenseman with offensive skill, Horton was killed in an auto accident on the way home from a game.

44. **Bill Cook:** A scorer with renowned toughness, Cook captained the New York Rangers for ten years and won two Stanley Cups.

45. **Johnny Bucyk:** Bucyk spent 21 season with the Boston Bruins and is the oldest player—at age 35—to have scored 50 goals in a season.

46. **George Hainsworth:** The first-ever recipient of the Vezina Trophy (and successor to the goalie for whom the award is named), Hainsworth won two Stanley Cups. He posted 94 career shutouts and finished with a career Goals-Against-Average under 2.0.

47. **Gilbert Perreault:** In a 17-year career with the expansion Buffalo Sabres, Perreault hit the 30-goal mark ten times.

48. **Max Bentley:** An outstanding puck handler who played with Chicago, Toronto, and New York, Bentley was a premiere finesse player and won the Art Ross Trophy twice.

Wayne Gretzky has turned the NHL record book into his personal resumé. That could explain why his nickname is simply "The Great One."

49. **Brad Park:** A rugged defenseman who finished second in Norris Trophy voting six times (behind either Bobby Orr, Denis Potvin, or Larry Robinson—all listed above), Park led his Rangers and Bruins teams to playoff in each season of his 17-year career.

50. **Jari Kurri:** The Finnish winger joined an elite group when he reached the 600-goal plateau during the 1997–98 season as a member of the Colorado Avalanche. A member of five Stanley Cup-winning teams, Kurri led the league in postseason goal-scoring four times.

The NHL has been known throughout its history for the colorful **nicknames** of its players, lines, coaches, teams, etc. Some of the most unique, personal nicknames over the years include The Flower, The Rat, The Great One, The Roadrunner, The Golden Jet, The Rocket, The Hammer, and The Pocket Rocket. Who were the players to whom these monikers referred?

The Flower was the Montreal Canadiens' Guy Lafleur: it was the literal English translation of his name. The name Rat was an honest, if disparaging, nod to Ken Linesman's feisty style of play. The Great One is none other than Wayne Gretzky, the NHL's all-time leading scorer. The Roadrunner, Yvan Cournoyer, was so named because of his speed. Bobby Hull was dubbed the Golden Jet because of both his blond hair and skating speed. Due to his quick acceleration, the Montreal Canadiens' Maurice Richard was christened The Rocket by his teammates. Dave Schultz's numerous fisticuffs earned him the label of The Hammer. As a member of Philadelphia's Broad Street Bullies, Schultz led the league in penalty minutes during the 1973–74 season. The Pocket Rocket was the logical name for Henri Richard, the younger—and smaller—brother of Maurice Richard.

What NHL all-time great had his **most productive season after turning 40**?

Gordie Howe reached the 100-point plateau the only time in his NHL career during the 1968–69 season (he turned 41 as the season ended).

Gordie Howe, one of hockey's all-time greats, had his most productive season after he turned 40.

Previous to that season Howe had scored 703 goals, 1,624 assists, and 2,327 points. In 1968–69 he tallied 44 goals and added 59 assists.

How many NHL All-Star games did Gordie Howe appear in?

"Mr. Hockey" appeared in an astounding 23 All-Star games. He was 51 years old when he played in his last All-Star game in 1980. The game, played at the Joe Louis Arena in Detroit featured the largest crowd ever to watch an NHL game at that time.

Who are the only NHL **goaltenders to score a goal**?

Philadelphia Flyer netminder Ron Hextall made history on December 8, 1987, when he became the first goalie to successfully shoot a puck into the opposition's net. Chris Osgood of the Detroit Red Wings joined Hextall in the record books when he scored an empty-net goal against the Hartford Whalers on March 6, 1996. Another goaltender, Billy Smith of the New York Islanders, is credited with scoring a goal, but this feat occurred on a technicality: Smith was the last Islander player to touch the puck before Colorado's Rob Ramage accidentally put the puck into his own team's net during a game on November 28, 1979.

What team featured the **Punch Line** and who were its members?

The Montreal Canadiens were the home team of this line, formed in the 1943-44 season, that consisted of Toe Blake, Elmer Lach, and Maurice Richard.

What team boasted the **Kid Line** and who were its members?

The Toronto Maple Leafs dubbed the forward line of 19-year-old Charlie Conacher, 23-year-old Joe Primeau, and 18-year-old Harvey "Busher" Jackson the Kid Line. Formed midway through the 1929-30 season, this trio is considered the league's first superstar unit. In the 1931–32 season, they finished first (Jackson), second (Primeau), and fourth (Conacher) in overall league scoring.

What players formed the NHL's Production Line?

The Detroit Red Wings line of Gordie Howe, Sid Abel, and Ted Lindsay was formed on November 1, 1947, and played together through the 1951-52 campaign. The trio reigned as the highest-scoring forward unit in the NHL in the early 1950s. The name was also a reference to the city's automotive industry, which Henry Ford had revolutionized by implementing the assembly line.

What players made up the famed "French Connection" line?

Gilbert Perreault, Richard Martin, and Rene Robert formed the high scoring line that would help take the Buffalo Sabres to the Stanley Cup finals in 1975, a mere five years after entering the league. The Sabres have not reached the finals since.

Who made up the Soviet Union's KLM Line?

This famous international unit of Vladimir Krutov, Igor Larionov, and Sergei Makarov was christened the KLM line, based upon the players' initials. After stellar international and Olympic careers, all three forwards were drafted by NHL teams. Krutov was a pick of the Vancouver Canucks; Larionov was also picked up by Vancouver in the eleventh round (214th overall) of the 1985 NHL Entry Draft; and Makarov was Calgary's 14th choice (231st overall) in 1983.

Who was the first non-North American to be voted into Hockey's Hall of Fame?

Vladislav Tretiak, a Russian goalie and later a coach. He led the Soviet team to three gold medals in the Winter Olympics and made a lasting impression on those who watched the 1972 Canada-Russian Summit Series as well as that year's Winter Olympics in Sapporo, Japan, where he led the Soviets to the gold medal. He was not the opposing goalie

Who was the first American to win the Hart Trophy?

Billy Burch of the Hamilton Tigers. The Yonkers, New York native scored 20 goals in 27 games in the 1924–25 season to win the second Hart Trophy ever awarded.

when the United States team won against the Soviets in the 1980 Olympics in Lake Placid. Tretiak was drafted by the Montreal Canadiens in 1983 and received offers to coach in the NHL, but Soviet authorities would not allow him to play outside the USSR. In 1991, Tretiak became a coach for the Chicago Black Hawks.

Who was the first European to win the Vezina Trophy as the NHL's best goalie?

Sweden's Pelle Lindbergh of the Philadelphia Flyers won the Vezina in 1984–85 with a 3.02 goals-against average and two shutouts.

Lindbergh was killed in a car accident during the 1985–86 season.

Who was the only player not named Gretzky to win the Hart Trophy as the NHL's MVP in the 1980s?

Pittsburgh's Mario Lemieux was the MVP in 1988, on the strength of his 70 goals and 98 assists in 77 games.

What rookie has scored the most goals and points in a season?

Teemu Selanne of the Winnipeg Jets (now the Phoenix Coyotes) scored 76 goals and had 132 points in his rookie year of 1992–93.

Selanne now teams with Paul Kariya to form a dangerous scoring tandem for the Anaheim Mighty Ducks.

What is the largest number of brothers playing in the same game at the same time?

Six Sutter brothers played in the NHL at the same time. During the 1983–84 season, four played in the same game (Darryl and Brent with the Islanders, Rich and Ron with Philadelphia). Brian was born in 1956 and scored 303 goals for the St. Louis Blues, with whom he played 12 seasons; Darryl was born in 1958 and scored 161 goals during eight seasons with Chicago; Duane was born in 1960 and scored 139 goals during 11 seasons, eight with the Islanders, three with the Chicago; Brent was born in 1962 and scored 305 goals, mostly with the Islanders, with whom he played 11 seasons; twins Rich and Ron were born in 1963, and Rich scored 124 goals and played 10 seasons with four teams, while Ron scored 156 goals during a 10-year career, nine with Philadelphia, one with St. Louis.

Who holds the NHL record for **career penalty minutes**?

Dave "Tiger" Williams spent 3,966 minutes (the equivalent of 66.1 games) in the penalty box during a 14-year career with the Toronto Maple Leafs, Vancouver Canucks, Detroit Red Wings, Los Angeles Kings, and Hartford Whalers. Williams had six seasons in which he surpassed the 300 minute mark, and another three seasons in which he was over 290.

The 6-1, 190 lb. left winger also racked up 455 penalty minutes in the post-season.

Who invented the **slap shot**?

Bernie Geoffrion is credited with introducing this now-standard shot. Geoffrion's nickname, "Boom Boom," is said to have mimicked the sound of his hard shot rattling off the end boards.

219

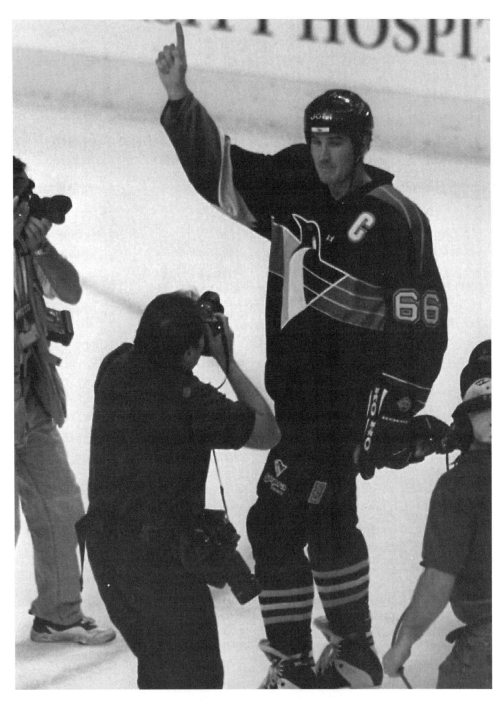

Mario Lemieux kept Wayne Gretzky from taking all the Hart Trophies of the 1980s by winning the MVP in 1988.

> ## Who was the only player to ever average two or more goals per game in a single season?
>
> Joe Malone of the Montreal Canadiens. In the 1917–18 season Malone scored 44 goals in a 20 game season. At that pace he would have scored 172 goals with today's 80 game schedule.

What **family** boasts the most NHL players?

The Sutter family of Viking, Alberta, Canada, produced six NHL players: brothers Brian, Darryl, Duane, Brent, Rich, and Ron. The first Sutter, Brian, came to the NHL in 1976. In 1982, all six of the brothers were active players.

Who are the only **father and son to win the Hart Trophy** as the NHL's most valuable player?

Bobby Hull won the award twice—in 1965 and 1966—as a member of the Chicago Black Hawks. His son, Brett Hull, won the award following the 1991-92 season, in which he recorded 131 points for the St. Louis Blues.

Who are the only **father and sons to play together** in professional hockey?

Gordie Howe and his sons, Marty and Mark, all played for the World Hockey Association's Houston Aeros during the 1973–74 season.

Who was the **youngest player** in NHL history?

Armand Guidolin played for the Boston Bruins as a 16-year-old starter in 1942. He had a nine-year career.

Teemu Selanne holds the rookie record for goals (76) and points (132) in a season.

Who was the first NHL player to become a **millionaire**?

Bobby Orr earned this distinction in the 1971–72 season.

Who was the first player to score **50 goals** in an NHL season?

Maurice "Rocket" Richard reached the 50-goal plateau in the 1944–45 season. Prior to that, no player had scored more than 45 goals in one year.

THE STANLEY CUP PLAYOFFS

Who is the **Stanley Cup** named for and what are its origins?

The cherished championship trophy is the namesake of Canadian Governor General Frederick Arthur, Lord Stanley of Preston. At an 1892 banquet honoring the Ottawa Hockey Club, which was Lord Stanley' favorite team, he announced: "I have for some time been thinking it would be a good thing if there were a challenge cup which could be held from year to year by the leading hockey club in Canada." Not long after the banquet, he was called back to England, but as a parting gift, he paid $50 to have a silver bowl handcrafted in London and sent to Canada. He named the bowl the "Dominion Challenge Trophy." The trophy was first awarded in 1893 amidst a swirl of controversy. The men in charge of awarding the trophy knew that Lord Stanley would like to see his favorite team win the cup, so they arranged for the Ottawa club to travel to Toronto to meet the Osgoode Hall Team for the championship. The Ottawa club felt it should have the home-ice advantage in the game, however, and refused to play. As a result, the cup was quietly awarded to the Montreal Amateur Athletic Association Hockey Club, which had won a smaller league title. By 1910, however, professionals vied for the trophy. The Stanley Cup is the oldest trophy for which North American-based athletes compete.

How big is the Stanley Cup?

The Stanley Cup weighs 32 pounds and stands almost three feet (35½ inches) tall.

The Stanley Cup. Hockey teams have been battling for the Cup since 1893.

During a 26-year span, 1962–1988, only six different franchises won the Stanley Cup. Who were they?

Toronto (1962–64, 1967), Montreal (1965–66, 1968–69, 1971, 1973, 1976–79), Boston (1970, 1972), Philadelphia (1974–75), New York Islanders (1980–83), Edmonton (1984–88).

In a 16 year period between 1972 and 1988 only five head coaches won the Stanley Cup. Who are they?

In an era of dynasties, Scotty Bowman won five Cups with the Montreal Canadiens, Fred Shero won two with the Philadelphia Flyers, Al Arbour won four with the New York Islanders, as did Glen Sather with the Edmonton Oilers, and Jean Perron won one with the Montreal Canadiens.

The 1973–74 season marked the first time an **expansion team won the Stanley Cup**. What was that team?

The Philadelphia Flyers, known as the "Broad Street Bullies" for their rugged play, was the first expansion team to win the cup. Proving it was no fluke, they repeated the feat the very next season.

In 1994, the New York Rangers won the Stanley Cup for the first time in 53 years; in 1997, the Detroit Red Wings won their first Cup in 41 years; what team going into the 1997–98 season has gone **longest**—36 years—**without winning the Cup**?

The Chicago Black Hawks last won the Stanley Cup in 1961. Toronto is next, having last won in 1967. Of the original six expansion teams, only Pittsburgh and Philadelphia have won Cups: Los Angeles, St. Louis, and Dallas (originally Minnesota) face passing 30 years Cup-less in 1998. Although they began play in the 1990s, the San Jose Sharks' lineage includes the original expansion California Golden Seals franchise, which relocated to Cleveland, then merged with Minnesota, then began play in San Jose after being allowed to take several Minnesota players with them.

Which teams have **won and played in the most Stanley Cup finals**?

The original six have made the most appearances in the finals through 1997, led by Montreal (32 finals, 23 Cups), Toronto (21 appearances, 13 Cups), and Detroit (20 appearances, 8 Cups). The Bruins have won five Cups, same as the Edmonton Oilers, the Rangers have four, same as crosstown rivals the Islanders (and also the original Ottawa Senators), and the Black Hawks have won three.

What was the **longest NHL game** ever played?

The Detroit Red Wings defeated the Montreal Maroons 1-0 on a goal by Mud Bruneteau in the sixth overtime of Game One of a 1936 semifinal series. The two teams had nearly played a tripleheader, as the goal came late in the sixth overtime—116 minutes and 30 seconds of play after the 60 minutes of regulation time.

That game eclipsed the old record of 104:46 of overtime in a 1933 semifinal game between Toronto and Boston, which Toronto won 1–0 in the sixth OT. More recently, the third longest game occured in a 1996 first round playoff contest between Pittsburgh and Washington, which featured 79:15 of overtime before Petr Nedved tallied the winner for Pittsburgh.

What player has been a member of the most **Stanley Cup**-winning teams?

Henri Richard of the Montreal Canadiens raised the Cup eleven times.

Who are the only two **rookies to win hockey's Conn Smythe award** as MVP of the playoffs?

Montreal Canadiens goalies Ken Dryden (1971) and Patrick Roy (1986). Dryden, in fact, qualified as a rookie the following season and went on to

What Hall of Fame defenseman played every position during a single Stanley Cup playoff game?

In the early days of the NHL, when a goalie drew a penalty, he had to serve it himself. That was the rule in 1923 when the Ottawa Senators faced the Edmonton Eskimoes in the final game of the Stanley Cup playoffs. When Ottawa's goalie was whistled off for a penalty, the Senators were in trouble. Injuries had already sidelined five starters, and the Senators had only dressed eight healthy skaters. Leave it to King Clancy to save the day. The star defenseman had already played center, both winger positions, and defense in the game, and he immediately volunteered to play goal during the penalty. Not only did he shut out the Eskimoes during the power play, but he nearly scored a goal himself, scooping up a loose puck in front of his own net and skating the length of the ice to take a shot that just missed. Thanks to Clancy's heroic efforts, Ottawa won the game 1–0 to clinch the Stanley Cup.

win the Calder Trophy (given to the outstanding rookie)—so he was Rookie of the Year the season after he led his team to the championship.

Who is the only **coach to win an NCAA college hockey championship and a Stanley Cup**?

Bob Johnson won three NCAA titles with the University of Wisconsin (1977, 1981, 1983) and led the 1990–91 Pittsburgh Penguins to Lord Stanley's Cup eight months before dying of a brain hemorrhage.

What was the **greatest team comeback in Stanley Cup** history?

The 1942 Toronto Maple Leafs were down three games to none in the finals to Detroit before rallying back with four straight wins to take the Cup.

What player won an Olympic gold medal and the Stanley Cup in the same year?

Through the 1996–97 season, only Ken Morrow has had the double pleasure. He was a member of the U.S. "Miracle on Ice" 1980 gold medal team and then went down the road from Lake Placid to help the New York Islanders win the Cup.

Which famous **coach was forced into action** during one of his team's playoff games?

In the 1928 Stanley Cup playoffs, the New York Rangers appeared to be in trouble when goalie Lorne Chabot was injured in the second period of the team's game with the Montreal Maroons. When Chabot had to leave the game, Patrick was stuck with no goaltender. Knowing that Alex Connell, talented goalie for the Ottawa Senators was at the game, Rangers' coach Lester Patrick asked the Maroons if he could use Connell as his goalie. Needless to say, the Maroons said no. "If you need a goalkeeper, why the hell doesn't Lester play?" shouted Montreal manager Eddie Gerard. Without another word, the 44-year-old Patrick did just that. During his professional career, Patrick had played goalie only once, but that didn't stop him. Somehow, Patrick made 18 saves and allowed only one goal, and the Rangers won the game in overtime. With a new goalie in place the next game, the Rangers would go on to win their first Stanley Cup.

What was **Yellow Sunday**?

The term refers to the Stanley Cup playoff game between the Boston Bruins and New Jersey Devils on May 8, 1988, that was officiated by replacement officials—Paul McInnis, Vin Godleski, and Jim Sullivan—wearing yellow practice jerseys (instead of the normal black-and-white striped shirts). In the previous game, Devils' coach Jim Shoenfeld had insulted NHL referee Don Koharski in front of live television cameras by shouting the now-infamous phrase, "Hey Koharski, have another donut,

Why do fans in Detroit
toss octopi onto the ice during playoff games?

The tradition, which has been discouraged by the NHL by allowing referees to penalize a home team when fans interrupt a game by tossing items to the ice surface, began during a 1952 playoff game: an octopus was tossed onto the ice to symbolize the eight playoff wins needed to capture the Stanley Cup at that time.

you fat pig!" Shoenfeld was suspended by the NHL for one game, but a New Jersey judge granted an order allowing Shoenfeld to take his regular spot behind the bench. As a protest, the NHL officials scheduled to work the game refused to take the ice, and the league had to scramble to find replacements. Although delayed more than an hour, the game took place with the substitutes keeping order. After a league hearing, Schoenfeld was suspended for the fifth game of the series, and the NHL officials returned to work.

ODDS AND ENDS

GENERAL

Which **coach** has won the most games?

With each win, Scotty Bowman adds to his lead—having passed the 1,200-win mark in 1997. Bowman has won seven Stanley Cups, five with Montreal, one with Pittsburgh, and one with Detroit.

Al Arbour ranks second with 902. Bowman also has the top winning percentage.

What are the **records** for most goals, assists, and points in one game?

Joe Malone scored seven goals for Quebec in a 1920 game against Toronto. Seven players have scored six goals in one game, the most recent being Darryl Sittler of the Maple Leafs in a 1976 game against Boston.

Seven is also the lucky number for assists in a game. It's been done four times, by Billy Taylor for Detroit in 1947 and by Wayne Gretzky of Edmonton on three occasions, 1980, 1985, and 1986.

In his six goal game, Darryl Sittler added four assists—a 10 point performance that is the most ever recorded in one game. On 12 occassions a player has recorded 8 points in a game, with Gretzky and Mario Lemieux performing the feat twice each.

Where is hockey's **Hall of Fame**?

Since 1943, Toronto, Ontario, Canada has been the home of the Hockey Hall of Fame and Museum. Originally, the Hall of Fame was in Kingston, Ontario.

How is one **voted** into hockey's Hall of Fame?

A person can be elected to the Hall of Fame in one of four categories: players, builders, referees or linesmen, and media. Players are selected by a special committee that includes former players, officials, and hockey writers. Originally a player had to wait five years before he was eligi-

Who is the first woman to play in one of the four major sports leagues (NHL, NFL, NBA, MLB)?

Manon Rheaume. On September 23, 1992, Rheaume started in goal for the Tampa Bay Lightning in an pre-season game against the St. Louis Blues.

ble for membership. As of the late 1990s there is a three-year waiting period that can be waived if deemed appropriate. Builders are selected by the Hall of Fame's board of directors. The media category includes writers and broadcasters; they are selected by the Professional Hockey Writers Association and the NHL Broadcasters' Association, respectively.

What is the significance of **September 28, 1972**, for Canadian hockey fans?

This date marked the clinching game of the Canada-Russia "Summit Series," which included eight games in each country. It was a confrontation between a country that took immeasurable pride in originating the sport and filling NHL rosters versus a country that, in only 25 years, had gone from introducing the game to its denizens to dominating competition at the world amateur level. The professionals and amateurs proved surprisingly well matched. Going into game eight, the series was deadlocked at three wins, three losses, and one tie; Canada had scored 25 goals, while the Soviets had put in 27. At least 7.5 million of Canada's 21.8 million population watched the afternoon broadcast of the series-clinching game (and another five million watched the replay). In the second period of the eighth game, the Soviets led 5-3. Canada came back to tie the game at five with less than a minute to play. And then, in a play emblazoned on the Canadian psyche, Paul Henderson scored a goal with 34 second to go to win both the game and the series. Henderson later remarked to Ken Dryden for the book *Home Game*, "I still talk about that goal 300 days a year...I mean, it's gotta die, but it's not going to die. I mean, it's just indelibly written in Canadians'

Manon Rheaume (in goal) prepares for a faceoff during her NHL debut as a member of the Tampa Bay Lightning.

What is the origin of "the Habs", the nickname of the Montreal Canadiens, and of their logo, the intertwined letters C and H?

There are several unofficial explanations for the Canadiens' nickname and logo. The nickname is generally regarded to be the shortened English pronunciation of les Habitants, the French term for "those who live there." The C and H that appear on the Montreal sweater are officially said to be initials standing for the name Club de Hockey Canadien. Other unofficial explanations are that the C and H stand for "Canadian habitants," or that the logo has its origins in a French-Catholic cursing expression— "p'tit criss d'hostie," meaning "tiny Christ of the host."

hearts." In 1997, the country marked the 25th anniversary of the "Summit Series" with a Canadian postage stamp.

Has the NHL **schedule** ever been interrupted?

Yes. The members of the NHL's Player Association went on strike on April 1, 1992, threatening that year's Stanley Cup playoffs. An agreement was reached, however, and the players returned to the ice on April 12th. During the 1994–95 season owners essentially locked out the players, although the NHL's wording was that the season was delayed. Play resumed on January 19, 1995, with all clubs playing a condensed 48-game schedule featuring only intra-conference games.

Another, more positive, break in play took place when the NHL voluntarily interrupted its schedule in February of 1998 to allow its players to take part in the Olympic games. The NHL did not suspend play, however, during either world war. Although the Winter Olympics were canceled during World War II, NHL officials decided to maintain their regular schedule, regardless of the fact that many players were pressed into service for their countries.

Who is the **Zamboni** machine named for, and what does it do?

The Zamboni is the creation and namesake of Frank Zamboni, an ice-rink operator from California, who introduced the revolutionary vehicle in 1949. The four-wheel-drive machine resurfaces the ice by scraping it and then laying down a thin layer of water. Previously, the maintenance of the ice during the game had consisted of flooding the rink between periods. The Zamboni makes its appearance during each of the two intermissions of a typical hockey game, but because it scrapes the ice before flooding it, the resulting sheet of ice is smoother and freezes more quickly than previous methods. This innovation improved the quality of play by allowing for more speed, because the ice was less likely to turn slushy, or melt in warmer weather.

What were the names of the NHL's **division and conferences** in the 1992–93 season and why is this significant?

In 1992–93, the Prince of Wales Conference consisted of the Adams and Patrick divisions, and the Clarence Campbell Conference consisted of the Norris and Smythe divisions. The 1992–93 season was the last in which historical hockey names were used to designate groupings within the NHL. Starting in 1993–94, the NHL adopted a generic and geographical system—the Eastern and Western conferences and the Northeast, Atlantic, Central, and Pacific divisions.

How much has it cost for teams to enter the NHL in each phase of **expansion**?

During the NHL's first expansion in 1967-68, prospective owners were charged $2 million. In each of the next four expansions—1970-71, 1972-73, 1974-75, and 1979-80—the price tag was $6 million(except for the New York Islanders, who were required to pay an extra $4 million to the New York Rangers for territorial indemnification). In 1990 the expansion fee climbed to $50 million, and those teams seeking to enter the NHL via the 1997 expansion were charged $80 million.

Which team did Wayne Gretzky once refer to as a **"Mickey Mouse Operation?"**

The New Jersey Devils. Gretzky made the controversial comment in 1983 after his team had inflicted a 13–4 drubbing on the hapless Devils. While creating controversy, Gretzky's words had unexpectedly done the troubled franchise a favor. The next time the teams played, the Byrne Arena was a sea of mouse ears and chanting fans. While not inspiring the team to change it's losing ways, his words did help at the box office as fans began to come out in larger numbers to see the home team.

RULES AND STANDARDS

Has the NHL always had **overtime periods** when games ended in ties at the end of regulation?

No. Overtime sessions were discontinued during the 1942-43 season because there were wartime restrictions on train scheduling, and trains were the form of transportation for NHL clubs.

When and why did the NHL change the rule on minor penalties, allowing the penalized team to return to full-strength following a power-play goal?

Up until the 1956–57 season, a penalized player had to serve his full 2-minute term regardless of how many goals were scored by the opposing

235

What are the dimensions of a hockey rink?

In the NHL, the standard rink is 200 by 85 feet. Olympic rinks may legally reach a length of 200 feet and width of 98.5 feet. The rink is enclosed by boards about four feet high. Goals are four feet high and six feet wide. The playing area is divided into three equal-sized zones, set off by the blue lines. The center red line divides the rink into halves. The five face-off circles each have a 15-foot radius.

team. The rule was changed because the Montreal Canadiens had such a powerhouse power-play unit that they frequently scored two or more goals during a power play, with a unit that featured Hall of Famers Jean Beliveau, Maurice "Rocket" Richard, Boom Boom Geoffrion, Bert Olmsted, and Dickie Moore, among others. Three of those players finished among the top four in league scoring during the 1955-56 season, and a fourth finished seventh (Beliveau led the league in goals and points, Richard tied for second in goals and finished third in points, Olmstead led the league in assists and finished fourth in points, and Geoffrion finished fifth in goals and seventh in points).

Who is the only member of an NHL team who can't serve as **captain**?

According to rule 14d of the NHL rule book, no goaltender is allowed to be either a captain or alternate captain. This rule came into effect in the late 1940s. Bill Durnan of the Montreal Canadiens was the last goaltender to serve as a captain of his team, a position he held during the 1947-48 season.

What are some **rule changes** under consideration for the 1998–99 season and beyond by the NHL?

Suggestions have been made for adopting the college and international rule of immediately stopping play for icing once the puck crosses the red

What are offsides and icing in hockey?

Offsides is called when an attacking player precedes the puck over the opponent's blue line and when a player passes a puck across two or more lines to a teammate. Icing occurs when one team shoots the puck from behind the center line and it slides untouched past the opponent's goal line; icing is waved off if, in the referee's opinion, a player on defense can play the puck before it reaches the line, if an offensive player touches it first, or if the defending goalie plays the puck. In college and international rules, play is stopped as soon as the puck crosses the goal line, while in the NHL icing is called only if a defensive player other than the goalie plays the puck first.

line and for discouraging players from using their sticks to slow, tie up, or hit at opponents. The alternative icing rule eliminates hot pursuit between a defensive and offensive player where one player might aggressively body check the other player who becomes vulnerable when reaching for the puck. The stick rule helps alleviate "clutch and grab" defensive techniques that slow action and the prevents the kinds of stick checks that can result in injuries, such as the meaningless hit Mighty Ducks' star player Paul Kariya endured during the 1997–98 season that knocked him out of the Olympics and led him to miss a significant number of games.

During the spring of 1998, the minor American Hockey League tested several possible NHL rule changes in live action during certain games. Those alternative rules include: 1) having penalized players serve the entire two-minutes for minor infractions instead of having the penalty terminated if the opposing team scores in their man-advantage situation; 2) not allowing goalies to go behind the net to stop a puck shot into the offensive zone by an opposing player, which would create more possibilities for the offensive team to gain possession and scoring opportunities; 3) not allowing players in possession of the puck in their defensive zone to stop behind the net, where they pause while time ticks away and can easily avoid possession challenges by offensive players; 4) having "hurry-up face offs," which under proposed new rules means immediately conducting neutral zone face-offs after play-stoppages instead of allowing players to skate around or teams to make line changes; 5) moving the red line up two feet, which increases behind-the-net play by creating more room and thus more offensive playmaking potential.

UNIFORMS AND EQUIPMENT

When did **numbers and names** first make their appearance on hockey jerseys?

In 1930 it became mandatory for players to have numbers on their jerseys. It was not until the 1977-78 season, however, that the league mandated that all players must have their names on the backs of their uniforms.

What other innovation, besides popularizing the facemask, was **Jacques Plante** responsible for?

A superior skater, Plante was the first goalie to leave the goal crease as a matter of strategy. Plante often skated behind the net when an opponent shot the puck into the corners. He would trap the puck and hold it in place for his defensemen. Gradually he became more courageous, skating out of his crease to deliver passes to his teammates.

When did NHL players first begin wearing **helmets**?

In the 1959–60 season, four players donned headgear: Charlie Burns and Vic Stasiuk of Boston, Warren Godfrey of Detroit, and Camille Henry of New York. By the 1979–80 season, all players entering the NHL were required to wear helmets.

Who was the first goaltender
to wear a mask during an NHL game?

Although Jacques Plante is credited with popularizing the facemask by proving that it did not adversely affect his play (he won the Vezina Trophy and Stanley Cup the year he began wearing it), he was actually the second goalie to don a mask when he took to the ice in one on November 1, 1959. Almost 30 years earlier, in 1930, Montreal Maroon goalie Clint Benedict wore a leather facemask during an NHL game in the hopes of protecting his broken nose from further damage.

Who was the **last helmetless player** in the NHL?

Craig MacTavish entered the league before the 1979–80 season and went hatless his entire career, which ended when he retired after the 1996–97 season.

COLLEGE HOCKEY

Who are some of the **great NCAA players** of all time?

During the 50th NCAA Tournament in 1997, the NCAA unveiled its All-Time Tournament team—21 players elected by a group of current Division I coaches, past coaches who participated in the NCAA Tournament, and members of the Division I Hockey Committee. Players named had to have participated in at least one tournament. The team included the following players with their university and year(s) in the tournament in parentheses:

Forwards
Tony Amonte (Boston University, 1981, 1983)
Lou Angotti (Michigan Tech, 1960, 1962)

239

Which teams have won the most NCAA hockey championship?

The U.S. Division I Hockey championship has been played since 1948. Through 1997, Michigan leads with eight championships, followed by North Dakota (six), Denver and Wisconsin (five), and Boston University (four). Lake Superior State, Michigan Tech and Minnesota have won three times, Colorado College, Cornell, Michigan State, and Renneslaer Polytechnic Intsitute each took the title twice.

Red Berenson (Michigan, 1962)
Bill Cleary (Harvard, 1955)
Tony Hrkac (North Dakota, 1987)
Paul Kariya (Maine, 1993)
Bill Masterson (Denver 1960–61)
John Matchetts (Michigan, 1951, 1953)
John Mayasich (Minnesota, 1954–54)
Jim Montgomery (Maine, 1990–93)
Tom Rendall (Michigan, 1955–57)
Phil Sykes (North Dakota, 1979–80, 1982).

Defensemen
Chris Chelios (Wisconsin, 1982–83)
Bruce Driver (Wisconsin, 1981–83)
George Konik (Denver, 1960–61)
Don Lodboa (Cornell, 1970)
Keith Magnuson (Denver, 1968–69)
Jack O'Callahan (Boston University, 1976–78).

Goalies
Marc Behrend (Wisconsin, 1981, 1983)
Ken Dryden (Cornell, 1967–69)
Chris Terreri (Providence, 1983, 1985)

What are the major **awards given to college players**?

The Hobey Baker Award has been given annually since 1981 to honor the outstanding college hockey player of the year. Hobey Baker was a Princeton hockey and football star killed in World War I. A Most Outstanding Player award is given annually for each NCAA tournament.

OLYMPICS

GENERAL

What are the **origins of the Olympic games**?

The Olympian Games date from 776 BC as one the four great national festivals of the ancient Greeks. The Olympian Games were celebrated in the summer every four years in the sanctuary of Zeus at Olympia. Greek city-states sent delegations to compete with one another and to celebrate athletic feats. The competitions included footraces, wrestling, boxing, and the pancratium (a combination of wrestling and boxing), horse racing (with owners competing as jockeys), the pentathlon (a series of five events described below). The victors were awarded crowns of wild olive. The Olympian Games were stopped late in the fourth century AD by the Roman emperor Theodosius I.

The Games were revived in Athens, Greece, in 1896. French educator Pierre de Coubertin had proposed the resumption as a means to promote a more peaceful world. The 1896 games featured summer events (the Winter Olympics was established in 1924). About 300 athletes competed in 43 events in nine sports. More than 10,000 athletes from more than 190 countries competed in 271 events in 29 different sports during the 1996 Summer Olympics in Atlanta, Georgia.

When did badminton become an Olympic sport, and what are its origins?

Badminton was a demonstration sport in 1972, an exhibition sport in 1988, and a full medal sport in 1992. Badminton most certainly began on the Asian continent, but the exact origins are unknown. In 5th-century BC China the game of *Ti Jian Zi*, or shuttlecock kicking, was played, and the modern version of badminton can be traced to India, where *poona* matches were contested during the 1800s. British military officers stationed in India during that time became interested in *poona* because of its similarities to lawn tennis. The officers brought the game with them when they returned home. The game became a popular pastime on the Gloucestershire estate of the Duke of Beaufort, beginning at a party he gave in 1873. The estate's name was "Badminton" and participants were given to referring to the sport as "that game at Badminton."

SUMMER GAMES

GENERAL

What is the world's **fastest racket sport**?

Competitive badminton is ranked as the world's fastest racket sport, featuring shuttlecocks zooming off the surface of lightweight rackets at speeds approaching 200 miles per hour. Players require dexterity and lightning-quick reflexes. Like the backyard version of badminton, the Olympic event involves hitting a shuttlecock (the bird) over a net with a racket.

The shuttlecock weighs less than two ounces and is just under three inches in length. The bird is constructed of 16 goose feathers, taken from the identical wing of four different geese to ensure that the shuttle flies true.

The base where the shuttle is struck is cork wrapped in kid leather. The accuracy and speed of the bird is paramount: hidden inside is a small metal screw that may be adjusted for weight and altitude considerations.

What are the three **weapons used in fencing** competitions?

The foil is the sword of choice for the majority of fencers. Designed as a training weapon, the foil still serves as the introductory weapon for virtually all fencers. However, it should not be regarded only as a beginner's weapon: the foil is often said to be the most difficult of the three to master.

Foils feature four-sided blades, rectangular in cross-section, a circular hand guard, and a handle that can vary according to the preference of the individual fencer. A foil can reach up to 1100 millimeters (43.307 inches) in total length and up to 500 grams (17.637 ounces) in weight, although the modern emphasis on quickness leads competitors to favor much lighter foils.

The épée (pronounced *eh*-pay in English, or eh-*pay* in proper French), like the foil, is a thrusting weapon only and is the same length as the foil. But the épée is considerably heavier, weighing up to 770 grams (27.16 ounces). The blade of an épée is triangular in cross section, making it quite a bit stiffer than a foil, and its hand guard is significantly larger.

The sabre is the only weapon that can score points by cutting, or slicing, in addition to thrusting. Its blade is V-shaped and narrow, fairly stiff when used with a cutting motion but quite flexible in the flat plane (that is, when moved side to side). The maximum overall length of the sabre is 1050 millimeters (41.338 inches) and it has the same maximum weight as the foil. While in the *en guard*, or "ready," position, a foil or épée fencer's arm is generally in line with the blade, while the sabre is held perpendicular to the arm. As a result, the sabre's hand guard sweeps around the back of the hand to the pommel and protects the fencer's knuckles against cuts.

What does one watch for in **fencing** competitions?

Foil: Foil fencing is characterized by a group of "conventions," rules that have evolved from the desire to make the sport resemble a real sword

How is scoring determined in Olympic judo?

After a ceremonial bow, the contestants await the referee's command of "*hajme*," which means "begin fighting." Olympic matches last 10 minutes and are won by a single point, which may be scored if one contestant throws his or her opponent to the mat so that the opponent's back strikes the canvas. If the throw is executed with perfect form, a point is awarded and the match is over. If the form is not perfect, half a point may be awarded; another half can be gained by holding the opponent on the mat 20 seconds. Thirty seconds of holding is worth a full point as well.

If no point is scored in the full 10 minutes, the decision is up to the referee and judges. An extra three minutes of competition may be held at the judges' request.

---

fight as closely as possible. Once an attack has been started, the defender must neutralize, or "parry" the thrust before beginning a counterattack. If a defender attacks into an attack (a very dangerous and foolhardy move that could, in a real duel, result in the death of both opponents), that defender does not score a legal touch. The determination of "right of way" is made by a tournament official called the president or director.

Épée: Since the épée evolved from dueling weapons, and since the object of many duels was to draw first blood and not necessarily deliver a fatal thrust, the épée has no invalid target. Hits from head to toe count as touches. It is, therefore, the simplest of the three weapons to follow in a bout, and it was the first of the three fencing competitions to be electrified—by adding a rudimentary plunger on the end of the blade. The only thing remotely sophisticated about electric épée equipment is its ability to "lock out" a second light within a split second, thus eliminating constant simultaneous touches and, incidentally, making this the easiest type of fencing for the novice viewer to understand: The light signals a point.

Sabre: Having evolved from the cavalry sabre, the fencing sabre takes as its target area the entire body above the waist, the most logical targets for a mounted warrior. As in foil competition, sabre bouts are regulated by conventions, with the same right-of-way rule in effect. Unlike foil and épée bouts, however, sabre matches until very recently were officiated manually, since this weapon proved to be the most complicated to electrify. The director presided over the bout with four judges watching for touches. But new advances in technology have finally allowed the sabre to catch up with the other weapons, and in the 1992 Olympic sabre matches were officiated with the aid of electrical equipment for the first time.

Sabre fencing is often considered the most exciting of the three weapons to watch. Since the sabre offers a wider variety of targets than the foil, as well as cutting attacks not possible with either the foil or the épée, sabre movements tend to be noisier and more flamboyant. The movements are also larger than the quick maneuvers of the other competitions, making sabre bouts easier for casual fans to enjoy.

What Summer Olympic athletes later became **U.S. Congressmen**?

Senator Bill Bradley (D-New Jersey), elected to Congress in 1978, played on the 1964 gold-medal basketball team in Tokyo. Bradley, a three-time All-American at Princeton and a Rhodes scholar, went on to play for the NBA New York Knicks. He averaged 10.1 points per game for the U.S. team in 1964.

Representative Tom McMillen (D-Maryland) was elected to Congress in 1986 and served six years. McMillen averaged 7.6 points and 4.3 rebounds for the 1972 silver-medal team that suffered a crushing, controversial, last-second defeat to the Soviets, 51–50, in Munich. McMillen played college hoops at Maryland, was a Rhodes scholar, and played in the NBA for 11 years, with stops in Buffalo, New York, Atlanta, and Washington. His book *Out of Bounds*, a critique of professional and youth sports, was published in 1992, and in 1993 he was named co-chairperson (with fellow Olympian Florence Griffith Joyner) of the President's Council on Physical Fitness.

Ben Nighthorse Campbell (R-Colorado) was elected to the House as a Democrat in 1986 and to the Senate in 1992. In 1995, he switched par-

What Olympic gold medalists
went on to become professional prizefight champions?

Among the most noted are Floyd Patterson (1952, middle-weight gold), Muhammad Ali, then known as Cassius Clay (1960, light heavyweight gold), Joe Frazier (1964, heavyweight gold), Sugar Ray Leonard (1976, light welterweight gold), brothers Michael (1976, middleweight gold) and Leon Spinks (1976, light heavyweight gold), Pernell Whitaker (1984, lightweight gold), Mark Breland (1984, welterweight gold), Virgil Hill (1984, middleweight silver), Evander Holyfield (1984, light heavyweight bronze), Riddick Bowe (1988, super heavyweight silver), and Oscar De La Hoya (1992, lightweight gold).

ties to become a Republican. Campbell, a member of the Black Belt Hall of Fame in Burbank, California, captained the 1964—and first—U.S. Olympic judo team.

What made New Zealand **archer Neroli Fairhall** different from all other athletes competing in Olympic history?

Competing in the 1984 Olympics, she was the first Olympic athlete to perform from a wheelchair.

BOXING

What was early **Olympic boxing** like?

It is unclear what kind of boxing was contested during the early Olympics, but in 688 BC, during the 23rd Ancient Olympiad, the boxers wore headgear and wrapped their fists with long leather thongs known as *caestus* to protect their hands and increase the power of their punches. The fights were not divided into rounds; the boxers fought until one combatant dropped or conceded by raising a fist in the air.

Swimming and Diving

How is scoring determined in **diving**?

There are seven judges in Olympic diving contests. After each dive, each judge determines the point total for the dive on a scale of 0 (lowest) to 10 (highest), in half or whole point increments. The seven point scores are displayed and the highest and lowest scores are eliminated. The remaining five scores are totaled and then multiplied by the degree of difficulty. The result is reduced by $\frac{3}{5}$ (0.6), in keeping with the tradition that a diver's score comes from three judges.

For example, a dive earns scores of 6–5–5–5–5–5–4. The sum, after high (6) and low (4) scores are eliminated, is 25. Let's say the degree of difficulty is 2.0: 25 x 2 = 50, 50 x 0.6 = 30—the score for the dive.

The degree of difficulty is a rating from 1.1 to 3.5. for executing a specific dive. Beginning with the 1996 Summer Games, divers no longer had to choose their dives from a list that had set degrees of difficulty. Instead, they can create their own dives using the different categories— forward, reverse, or twisting. With the new dives, competitors can potentially raise their scoring ability, since they are choosing as much difficulty as they desire.

At the beginning of a dive, the diver's body should be straight, head erect, heels together and arms straight to the sides. Once the diver stands on the front end of the board to perform a standing dive, the judges assume the dive has begun. The parts of each dive are analyzed and evaluated by the judges.

Who is considered the **greatest diver of the late 20th century**?

Greg Louganis had a record-breaking two gold medals in each of two successive Olympic diving competitions, an unprecedented platform

What are the Olympic medley swimming competitions?

The individual medley features all four competitive strokes. The swimmer begins with the butterfly, changes to the backstroke for another quarter, then breaststroke, and finally finishes with the freestyle. The new "no-touch" backstroke turn may not be used in the backstroke to breaststroke exchange in an individual medley race. Both men and women swim 200m and 400m individual medleys.

In the medley relay, all four strokes are swum by four different swimmers, covering 100m each. No swimmer may swim more than one leg of the relay, which is swum in backstroke, breaststroke, butterfly, then freestyle order. The men and women each compete in their own 400m race. An important part of any relay race is the exchange between the swimmer in the water and the next swimmer on the relay team. In a perfect exchange, the finishing swimmer's hand will alight on the touch pad at the same time as the starting swimmer's feet are still just touching the starting block, with the body extended over the water in the last instant before takeoff.

score of more than 700 points, and gold-medal success in every major national and international diving event he entered during the 1980s.

Though he couldn't compete in the 1980 Olympics in Moscow, which the United States and other Western nations boycotted to protest the Soviet invasion of Afghanistan, he had already begun building his reputation as the greatest diver in the world.

Having won twenty-six U.S. championships, four Pan American events, and three world championships, Louganis was clearly favored to win the platform and springboard diving contests in the 1984 Olympic Games. Louganis won gold medals in both events (becoming the first man to do so in fifty-six years). He won the springboard competition by more than ninety points over the silver medalist, and he set a record for points scored in the platform event.

Four years later, at the Summer Olympics in Seoul, Louganis' competitive edge was complicated by physical problems, including an injured wrist, a fever, and a three-inch head wound he sustained by striking the springboard during a preliminary competition dive. Nonetheless, Louganis finished the springboard event and won the gold, and he performed a superior final platform dive, which ensured him that gold medal, too. For his gutsy performance at the 1988 Olympics, Louganis was also given the Olympic Spirit Award.

What are the different **swimming styles** used in Olympic competition?

In the freestyle, competitors may use any stroke they wish, and their wish is usually the Australian crawl, characterized by the alternate overhand motion of the arms. Individual freestyle events for men and women include 50m, 100m, 200m, and 400m. Women also swim an 800m individual race, while the men engage in a 1500m event. Additionally, both women and men swim 400m and 800m freestyle relays in which no individual may swim more than one leg of the race.

The butterfly features the simultaneous overhead stroke of the arms combined with the dolphin kick, and both the arms and legs move up and down together. No flutter kicking is allowed. The butterfly, perhaps the most beautiful and physically demanding stroke, was developed in the early 1950s as a loophole in the breaststroke rules and in 1956 became an Olympic event at the Melbourne Games. Butterfly races include a men's and women's 100m and 200m.

Popularized by Harry Hebner of the United States in the 1912 Olympics, the backstroke requires the swimmer to remain on his or her back at all times. The backstroke is the only race in which the competitors are in the water at the start, taking a handgrip on the edge of the pool while resting on their back. The stroke is an alternating motion of the arm, resembling an upside-down crawl. Starting in 1991, a swimmer no longer must touch the wall with his or her hand before executing the turn maneuver, a change that may cause many Olympic backstroke

Mark Spitz entered seven events in the 1972 Olympics—four individual and three relays—and took the gold in all of them, setting world records every time.

records to fall. Backstroke events include the men's and women's 100m and 200m races.

One of the most difficult strokes to master is the breaststroke, which requires simultaneous movements of the arms on the same horizontal plane. The hands are pushed forward from the breast or under the surface of the water and brought backward in the propulsive stage of the stroke simultaneously. The kick is a simultaneous thrust of the legs called a "frog" or breaststroke kick. No flutter or dolphin kicking is allowed. At each turn a swimmer must touch with both hands at the same time. The breaststroke races include a men's and women's 100m and 200m.

What is considered the **greatest individual accomplishment in Olympic swimming** history?

Limited to two gold medals for his work on the 1968 relay teams, Mark Spitz stormed the 1972 Games in Munich, capturing gold medals for four individual races (the freestyle sprints and both butterfly events) and

Why is the order of competitors crucial in women's gymnastics?

As gymnastics routines become more complex and difficult, the maximum score of 10 does not mean perfection so much as it means a better and harder performance than the previous competitor's. For that reason, the order in which gymnasts compete is crucial: coaches send out their lineups of six team members in inverse order of accomplishment. The weakest competitor in an event goes first, and her score becomes the base against which the rest are compared. If the first scores well and the second a bit better, the judges' scores escalate until, finally, the top performer goes out last in hopes of building on a base now escalated to 9.90 or 9.95.

three more on successful relay teams. As if that weren't enough, all seven events broke world record times.

GYMNASTICS

How are **gymnastic** competitions scored?

Artistic gymnastic competition is divided into compulsory and optional movements. For each routine, the gymnast begins with less than a perfect score (for women, 9.40, and for men 9.00). In awarding their scores, judges take into consideration the degree of difficulty of a gymnast's program along with aesthetic appeal. Points are deducted for such faults as poor execution, lack of control, falling, missing requirements, or exceeding the time limit. Judges may award up to 0.60 bonus points for women and up to 1.00 for men. The "perfect 10.00" score was first awarded in world-class competition to Nadia Comaneci at the 1976 Olympic Games.

The individual all-around (combined) champions for men and women are determined by totaling scores on all the apparatuses. For the men's and women's team combined, the total of the top six scores on each apparatus is the team's score.

What are the different **exercises** in a gymnastic competition?

Floor Exercise: Floor exercise routines for men consist of tumbling skills that only a few years ago were performed solely on the trampoline. Multiple saltos (flips or somersaults) and twists are increasingly common. The best will incorporate three or four tumbling passes of substantial difficulty, performing twisting double saltos on the second or third passes. Unlike the women's competition, the men's floor exercise is not performed to music.

Always a crowd favorite, women's floor exercise is best identified with Nadia Comaneci's perfect precision and Mary Lou Retton's powerful tumbling. The most important aspect to the floor exercise is grace. Look for dancer-like command of music, rhythm, and space. The gymnastics elements should flow freely into each other—the leaps covering impressive distances, the pirouettes and turns adding excitement to the music, the displays of strength, flexibility and balance all complementing each other. Difficult tumbling, ranging from triple twists to double-back somersaults with a full twist, are expected.

Vault: Men's and women's vaults begin with a strong, accelerated run. The best vaulters explode off the board, getting their feet up over their head with tremendous quickness during the first flight phase of the vault—from the springboard to contact with the horse. The judges are looking for proper body, shoulder, and hand position and instantaneous repulsion. The second flight phase and the landing are critical. Watch for height and distance of travel, as well as the number of saltos and twists—usually the more of each, the higher the difficulty value of the vault. The sudden impact of a no-step, "stuck" landing creates a favorable impression. Note that male gymnasts are not allowed to perform the round-off vault, or Yurchenko, named after the Soviet woman who invented the maneuver. The women's horse is set perpendicular to the approach while the men's horse is set in line with the launching board.

Pommel Horse (men only): Considered by many to be the most difficult of all men's gymnastics events, the pommel horse is also the most subtle. Each move is defined by complex hand placements and body positions. The difficulty stems from two factors. First, the gymnast is performing moves that differ from the swinging and tumbling skills of the other five events. Second, he spends most of each routine on only one arm, as the free hand reaches for another part of the horse to begin the next move. Look for a long series of moves in which the gymnast reaches his hands behind his back, or places both hands on a single pommel. The hand placements should be quick, quiet, and rhythmic.

Rings (men only): The rings are the least stable of the men's apparatuses. Stillness is paramount and those with the best command of the event will display extraordinary skill in arriving at all holds with absolute precision. The rings should not wobble or swing, the body should not sag or twist, and the arms should not waver or shake.

Parallel Bars (men only): Although not a requirement, some of the better gymnasts move outside the two rails, performing handstands, presses, kips, and hip circles on only one bar. The most difficult skills require the gymnast to lose sight of the bars for a moment, as in front and back saltos.

Horizontal Bar (men only): Watch for blind releases, in which the gymnast loses sight of the bar while executing a salto or twist. One-arm giants are extremely difficult, and if the gymnast performs several in succession as he changes directions, or if he performs a blind release out of one-arm giants, he has performed admirably.

Uneven Bars (women only): The most spectacular of the women's events. Watch for the big swings that begin in handstands on the high bar—two, three, or four in succession, incorporating multiple hand changes, pirouettes, and release/flight elements.

Balance Beam (women only): The overall execution should give the impression that the gymnast is performing on a floor, not on a strip four inches wide. The beam is sixteen feet, three inches long, four inches wide, and almost four feet off the floor. Watch for variations in rhythm, changes in level (from sitting on the beam to jumping head-height above it) and the harmonious blend of gymnastics and acrobatic elements.

257

Nadia Comaneci's 1976 performance is one of the reasons for the surge in popularity of women's gymnastics

When did **women's gymnastics** become so popular?

The popularity in participation and viewing women's gymnastics erupted during the 1970s and was fueled further by dynamic competitors of the 1980s and 1990s. Olga Korbut injected new daring and dash into the sport in the 1972 Olympics, and Nadia Comaneci followed in 1976 with her flawless work on the uneven parallel bars and the balance beam. Mary Lou Retton, watching those performances on television as a child, vowed to do the very same thing, and did so during the 1980s.

Olga Korbut was perhaps the first notable example of a changing trend in women's gymnastics. As international competitions intensified during the 1960s, coaches began to look for younger and younger children who could be trained to perform daring stunts before natural fear processes set in. Korbut, born in 1955, was nine when she began to work out at a gymnastics club in Grodno, near the Polish border. A mere five years later she was a national star, the first athlete ever to perform a back flip on the balance beam. She became the entire world's darling at the 1972 Olympics, earning gold medals for Soviet team victories in the balance beam and floor exercises, and she won a silver medal for her performance on the uneven bars.

Nadia Comaneci's daring in the Olympics in 1976 on the uneven bars and balance beam made history with the first perfect scores ever awarded. Comaneci left Montreal that year with two gold medals, a silver for team finish, and a bronze for floor exercise. As Walter Bingham put it in *Sports Illustrated*, the youngster compiled routines "that had the audience first gasping, then roaring with applause."

Retton's showdown in the 1984 Olympics was one of the closest ever. With her scores hovering within .10 of opponent Ecaterina Szabo—and coming off knee and wrist injuries—Retton earned the all-around gold, silver in team and vault, and bronze in uneven bars and floor exercise, earning a place in the record books next to the champions who had inspired her.

Youth is an absolute premium now in gymnastics, thanks to the exploits of Korbut, Comaneci, and Retton. It is no coincidence that each of the three champions retired before the age that most people go to work. As Retton declared in 1989: "I just can't do it [anymore]. My body's strong enough, but I don't have the discipline. The girl who won those medals was a machine. Gymnastics was her life. I've found other things now—

How does the modern pentathlon differ from the pentathlon?

Five events comprise the modern pentathlon: equestrian, fencing, pistol shooting, swimming, and cross-country running. The only contemporary event of the five that has changed significantly from the 1912 Olympic format is the equestrian competition, which is now a 350-to-450-meter stadium-jumping course instead of a 5000-meter cross-country course. The scoring system has been completely revised to produce a points award for each individual performance, and the highest point total after five events is the winner. Both individual and team competitions have traditionally been held, but only the individual competition survives for the contemporary Olympic Games.

that you actually can go to a movie on a Thursday night, and it can be very nice. Just go to a movie."

TRACK AND FIELD

What are the origins of the **pentathlon**?

The pentathlon was designed for the soldier athlete and included discus, spear or javelin throwing, broad jumping, running, and wrestling. Unlike the modern pentathlon, in which every person competes to the end, the original pentathlon was an elimination contest. All participants took part in the broad jumping contest. Those who jumped a certain distance entered the second event, spear or javelin throwing. The four best in that event qualified for the sprint. The top three in the sprint entered the discus throw, and the two surviving athletes wound up the grueling competition wrestling each other to a finish. The exhausted winner was crowned the Olympic pentathlon champion.

What is the Fosbury Flop and when did it become popular?

The Fosbury Flop was invented by high-jumper Dick Fosbury during the 1960s. It involves the jumper twisting his body during flight over the bar so that he clears it while manuvering his back over the bar, rather than the more traditional side twisting. The "Fosbury flop" became the talk of the town at the 1968 Games when Fosbury won the gold medal with an Olympic record-breaking jump of 7ft, 4.25in. Soviet Yuri Tarmak won the gold in Munich in 1972, but still fell one inch short of Fosbury's mark. At Montreal in 1976, Dwight Stones, who had placed third in the Munich Games, placed third again, although the world record he had set prior to the 1976 Games remained untouched. Poland's Jacek Wszola set a new Olympic record that year with his gold-winning 7ft, 4.5in jump. Between 1972 and 1992, 13 of the 15 men's Olympic high jumping medalists used the Fosbury Flop.

How are **Pentathlon events** structured?

Shooting: Competitors fire air pistols. The targets, 10 meters away, face the shooter for three seconds, then rotate away for seven seconds. During the three seconds, the contestant must raise the pistol, aim, and fire one shot. After four rounds of five shots each, the scores are totaled. Each bullet is worth up to 10 points, with the highest possible target score being 200 points. Only twice in Olympic history has a perfect score been achieved.

Fencing: This is the only event of the five in which the athletes engage in one-on-one competition. The dueling sword, or épée, is used in one-hit, sudden death bouts, which are limited to two minutes but often end in a matter of seconds. Scoring is determined by percentage of wins.

Swimming: A three-hundred-meter freestyle heat in which athletes are swimming against the clock: the faster the time, the more points the pentathlete earns.

Riding: On horses selected by random draw immediately before the competition, the riders are allowed a maximum of 20 minutes to practice with their mount. Horse and rider take on a 350- to-450-meter course of 15 obstacles. Points are taken off for refusals, falls, knockdowns, and for riding too slowly.

Running: A 4000-meter cross-country course is run, which begins with a staggered start: competitors take their places according to their standings going into this final event. Whoever crosses the finish line first is the winner of the entire Pentathlon event.

Has anyone **won the decathlon and the pentathlon**?

Jim Thorpe won both at the 1912 Summer Olympics in Stockholm. At the medal ceremony, King Gustav V of Sweden presented him with the golds and said, "You, sir, are the greatest athlete in the world," to which Thorpe replied, "Thanks, King." A 1950 poll of Associated Press sportswriters agreed, voting Thorpe the greatest athlete of the first half of the twentieth century.

What is a **discus** made of, and how is the discus competition arranged?

Today's discus is made from wood and metal and shaped like a saucer. It has a metal rim and metal center for added weight. The men's discus is about 22 centimeters (0.66 inches) and weighs two kilograms (4 pounds, 6.5 ounces). The women's discus weighs one kilogram and measures 18 centimeters (7.13 inches).

The athlete holds the discus flat against the palm and forearm while standing in the 2.5m (eight foot, 2.25-inch) throwing circle. The throw begins with one and a half spins that leads to a sidearm release. The discus spins through the air at an upward angle, the spin helping to propel it further. Throws with a strong wind will carry the discus further, but there is no rule against wind-aided throws. This makes it difficult to compare the distances of throws. Once the athlete enters the throwing circle, he or she must not leave until the discus has landed. Throws are measured from the landing point to the inside edge of the circle.

Who was the most
dominant athlete in a track and field event?

Hurdler Edwin Moses won the World Cup 400m hurdles in Dusseldorf, West Germany, in 1977, beginning a string of 122 consecutive victories and setting a record for dominance in a track event. It was ten years later, in June 1987, when he finally lost a race. Moses won two gold medals at the Summer Olympic Games (1976 and 1984). In the 1976 Summer Olympics in Montreal, he won in record time—47.64 seconds—then went on to break that world record three times, reaching 47.02 seconds in 1983.

Too much spin on the thrower's part causes an uneven launch. Early discus throwers were strong but slow athletes who depended on pure power for throw length. Smaller but quicker athletes began to get better results by concentrating on form and spin. The winning distance for the discus has more than doubled since the modern Games began in 1896, when the winning throw was 95 feet, 7.5 inches.

Al Oerter is probably the greatest discus thrower of modern times. He favored a controlled spin in his throws, and he won four Olympic gold medals, beginning in 1956 at age 20.

What is a **shot put** made of, and how is the shot put competition arranged?

The shot is a ball of solid metal that weighs 16 pounds for men, and eight pounds, 13 ounces for women. The goal of this event is to "put" the shot as far as possible.

Because shots lose weight in use—tiny particles get chipped off when they land—the balls are weighed before each use. Additional tungsten chips can be added through a plugged hole to bring the shot back up to legal weight.

263

The shot must be pushed, or put, not thrown. The shot must not drop during the put below the athlete's shoulder. The putting technique begins with the contestant holding the shot in his or her hand, which rests against the shoulder. This is followed by a series of hops inside the putting circle, which is seven feet (2.1m) in diameter. The athlete then springs powerfully from a near-crouch, unleashes his or her arm, and lets loose the shot with a powerful push.

The athlete must remain within the circle during the throw. The ring is bounded by a board four inches (10cm) high at the top of the circle. The purpose is to allow the competitor's foot to hit the board without pushing beyond the circle. Measurement is from the point of impact to the inside circumference of the putting circle.

Like discus throwers, shot putters were originally physically powerful athletes who lacked technique. That changed as speed became important and as weight training improved performances. Additionally, shot putters were among the first athletes to abuse steroids, and many performances improved accordingly. Up until the early 20th century, most shot putters used the side-on hop favored by Scottish athletes since the beginning of the 19th century. A new putting technique was developed by American Parry O'Brien, who started with his back to the putting field to give more momentum before releasing the shot. He won gold medals in 1952 and 1956. Some putters use a relatively new technique of making one complete spin in the ring before putting.

What is the **hammer**, and how is the **hammer throw** competition arranged?

The hammer is a 16-pound metal ball attached to nearly four feet (121.5cm) of a spring steel wire that leads to grips. The name apparently derives from the Scottish and English sport of sledgehammer throwing.

The throwing circle is seven feet (2.1m) in diameter. Inside the circle, with his feet stationary, the thrower grasps the handle in both hands and begins to swing the hammer. He swings the hammer in an arc so it passes below his knees and above his head several times. Before releasing the hammer he swings his body around to build up even more force, up to 500 pounds (227kg). Measurement of the throw is from the dent in the ground where the hammer landed to the inside circumference of

What are the origins of the marathon?

Though not part of the ancient Games, the marathon commemorates the 25-mile run by Greek soldier and Olympic star Pheidippides. He ran that distance from Marathon to Athens with news of the Athenian victory over the Persians. "Rejoice, we conquer," he announced. Then, according to legend, he fell over dead.

the circle. A cage protects spectators from wild throws. Throws that land outside a marked field are not allowed.

Irish Americans won the hammer toss at the Olympics from 1896-1924. John Flanagan, a New York City policeman and Irish emigrant, won three golds, and Matt McGrath, also a policeman, won a gold and a silver. Europeans dominated the sport then until the mid-1950s. Soviet hammer throwers swept the event in the 1976, 1980, and 1988 Olympics, and again as the Unified Team in 1992.

How is the **javelin** competition organized?

A men's javelin must weigh at least 800 grams (one pound, 12.25 ounces) and measure 2.6-2.7 meters (eight feet, 6.25 inches and eight feet, 10.25 inches). A women's javelin weighs at least 600 grams (26.16 ounces) and measures 2.2-2.3 meters (seven feet, 2.66 inches and seven feet, 6.5 inches). The shaft can be either wood or metal, though the tip is always steel. For a throw to be counted, the metal tip must break the turf, and the distance is measured from the first touch-down point to a scratch line at the end of the thrower's runway.

Unlike competitors in other throwing events, javelin throwers wear spikes. They begin with a sprint down a runway, carrying the spear-like instrument by a grip in the shaft's center. As they near the line, throwers turn to one side, pull back the javelin and throw. Crossing the scratch line disqualifies the throw, and spinning before throwing the javelin is illegal because it endangers spectators.

265

How do Olympic and NHL rules differ?

Olympic hockey rules differ in several respects from those of the National Hockey League. An offside pass crossing the center, or red line, is called immediately in the NHL and play stops. In the Olympics, extenuating circumstances may permit play to continue at the referee's discretion. Similarly, play is stopped in the NHL for any offside or when a player enters the faceoff circle at the time of a faceoff. But in the Olympics, no whistle is blown if the non-offending team gains possession of the puck.

In Olympic hockey, a second major penalty carries an automatic game misconduct and a trip to the locker room. Any Olympian starting a fight is assessed a match penalty.

In the Middle Ages, the javelin was thrown for accuracy. Throwing for distance was developed in Hungary and Germany in the mid-1800s. Most modern developments in the sport came in Sweden and Finland. Throwers from those two countries won all the Olympic competitions in javelin until 1936.

Franklin Held, an American, helped develop a more aerodynamic javelin. It floated farther but sometimes landed flat rather than at the point. He used this javelin to extend the world record to 263 feet. An East German athlete threw the javelin 16 feet, eight inches beyond the world record at the time, and in 1986 an amateur sports federation placed limits on javelins that emphasize aerodynamics over distance.

How do fellow Alabamans **Carl Lewis and Jesse Owens** compare in their **Olympic achievements**?

James Cleveland (Jesse) Owens, who was born in Danville, Alabama, and later attended Ohio State University, set a world record of 26 ft 83 in. for the running broad jump as a member of the Buckeyes' track squad in 1935, and the following year he set a new world record of 10.2 seconds for the 100m dash. At the 1936 Olympic Games held in Berlin, Owens won four gold medals: he ran the 100-m dash in 10.3 seconds, equaling the Olympic record; he ran the 200m dash in 20.7 seconds, setting a new world and Olympic record; he won the running broad jump with a leap of 26 ft 51 inches, setting a new Olympic record; and he was a member of the U.S. 400m relay team that set a new Olympic and world record of 39.8 seconds.

Frederick Carlton (Carl) Lewis, who was born in Birmingham, Alabama, and later attended the University of Houston, won nine gold medals spanning the Olympic Games of 1984, 1988, 1992 and 1996 (he had also qualified for the 1980 games in Moscow but was unable to compete because United States participation at the games was canceled to protest against the Soviet invasion of Afghanistan). At the 1984 Olympics in Los Angeles, Lewis won gold medals in the 100-meter and 200-meter dashes, the long jump, and the 4 x 100-meter relay—a feat that had only been accomplished once before, by Jesse Owens at the 1936 Olympics.

Lewis placed second in the 100-meter dash at the 1988 Olympics, but was declared the winner of this race when Ben Johnson was disqualified. Lewis also won the long jump. He won two more gold medals at the 1992 Olympics in Barcelona, Spain, in the 4 x 100-meter relay and in the long jump.

WINTER GAMES

HOCKEY

What countries have won the most Olympic hockey medals?

Since hockey debuted as a full-medal sport at the Winter Olympic Games in Chamonix, France, in 1924, Canada and Russia (the former Soviet Union) have won the most medals, garnering 11. Canada's yield includes five golds, four silvers, and two bronzes, while Russia has earned eight golds. The United States and the Czech Republic have both won eight medals (with the Czechs earning their first gold in 1998), and Sweden has earned seven.

What was the "Miracle on Ice"?

In the 1980 Winter Olympics at Lake Placid, New York, an upstart group of young Americans defeated the heavily favored Soviet team on their way to claiming the gold medal. At the time, the U.S. team was composed of amateurs, while the Soviets were, essentially, professionals. Announcer Al Michaels immortalized the moment as the game clock ticked down by shouting, "Do you believe in miracles? YES!"

Women's hockey became a full-medal sport in 1998, so three countries—the United States with gold, Canada with silver, and Finland with bronze—share the lead with one medal apiece.

How is the 12-team **Olympic** field determined?

For the Winter Olympics, ten countries are eligible based on their finish in the previous year's world championships. The defending Olympic champion is given an automatic berth, as is the host nation. The 12 countries are split into two groups, with each group engaging in a five-game round-robin series. The two teams with the best records from each division advance to the semifinals, where the winner of each group meets the second place team of the other group. The two survivors then play for the championship.

SKIING AND SNOWBOARDING

What are the different types of **downhill skiing**?

Alpine, or downhill, takes place on steep slopes where the skiers follow a route and the best time wins. There are four types of Alpine races, plus a combined contest:

The U.S. hockey team stunned the world when it won the gold medal at the 1980 Winter Olympic Games in Lake Placid, NY.

Downhill Racing—skiing down a sharply descending slope on a relatively straight course made up of poles with marker flags, placed in pairs. The racer passes through the gates while reaching speeds of 130 km/h (about 80 mph).

Slalom Racing—skiing in zigzags down and across the surface of a sloping course (in Norwegian, slalom means "sloping track") of about 536 m (about 1760 ft), maneuvering through 45 to 75 gates. A slalom race is run over two different courses and the winner is determined by who has fastest combined time for the two runs.

The Giant Slalom—a longer slalom, usually 1.6 km (1 mile) in length for men, run over two different courses, and the winner is determined by who has the fastest combined time for the two runs.

The Super Giant Slalom—also known as the Super G, this race combines downhill and giant slalom and features long, high-speed turns. The winner is decided in one run.

The Combined—skiers compete in downhill and slalom runs, with the best cumulative time over the two runs determining the winner.

What are the different kinds of **Freestyle Skiing**?

The Ballet—a 2 minute, 15 second program of jumps, spins, and gliding steps performed to music while the skier moves down a smooth slope. The routine is judged on its technical difficulty and the skier's overall performance and choreography.

Mogul—high-speed turns on a snow-bumped slope, where competitors are judged on the quality and technique of turns and their line down the slope, upright aerial tricks, and speed.

Aerial competitions—the skier makes an acrobatic leap from a specially prepared ski jump; the scoring is based on the takeoff, form and execution in the air, and landing, with the judges' scores multiplied by the degree of difficulty and the lowest and highest scores discarded.

Snowboarding's cool. What am I looking for?

Snowboarding, a cross-breed of skateboarding and surfing, debuted as an Olympic sport in the 1998 Games at Nagano, Japan, with two events—the half-pipe and the giant slalom. The sport began in the United States in the late 1960s when skis were tied together to create a winter surfboard. The equipment became more sophisticated, with symmetrically-shaped boards (for easier movement) made of fiber-

What is the biathlon, and what are its origins?

Perhaps the most unknown Olympic sport as far as Americans are concerned, the biathlon is a grueling discipline that combines furious cross-country skiing with expert marksmanship. Although not a Winter Olympic event until 1960, biathlon has its origins in ancient Scandinavian society. Early Scandinavians, after inventing skis for transportation across the snowy terrain, soon discovered that stalking prey was easier on skis than afoot. Later, when survival became less of a day-to-day struggle, the combination of skiing and shooting was included in the training of infantry soldiers, particularly in Finland. This led to the military ski patrol race, which began early this century among European armies.

In 1958, the first world biathlon championship was held in Austria. The 2km biathlon was added to the Olympics program in 1960; in 1968, the 30km relay was added. The 10km race made its Olympic debut in 1980. Olympic biathlon had been an all-male preserve, but in 1992 women made their skiing and shooting debut in three events: the 7.5km, 15km, and the 3 x 7.5km relay.

glass and wood and two bindings. Snowboarding grew rapidly in the late 1980s and the 1990s, and an estimated 40 percent of people who go to the snow will be snowboarding, rather than skiing, by the year 2000.

Beside the wild colors of gear and hair, look for similarities in giant slalom snowboarding with its skiing namesake, with the boarder passing through gates. The fastest boarder who doesn't miss a gate is the winner.

The half-pipe features a U shaped course, the name referring to its shape—like a pipe cut in half: boarders ride up to the lip of the pipe, leap off the edge, and perform aerial tricks—the more original and intricate the better. Judging categories include Standard Maneuvers, Rotational Maneuvers, Amplitude, Landings, and Overall/Technical Merit. Unlike figure skaters, snowboarders are not expected to execute pre-arranged jumps or rotations.

BOBSLEDDING AND LUGE

Why is it called **Bobsledding**?

Bobsleds are named after the bobbing of crew members on straight-aways to gain speed.

What factors affect **bobsled speed**?

The chief attractions of bobsledding are the speed of the sleds (approaching 90 miles per hour) and the danger to the crew (resting on a sled less than a foot above the ground while flying down an icy, mile-long course containing a series of curves designed to control speed as well as increase it). Bobsled speed is affected by three main factors: weight, air resistance, and friction. All things being equal, the heaviest sled/crew combination will run the fastest. Therefore, a maximum weight is set for each sled and crew combination. A four-man sled cannot exceed 630 kilograms (approximately 1,389 pounds), while two-man sleds cannot exceed 390 kilograms (859 pounds). Lighter crews can add weight to their sleds before a race, but heavier sleds can prove more difficult to start, a critical element to racers. Explosive starts result in fast finish times. Racers who beat a competitor's time by a fraction of a second at the beginning of the race can finish up to two or three seconds faster at the bottom. Considering this, adding weight to a sled for competition can be more detrimental than helpful to a lighter bobsled team.

Push time is the crucial factor—how long it takes the sledders to propel their craft and leap into it over the 50-meter starting run. A tenth of a second of saved push time can earn a third of a second off the entire run.

What speeds are attained in the luge event?

Luge has been described as the most dangerous of Olympic sports, with the sleds careening downhill at speeds up to 80 mph, the riders flat on their backs, feet extending beyond the runners of the sled. For roughly 40 seconds the pressure that flattens them against the sled could be up to five times the force of gravity, or twice that exerted on an astronaut during a shuttle launch. From a spectator's point of view, it looks like a mighty uncomfortable ride. A luge is so flexible that even a slight repositioning of the head can cause the sled to veer into a wall or off the track altogether.

Because bobsled requires a lot of upper-body strength and foot speed, it attracts cross-overs from football and track.

SKATING

What are the **various maneuvers in figure skating**?

Axel: the easiest jump to recognize because it is the only jump taken from a forward position. The skater glides forward on one foot, takes off from a forward outside edge, rotates (1.5 revolutions for a single, 2.5 for a double, and 3.5 for a triple axel), and lands on the opposite foot skating backward.

Loop: take off and landing on the same floor and edge. At the point of take-off, the skater's feet may look as if they are together. The free leg is then thrown sideways and upward in the direction of the jump.

Lutz: one of the few jumps that takes off counter to the natural rotation of the edge. The skater usually approaches in a long curve, takes off from the left back outside edge with assistance from the right toe, and turns counterclockwise, landing on the outside back edge of the right foot.

Who is the United States' most successful Olympic speed skater?

Bonnie Blair won one gold medal at the 1988 Winter Olympics in Calgary, Alberta, Canada; two gold medals at the 1992 Winter Olympics in Albertville, France; and two gold medals at the 1994 Winter Olympics in Lillehammer, Norway.

She also won a bronze medal in the 1000m (1093 yard) race at the 1988 Winter Olympics. Her gold medal triumph in 1992 in the 1000m race was by an incredibly close two-hundredths of a second. Her five gold medals are the most for any American female Olympic athlete.

Salchow: a jump with a wide leg swing. At the moment before takeoff, the back inside edge of the skating foot curves sharply and the free leg is brought forward to initiate rotation. The skater lands on the back outside edge of the opposite foot of takeoff.

Split jump: the skater jumps and performs the splits in the air with hands touching the ankles or toes.

Who was the **youngest-ever Olympic gold medalist**?

Figure skater Tara Lipinski won the gold in the 1998 Olympics. She is younger by one month than the previous record holder, Sonja Henie, also a figure skater.

What techniques are used in **speed skating**?

The speed skater's body position—knees and waist bent, head lifted just enough to see down the track—reduces wind resistance. A top skater usually has his/her knee bent at a 90 degree angle, but Dan Jansen used

Bonnie Blair won five gold medals while participating in three Olympics—1988 in Calgary, Canada; 1992 in Albertville, France; and 1994 in Lillehammer, Norway.

a 78-degree bend and short-track skaters sit at a thigh-burning 70- to 75-degree angle.

The start is critical to the race's outcome. Racers run on their skates, lurching toward the first turn with a furious duck walk. Some races are decided within the first 100 meters: Bonnie Blair's wins, for example, are credited to her great starts.

While racing on a speed-skating oval, the racer's skates are almost constantly turning, usually with the skater not taking more than 10 strokes between curves, and a skater hits top speed when coming out of a turn: as both legs stroke outward, the skater creates an inward force through the turn. Leaning into the 180-degree turn, the skater pivots his left leg against centripetal force—which is why a speedskater's left leg is sometimes more than an inch larger in circumference that the right. The inward force coming out of the turn translates into speed, as the skater slingshots out of the turn with a burst of forward momentum.

A skater who's found a sweet spot seems to be hardly working: movements are measured, fluid, methodical. Signs that a skater is fading include more labored strides, elbows slipping away from the back, head lifted higher, and lack of full extension of the legs.

SOCCER

ORIGINS AND HISTORY

What is the **origin** of soccer?

References to soccer-like games date back to ancient times in Greece and Rome. In these various contests, the use of hands was still allowed. Legend has it that the game developed further after a conquering army celebrated by booting a foe's severed head into a makeshift goal. Students in England organized games in the twelfth century, by which time the use of hands was forbidden. In the 1400s, the game itself was forbidden by Edward III, who deemed it a frivolous practice. Soccer flourished again during the Restoration and was introduced outside Britain as England developed into a global empire. The word "soccer," by the way, derives rather obscurely from the term "association football," used to distinguish the game from rugby.

What are the **dimensions of a soccer field,** and what do the markings signify?

The length of a soccer field is 100 to 130 yards. The width is 50 to 100 yards. Goals are eight yards across and eight feet high. The goal area extends six yards either side of the goal and another six yards in front, stretching twelve yards across. The goal area lies within the penalty area,

The Laws are a set of seventeen rules (with many amendments and clauses) dictating everything from field dimensions to game duration and player conduct. These laws distinguish various infractions and dictate their consequences.

which is eighteen yards long and twenty yards wide. Infractions committed within this area are punished by penalty kicks taken from a spot centered twelve yards from goal. An arc with a radius of ten yards extends from the top of the penalty area to keep players away from the penalty kicker. In the center of the field, there is a circle with a ten-yard radius that opponents cannot enter until the ball has been kicked into play to commence the half or to resume play after a goal. In addition, there are corner arcs with one-yard radii: when the defending team kicks the ball out of bounds across the goal line, the attacking team kicks the ball back into play from the corner arcs. The ball is thrown back into play when it goes out of bounds from the sidelines, or touchlines.

How are **infractions** punished?

Minor fouls are punished by awarding the injured team an indirect kick, in which two players must touch the ball before a goal may be scored. More serious fouls are punished by a direct kick, in which only player taking the kick must touch the ball before a possible goal is scored. Extreme fouls are punished by a yellow card. Finally, the most extreme fouls are punished with a red card, which constitutes immediate expulsion from the game. Two yellow cards also result in expulsion.

What is **"offsides?"**

Offsides is to soccer as cherry picking is to basketball, except that in soccer it isn't allowed. The furthest forward attacker cannot be closer to the

What are the player positions?

The essential positions in soccer are goalkeeper, defender, midfielder, and forward. Most contemporary formations use four defenders, with the central defenders marking (guarding) the opposition forwards. Flanking defenders may support the midfield, funnel play towards the center, and even attack. Central midfielders usually include a playmaker and a tackler capable of winning possession. Flanking midfielders may serve as wingers to hit crossing passes to the centered attackers. Forwards, also called strikers, are expected to score. They may play back to goal and jockey for position or face goal and pounce onto passes played through the defense.

opponent's goal than the furthest back defender when a ball is played forward. Intelligent players time their advances to avoid being offsides. Intelligent defenders will anticipate play and actually move forward to render the opponent offsides. This ploy is called "the offsides trap." When defenders incorrectly execute the trap, attackers find themselves with open space between them and the goal.

What can **goalkeepers** do?

Goalkeepers can use their hands on the ball provided it doesn't come to them from a teammate's foot. They can catch the ball or punch it away. They can pick it up and punt it downfield.

What **tactics** are employed?

Tactics have changed throughout soccer's history. Early in the century, teams favored a 2–3–5 setup light on defenders and strong on attackers. In the late 1950s, Brazil developed a 4–2–4 formation that still allowed for plenty of offense and short passing. Italy, meanwhile, developed an

281

How long are games?

Soccer games are played in two forty-five minute halves totaling ninety minutes. The referee, who maintains the only game clock, adds time at the end of each half if play had previously been interrupted (usually due to injuries). If tied at the end of regulation play, World Cup games continue for two fifteen-minute halves. If tied after extra time, games are resolved in penalty shootouts, with each team selecting five players to take penalty kicks. If tied after each team has taken five penalty kicks, teams take one kick each, continuing until the tie is ended.

extremely defensive 1–4–3–2 formation with a safety valve called a sweeper playing behind the defense. Offensive play from this setup usually derived from swift counterattacks instead of systematic buildups. During the 1970s Holland played a freewheeling style called "total soccer" wherein players were required to be proficient in all positions. In more recent years, 4–4–2 and 4–3–3 formations have been most popular, with the defenders playing in unison to execute the offside trap.

WORLD CUP

What is the **World Cup?**

The World Cup is a championship contested every four years by more than 100 countries. Various geographic regions conduct qualifying rounds, then send representatives to compete in the finals. The first World Cup was held in 1930 in Uruguay, where 13 nations competed. The locations of ensuing competitions have been in both Europe and North and South America. More than 100 nations competed in qualifying games for the 1998 World Cup, held in France. The World Cup is routinely one of the most popular sporting events in the world.

What are some of the greatest World Cup games?

In 1950, Uruguay overcame their favored hosts Brazil 2–1. Four years later, West Germany upset Hungary 3–2 in another thrilling final. Brazil won impressively in 1958, thrashing hosts Sweden 5–2, with Pelé scoring twice. England's victory in 1966, when they downed West Germany 4–2, came after extra time. The foremost match of the 1970 cup came in the semifinals when Italy defeated West Germany. In 1982 Italy overcame Brazil 3–2 in a quarterfinal and West Germany advanced to the final on penalties after tying France 3–3. In 1986 France went through on penalties after tying Brazil 1–1. The same score occurred in an enthralling 1990 semifinal between West Germany and England, with the German advancing on penalties.

What are the **top World Cup teams?**

Brazil, the 1994 world champion, is the only country to win four World Cups. West Germany and Italy have each won three, while Argentina and Uruguay have each won two. England won the only other World Cup. Argentina, Czechoslovakia, Holland, Hungary, and West Germany have all lost the final game on two occasions. Sweden is the only other team to lose a final game. Brazil, West Germany, and Italy have all played in five final games, and Argentina has played in four. Brazil is the only nation to triumph in a Cup held outside its own hemisphere.

What is the **history of the trophy** given to the World Cup champion?

The original trophy was named for the first president of FIFA (soccer's international governing body), Jules Rimet. After Brazil won the trophy three times—in 1958, 1962, and 1970—the original trophy was retired and the new trophy was called simply the World Cup.

What is the **highest scoring game** in World Cup history, and what is the **most lopsided** game?

In 1954, Austria defeated Switzerland 7–5 in the highest scoring game in Cup history. The score was 5–4 Austria at halftime. Three other games have totalled 11 goals, the most recent being Hungary's 10–1 win over El Salvador in the 1982 tournament. That game also represents the most goals scored by one team in a single game and is tied for the most lopsided win ever with Hungary's 9–0 win over South Korea in 1954 and Yugoslavia's 9–0 whitewashing of Zaire in 1974.

Who is the leader in **career goals in World Cup** competition?

Gerd Muller scored 14 goals for West Germany in back-to-back Cup appearances in 1970 and 1974; the Germans won the Cup the latter year. In second place in career scoring is Just Fontaine of France, who is notable because all 13 of his career goals came in a single World Cup, the 1958 tournament.

What other **important tournaments** exist for national teams?

The South American championship, the Copa America, commenced in 1910 and has been held irregularly in the ensuing years. In recent times, it has been played every two years. Argentina and Uruguay have each won this tournament on fourteen occasions. The European Championship began in 1960 and has since been held every four years. The Germans have won this tournament three times. No other country has won more than once. The African Nations Cup began play in 1957 and has continued irregularly; in recent times it has been contested every two years. Egypt has won the African Nations Cup three times. The Asian Cup began in 1956 and has since been played every four years, with Iran as three-time winners. The CONCACAF Cup, contested by members of the Confederation of North, Central American, and Caribbean Football, has been held since 1941. Costa Rica leads the CONCACAF field with ten titles. Other prominent tournaments include the Olympics, where Hungary is a three-time winner of the gold medal. Women's tournaments include the World Cup, won by the U.S. in 1991, and the Olympics, in which the U.S. team scored the gold medal in 1996.

Who are the only men to win World Cup titles as both a player and a coach?

Mario Zegalo was a left wing on the great Brazilian team that won back-to-back World Cup titles in 1958 and 1962. In 1970, he was the coach of a victorious Brazilian team that many consider to be the finest national team ever. He was the only man to pull off the player-coach double until the legendary West German soccer star Franz Beckenbauer coached his team to a 1–0 victory over Argentina in 1990. As a player, Beckenbauer was an attacking sweeper who served as captain of the squad that defeated Holland for the title in 1974.

LEAGUES AND TOURNAMENTS

How are **domestic leagues** organized?

In Europe, most leagues usually hold between ten and twenty teams. One league is reserved for the very best teams, with other leagues also arranged based on talent. In a season, teams play each other home and away, earning three points for wins and one point for ties. The team with the most points at the end is the champion, period. At season's end, the bottom teams—anywhere from one to four—are relegated to the league that is one level below the teams' previous league. In turn, the top one to four teams from that league are elevated to the higher league. While competing in their domestic leagues, top teams may play other European teams in various competitions. South American leagues are organized in a similar manner, with the exception of Brazil, which has two top leagues. Major League Soccer, the top American league, holds playoffs to determine a champion. Many leagues conduct cup tournaments concurrent with league seasons. These tournaments, which include teams from lower leagues, may be held as a series of home-and-away or one-game rounds, with winners advancing.

What are the most important tournaments in each region of the world?

In Europe, the most significant prize is the Champion's Cup, which is contested annually by the winners of the various leagues. Since the 1997–98 season, second-place teams from the eight highest-ranked leagues are also allowed to compete. Real Madrid lead the Champion's Cup field with six prizes, including the first five! The Cup-Winners Cup is played by the winners of the various leagues' cup competitions. Barcelona is the only four-time winner of this event. The third major tournament among European clubs is the UEFA Cup, which is contested by the best clubs absent from the other two competitions. Barcelona and Juventus of Turin have each won the UEFA Cup three times. South American champions vie for the Copa Libertadores, which has been in existence since 1960. Argentine teams have dominated this tournament, winning roughly as many titles as Brazilian and Uruguayan teams together. Other key competitions are the African Champions Cup and the CONCACAF Champions Cup.

What are some of the **world's greatest clubs?**

Among the most distinguished teams is Spain's Real Madrid, winner of six Champions Cups. Real's chief rival in Spain is Barcelona, past winners of all three of the major European tournaments. Among the most prominent Italian teams is A.C. Milan, five-time champions of Europe, and Juventus of Turin, which holds a record 25 domestic titles to add to two Champion's Cups. England's most accomplished club is Liverpool, which holds four Champion's Cups. Holland's most prominent team is Ajax of Amsterdam, four-time winners of the Champion's Cup, while Germany's most successful team is probably Bayern Munich, three-time winners of the same prize. Portugal's Lisbon club Benfica have a pair of Champion's Cup in addition to 30 domestic titles. In South America, many of the most accomplished clubs hail from Argentina. Notable here is River Plate, winner of more than 20 domestic championships. In Brazil, the most successful teams include Flamingo and Fluminense in Rio de Janiero and both Sao Paolo and Santos in Sao Paolo. Uruguay's greatest teams are Nacional and Penarol. Major League Soccer's best team has been D.C. United, winner of both league titles.

PLAYERS

Who are the **greatest players in soccer history?**

The Brazilian Pelé is likely the most significant player in soccer history. His scoring exploits are astounding, and his success—both at national and club levels—is profoundly impressive. Alfredo di Stefano, the versatile Real Madrid forward, is also prominent, as is his Hungarian teammate, Ferenc Puskas. Diego Maradona, who led Argentina to the 1986 World Cup prize, and Dutch master Johann Cruyff, also figure among the all-time greats. The game's finest defensive player was probably Franz Beckenbauer, the West German sweeper who hoisted the World Cup, the European Championship Cup, and the Champion's Cup during his illustrious career. Among England's greatest players are Stanley Matthews, an astounding dribbler with Blackpool in the 1950s, and Bobby Charlton, a powerful forward for Manchester United in the 1950s and 60s. Charlton's flamboyant clubmate George Best also ranks at the top. Among the game's most celebrated goaltenders are Soviet Lev Yashin, credited with saving more than one hundred penalty kicks, and England's Gordon Banks, member of the 1966 world champions. Among female players, American Michelle Akers-Stahl is considered to be one of the best ever.

Who are among the **best players in the game today?**

The Brazilian Ronaldo is widely considered the game's greatest player in the late 1990s. He has been a top scorer in the Dutch and Spanish leagues, and he currently plays for Italy's Internazionale Milan. Fellow Brazilian Roberto Carlos, who plays for Real Madrid, is among the

Pele is one of the best-known soccer players in the world

What makes Pelé so special?

Pelé is credited with 1280 career goals! He holds the world record for most three-goal games (92) and the most international goals (97). He led the Brazilian Sao Paolo league in scoring from 1957 to 1965, with 127 goals in 1959 and another 110 in 1961. On nine occasions his club, Santos, won its league championship. Pelé inspired soccer enthusiasm in the United States when he emerged from retirement in the 1970s and led the New York Cosmos to three consecutive titles in the now-defunct North American Soccer League. He is widely regarded as an engaging, generous public figure, and he serves as an extraordinary goodwill ambassador for the game.

game's finest defenders. Eric Cantona, a versatile playmaker and scorer, has led Manchester United to four English titles, while fellow Frenchman Youri Djorkaeff stars with Ronaldo at Internazionale. Liberian striker George Weah leads the attack at rivals A.C. Milan. Argentine striker Gabriel Batistuta is a feared scorer for Italian club Fiorentina, and Alessandro Del Piero is equally respected at rivals Juventus. In England, Alan Shearer is prominent at Newcastle United, while Dutchman Dennis Bergkamp impresses at London's Arsenal. Among the greatest goalkeepers are Peter Schmeichel, whose play spurred Denmark to a stunning triumph at the 1992 European Championship, and Paraguayan Jose Luis Chilavert, who even takes free kicks and penalties for his Argentine club Velez Sarzfeld. Stars of Major League Soccer include Colombian Carlos Valderrama, Bolivian Marco Etcheverry, and Americans John Harkes and Eric Wynalda. Perhaps the top female player today is American Mia Hamm, who starred at the 1996 Olympics.

Alexi Lalas has a distinctive look for the U.S. men's soccer team.

OFF–FIELD CONCERNS

What are some of the most **disastrous soccer incidents?**

There have been many, many well-publicized disasters related to soccer. In 1967, for example, a disallowed goal in a Turkish game triggered a riot that left 41 people dead and 600 injured. In 1982, a spectator urinated from an upper deck in Cali, Colombia, and sparked a panic in which 22 died and 100 were injured. In one of the game's most notorious riots, 39 fans died and six hundred were injured when Liverpool supporters charged Juventus fans at the 1985 Champion's Cup final. Four years later, 95 Liverpool fans were crushed to death and nearly 200 were injured during crowd-control problems at Hillsborough in Sheffield.

How does the **United States** rate?

The U.S. has a surprisingly impressive history. The U.S. team played in the semifinals of the first World Cup, held in 1930, and beat highly-rated

What are some of the largest stadiums and crowds?

The Maracana in Rio de Janeiro has held 200,000 spectators. The Morumbi, home to Sao Paolo, is likewise vast, holding 150,000. Among Europe's biggest stadiums are Barcelona's Nou Camp, which holds 130,000, and rival Real Madrid's Bernebau, which handles 105,000. In Italy, A.C. Milan and Internazionale share the Stadio Guiseppe Meazza, which holds 83,000, while Napoli's San Paulo holds 85,100 and Rome's Olimpico manages 80,000. In Lisbon, 130,000 have gathered to watch Benfica at the Estadio da Luz ("Stadium of Lights"). Glasgow's Hampden Park, meanwhile, held nearly 150,000 for a 1937 match in which Scotland beat England 3–1. London's Wembley, however, held more than 200,000 for a 1923 match in which Bolton beat West ham 2–1. Seating capacity for Wembley is now 80,000.

England 1–0 in the 1950 tournament. The U.S. also played in three consecutive World Cups in the 1990s. In addition, the team has twice won the U.S. Cup, once in a field featuring Italy, Ireland, and Portugal, and beat England 2–0 in the 1993 competition. The U.S. has also fared well as an invited team in the Copa America. In the 1995 tournament, the U.S. upset mighty Argentina 3–0 then advanced on penalties against Mexico before succumbing 1–0 to eventual winners Brazil in the semifinals. The current team, led by Alexi Lalas and John Harkes, has achieved such notable successes as the team's recent upset of Brazil. The women's team has enjoyed even greater success, winning the World Cup in 1991 and the Olympic gold medal in 1996.

What is the likely **future of soccer**?

Soccer continues to increase in popularity throughout the globe. Television, especially satellite broadcasting, has made the game accessible everywhere. As the networks and broadcasting groups pump astounding sums into the game, salaries rise accordingly. The game, which has

Mia Hamm of the United States is perhaps the best female soccer player in the world.

been largely attendance driven, even into the early 1990s, will doubtless become more similar to American sports, wherein the television-viewing fan is more valued than the paying spectator. In the United States, meanwhile, participation continues to increase, especially among children. If these same children develop an interest as spectators, then professional soccer will surely succeed in the United States. Otherwise, as the joke goes, "Soccer is the future of sports in America, and it always will be."

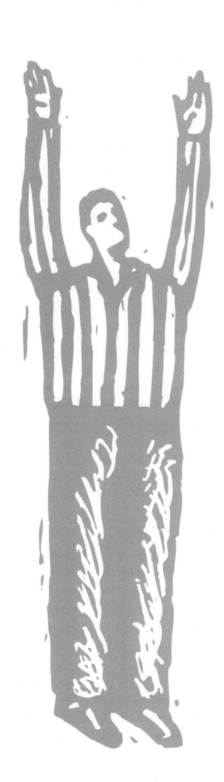

OTHER SPORTS

OFF TO THE RACES

FOOTRACING

What is the **oldest regularly-contested foot race in the United States**?

The Boston Marathon was first run in 1897 and continues to be held annually on Patriot's Day in April. Since World War II the race has taken on a strong international flavor after being won by Americans and Canadians before then. Kenyans have won from 1991 through 1997. The last Americans to win were Greg Meyer in 1983 and Lisa Larsen Weidenbach in 1985. The first Boston Marathon run under 2 hours, 20 minutes occured in 1921. Bill Rodgers of Massachusetts was the first to break the 2 hour, 10 minute level (1979), and Cosmas Ndeti of Kenya set the all-time low of 2 hours, seven minutes, 15 seconds in 1994.

The Women's competition in the Boston Marathon began in 1972 with the winner's time over three hours. The 2 hour, 50 minute mark was broken in 1974, and the all-time best time occured in 1994 when Uta Pippig of Germany ran in 2 hours, 21 minutes, 45 seconds.

What race was increased by 385 yards so King Edward VII of Great Britain could see the finish line better?

At the 1908 Olympic Games in London, the marathon distance was increased slightly so the finishers would pass by British royalty.

What did **Forrest Smithson** carry for inspiration while running hurdles at the 1908 Olympics?

The Holy Bible. He set a world record in the 110 meter hurdles by running that race in 15 seconds. The current world record was set by Rod Milburn of the United States in 1972 at 13.24 seconds.

Can a pole vaulter who **knocks off the crossbar during a vault** still get credit for a successful vault?

He can by pushing the crossbar back onto the support poles before touching the ground.

Cheaters never win and winners never cheat. What are two famous incidents of people **cheating during running races** and later being caught?

In 1980, the running world was stunned when an unknown named Rosie Ruiz came out of nowhere to win the women's division of the prestigious Boston Marathon. "How could she have done it?" people wondered. By cheating, turned out to be the answer. With only a little investigative work, it was discovered that Ruiz did not run the entire race, possibly taking the subway or a taxi to shorten the course. Once her sin was uncovered, she was stripped of first place and Canada's Jacqueline Garreau was declared the winner.

Who was the first man to run a four-minute mile?

Roger Bannister was the first to run a mile in less than four minutes. His mile, run in 3 minutes, 59.4 seconds, at a meet in Oxford, England on May 6, 1954, was bettered less than two months later by John Landy, an Australian who set the new record at 3 minutes, 58 seconds. Bannister later defeated Landy in a mile race held in Vancouver, Canada, in August 1954. Bannister retired from athletic competition in December 1954 at age 25 to practice medicine.

The 1,500 Meter Race contested regularly at the Summer Olympics and at track and field competitions is 120 yards short of a mile. Arnold Jackson of Great Britain ran a sub-four minute race back in 1912, and the world record was last broken in 1960 by Australian Herb Elliott, who won Olympic gold with 3:35.6.

A Canadian was also involved in the second incident, but less successfully. At the 1988 Olympics in Seoul, South Korea, Ben Johnson was declared the "World's Fastest Man" after he won the 100-meter dash in the world record time of 9.79 seconds. Unfortunately, the record didn't stand for long. It was discovered shortly after the race that Johnson had tested positive for performance-enhancing anabolic steroids, and, as a result, he was stripped of his record and his medal and his name was erased from the Olympic record books.

HORSE RACING

How many yards are in a furlong?

The furlong, which is a standard unit of measurement in horse racing, is 220 yards.

297

Eleven. In addition to Sir Barton and Gallant Fox, Triple Crown winners include Omaha (1935), War Admiral (1937), Whirlaway (1941), Count Fleet (1943), Assault (1946), Citation (1948), Secretariat (1973), Seattle Slew (1977), and Affirmed (1978).

What is the history of **horse-racing's Triple Crown**?

The Kentucky Derby, held at Churchill Downs in Louisville, Kentucky, was first run in 1875. The Preakness Stakes, held at Pimlico Race Course in Baltimore, Maryland, started in 1873. The Belmont Stakes, held at Belmont Park in Elmont, New York, was first held in 1867. The Kentucky Derby is held during the first Saturday in May, the Preakness is held two weeks after the Derby, and the Belmont is held three weeks after the Preakness. The length of the Kentucky Derby is $1\frac{1}{4}$ miles ($1\frac{1}{2}$ miles from 1875–1895), the Preakness has been at $1\frac{3}{16}$ miles since 1925, and the Belmont has been $1\frac{1}{2}$ miles since 1926.

The first horse to win all three races in one year was Sir Barton in 1919, but the term Triple Crown was coined in 1930 by sportswriter Charles Hatton to describe the three wins of Gallant Fox, the second horse to win the three races.

How many horses have **won two jewels of the Triple Crown**?

42. 15 horses won the Derby and Preakness but not the Belmont (two didn't race because of injuries). Zev, in 1923, won the Derby and the Belmont but finished 12th in the Preakness (which was the first of the three races run that year), and Hansel finished tenth in the Derby, then won the Preakness and Belmont. A horse has won the first two legs of the Triple Crown only to finish second in the Belmont 14 times, including Silver Charm in 1997. Through 1922, eleven horses won the the Preakness and Belmont but did not race in the Derby, including the legendary Man o' War (1920). Alydar in 1978 finished second to Triple Crown winner Affirmed in each race.

How many times has the chalk (favorite) won the Kentucky Derby?

Through 1997's 123rd run for the roses, 48 favorites finished first. Thirty-nine did not even pay, finishing fourth or worse. Spectacular Bid in 1979 was the last favorite to wear the roses in the winner's circle.

Which horse has **record times in two of the three races**?

Secretariat (1973) is the only horse to run the 1¼ mile Derby in under two minutes, and his 2:24 in the Belmont is still two seconds faster than any other horse has run since 1926—when the length of 1½ miles became standard—through 1997.

How many **fillies have won the Triple Crown**?

None. Three have won the Derby, four took the Preakness, and two at the Belmont.

What is the **Breeder's Cup**?

The Breeder's Cup has been held since 1984. Seven races are held at a different track each year to determine the year's champions in seven categories.

What does it mean to **win "hands down"** in horse racing?

The term originated in horse racing and means to win without using the whip. To win hands down has since been used more generally to refer to a win without significant challenges from competitiors.

What is the attendance record for a Triple Crown event?

163,628 showed up at Churchill Downs in 1974. Capacity for the Downs is 148,500 (48,500 seats, 100,000 in the infield). Pimlico holds 100,000 (40,000 seats, 60,000 infield) and Belmont holds 82,491 (32,491 seats, 50,000 infield).

AUTO RACING

What are the **different kinds of auto racing**?

Auto races are held on three types of courses: the oval track, which can be dirt, asphalt, or concrete, can range in length from .16 to 2.5 miles, and can be banked (high-banked tracks are called superspeedways); road courses, which follow twisting routes on city streets or courses that duplicate conditions of country roads; and the straight-line course—a strip of asphalt or concrete used for drag racing.

Major types of oval track racing include Indy Car, Stock Car, Dirt-Track, Sprint Car, Midget-car, and Sports Car racing; Formula racing (usually called Grand Prix races), Rallying, and Off-Road races are held on road courses; and Drag Racing and other sprint races are held on straight-line courses.

What is the difference between **Formula racing and Indy racing**?

Formula racing is strictly regulated by an international governing body, Fédération International de l'Automobile (FIA; International Automobile Federation), which sets technical regulations for building, maintaining, and racing many different classes of cars. Formula One (F1) vehicles are single-seat racing cars designed to allow the flow of air over and under the car to create a downward force that holds them close to the ground

What two auto racing "firsts" occurred during the 1895 Paris to Bordeaux race?

The first racing fatality—a dog hit by a Panhard car—and domination by gasoline-powered cars (propelled by Daimler engines) occurred during that 1895 race. Gasoline-powered engines finished in the first four spots, effectively ending the superiority of electric-powered automobile engines.

despite high speeds. Slower and less sophisticated single-seat racing cars compete in such categories as Formula Two (F2), Formula Three (F3), Formula Atlantic, Formula Renault, and Formula Ford.

These cars are run on Grand Prix circuits, a term that refers to the principal F1 auto race in a nation; in the United States, however, the term is used by several cities hosting annual Formula 1 races. The World Championship of Drivers was established in 1950 to honor the winner in points from the various F1 races each year.

Indy Car Racing developed with the establishment in 1911 of the Indianapolis 500 and has since become a circuit of races with the winner determined by a points-per-finish system. Indy cars are similar to F1 cars but were originally designed to only turn left since they were raced on oval tracks, while F1 cars could turn in either direction for racing on road courses. F1 cars also required more efficient braking systems because Grand Prix tracks have corners and a variety of turns. F1 designs began influencing Indy cars during the 1960s and 1970s, and since the 1980s, Indy car races have been held on ovals and road courses. Indy car circuit racing is governed by IndyCar, known from its formation in 1979 until 1992 as Championship Auto Racing Teams (CART).

What distinguishes the other kinds of **automobile racing**?

Drag Racing features two cars racing on a straight-line course—the drag strip. Drag racing originated with hot rods, modified for improved

Which legendary auto racer was the first to break the one-minute mile in a gasoline-powered vehicle?

Barney Oldfield reached the speed of 64 mph in 1903 in a car called the 999 built by Henry Ford. The next year, Louis E. Rigolly, a Frenchman driving a Gabron-Brille, became the first to exceed 100 mph when he reached a top speed of 103 in Ostend, Belgium. Back in April 1899, Belgian driver Camille Jenatzy ran an electric car at 65.79 mph.

acceleration, first built in southern California in the late 1930s. The first drag racing organization, the Southern California Timing Association (SCTA), was formed in 1937. The first paved strips for drag racing were runways at air bases and airports, and the first formal drag strip was opened in Goleta, California, in 1948.

The Rally is a test of endurance and speed over great distances and in tougher conditions than those of a closed course. Professional international rally drivers and teams use racing cars to negotiate routes in deserts and other rough terrain in Africa, Australia, and Europe; the annual Monte Carlo Rally, begun in 1911, is the most famous race of this kind. Each year the Monte Carlo rally begins in a different European city and winds down to Monte Carlo, Monaco. FIA is a major sanctioning body in international rallying.

Rallying in the United States generally features amateur drivers using tuned production vehicles on streets and country road routes. Competitors try to reach checkpoints at specified times while maintaining a speed set by the race's organizers (penalties for arriving early or late help ensure fairness).

Off-Road Racing is run on rudimentary trails, with major events being the Baja 500 and the Mexican 1000. Dirt-track racing, which originally served as a means for Indy car training, has evolved from use of miniature Indy cars to other specific forms.

When did Indianapolis open, and why is it dubbed "the Brickyard?"

Indianapolis was opened in 1909 as a testing ground. The oval track surface was laid with 3,200,000 bricks. The first Indianapolis 500 was run in 1911; even though the race is run on one day, testing, practice, and qualifying continue to occur over a three-week period preceding the race.

When was the **first major organized automobile race in the United States**, and what made it important?

The first widely publicized auto race in the United States occurred on Thanksgiving Day in 1895 and was organized by the *Times Herald* newspaper of Chicago. The race was won by an American vehicle made by Charles and Frank Duryea, who in 1896 would be credited as the first American manufacturer of gasoline-powered automobiles. The Duryea car finished ahead of a Benz, the most noted carmaker in the world at the time, further inspiring many American tinkerers, including Henry Ford, Ransom Olds, and others, to continue their experiments with the new-fangled horseless carriage.

The first American race was preceded in early November 1895 by a reliability demonstration that ran from Chicago to Waukegan, Illinois, and back (92 miles). The official race of 52 miles on Thanksgiving Day was won with an average speed of 5.1 miles per hour.

When was the **first long-distance auto race held in the United States**, and why was it stopped?

The Automobile Club of America organized the first long distance race—500 miles, from Cleveland to New York—in 1901. News that President William McKinley had been assassinated led to the race being

When was the first NASCAR race held?

Up until 1948, stock car racing was full of uncertainty: Would the next race be held? Would the track owner be able to afford to pay the winning driver? Would there be enough drivers to hold a race? With no governing body, there was chaos. Into that disorganized scene stepped Bill France Sr., who founded the organization known as the National Association of Stock Car Auto Racing in late 1947. France had some success running races in 1948 with what were known as Modified cars, but on June 19, 1949, he hit paydirt when he held a race in Charlotte, NC for fresh-off-the-showroom-floor "stock" cars. Crowds showed up in record numbers to watch Jim Roper claim victory in that race. The Strictly Stock races, as they were known, evolved into the Grand National series and then into today's wildly popular Winston Cup circuit.

canceled as the leaders reached Buffalo, New York. McKinley, incidentally, had been the first American president to ride in an automobile.

Why do they call the service area on racetracks the **pits**?

The first service areas actually *were* pits—two trenches separated by a counter beside the track where crews could quickly service race cars. The first pits were used in a Grand Prix race in Dieppe, France, in 1908.

What is the **largest sporting venue** in the United States?

The Indianapolis Motor Speedway in Indianapolis, IN, which has room for more than 300,000 fans. For years, the Indianapolis 500 was the main attraction at the track, but in 1994, NASCAR brought its stock cars to the historic site and ran the inaugural Brickyard 400, which was won by Jeff Gordon.

Who won the most races in a single NASCAR season?

In 1967, Richard Petty was already known as "The King" and was widely considered to be one of the top stock car drivers in the country. That season, however, he made it clear that he was the unquestioned No. 1 driver when he won 27 of the 48 races he started, finishing in the top-five 11 other times and the top-10 once. To top all that off, Petty is also considered to be one of the nicest people in the world of sports. His easy-going manner and great sense of humor made him a fan favorite and helped turn NASCAR into the huge sport that it is today.

Who was the first **four-time winner** of the Indianapolis 500?

Three drivers have won the race four times: A.J. Foyt, Jr., Al Unser, and Rick Mears, with Foyt the first to win four times. Foyt also won two Daytona 500s, the 24 Hours of LeMans, the 24 Hours of Daytona, and the 12 Hours of Sebring, as well as races on the dirt and midget circuits. Foyt's feats were encouraged by his father, a garage owner and racer of midget cars who gave his son an engine-equipped red racer at about the time young Foyt learned to walk. After years of experience racing around the yard, Foyt, at age five, competed against an established midget car driver in a three lap exhibition and won.

Which driver **won an Indianapolis 500, a Daytona 500, the 12 Hours of Sebring, a Formula One World Championship, and four USAC Indy Car championships**?

Mario Andretti, who first began racing competitively during the late-1950s in a 1948 Hudson he and his brother, Aldo, adapted for racing, is among racing's most versatile drivers. His family, which had been interred in a displaced person's camp during World War II in Italy, had emigrated to the United States in 1955. Since their father forbade the brothers to race, Mario and Aldo tinkered and raced secretly but were

305

exposed when Aldo was injured in a crash. Mario kept racing, against
his father's wishes; he himself proved a more encouraging father when it
came to auto racing, considering the successes of his race driver sons,
Michael and Jeff. Mario was USAC Champion and Rookie of the Year in
1965. He finished third at Indy that year but won the race in 1967, and
two years later he won at Daytona.

Who won the most **world driving championships on the Formula One** racing circuit

Juan Manuel Fangio won five titles in the 1950s driving four different
makes of automobile. He won his first title in 1951 driving an Alfa
Romeo, then won four straight titles between 1954 and 1957. The first
two were in a Mercedes, while the 1956 crown was won with a Ferrari
and the final championship behind the wheel of a Maserati.

What are the **Crown Jewels of NASCAR** racing?

The Daytona 500, Winston Select 500, Coca-Cola 600, and the Mountain Dew Southern 500. Between 1985 and 1997, R.J. Reynold's Winston brand cigarettes offered drivers a shot at the Winston Million—a
$1 million bonus that would be paid to any driver who could win
three of the big four races in a single year. It didn't take long for
someone to claim the prize—Bill Elliott won the Daytona, Winston,

> ## Who are the only two men to win the crown jewels of American automobile racing, the Indianapolis 500 and the Daytona 500?
>
> Indy-style cars and NASCAR stock cars have absolutely nothing in common, with the exception that they both travel nearly 200 miles per hour. That being said, there were two legendary drivers who were able to do the improbable and not just race both types of cars, but win in both types of cars. Mario Andretti won at Daytona in 1967 and at Indianapolis in 1969, while A.J. Foyt won at Daytona in 1972 and claimed victory at the Brickyard a record-tying four times.

and Southern races the very first year. Only Jeff Gordon was able to repeat the feat in 1997 before Winston changed the format of the bonus offer. Before the Winston Million, only two other men had won three of the races in a single year: Lee Roy Yarborough in 1969 and David Pearson in 1976. The Daytona 500 has been run since 1959, with Richard Petty winning seven times and Cale Yarborough four times; the Winston Select 500 has been run since 1970, with four drivers winning the race three times; the Coca-Cola 600 has been run since 1960, with Darrell Waltrip finding Victory Lane five times; and the Southern 500 has been run since 1950, with Cale Yarborough winning five times.

Why is the **1979 Daytona 500** considered to be such an important race?

At the time, auto racing was just beginning to gain in popularity on a nationwide basis. The sport was wildly popular in the South, where more than 100,000 people would show up to watch a race, but the people who ran the television networks didn't think that people in the rest of the country would enjoy the sport. CBS decided to gamble on the

307

sport and agreed to televise the Daytona 500 live from start to finish, the first time that had ever been done for a NASCAR race. The results were amazing. With a huge snowstorm forcing many people inside in the Northeast, millions of fans saw one of the most exciting races of all-time. Cale Yarborough and Donnie Allison battled it out side-by-side for much of the race, and on the final lap, second-place Yarborough tried to pass Allison, causing both to crash in the infield. As the nation watched, Richard Petty sped by to claim his sixth Daytona crown while Yarborough and Allison staged a memorable fistfight on the infield grass that was joined by Donnie's brother Bobby. It was great television, and the ratings soared, proving that NASCAR was ready for the big-time.

Just how many **major NASCAR records does Richard Petty own?**

Just about all of them. Not only did The King have one of the longest careers, but he had the most successful. Among the major career records Petty holds are: career victories (200), races started (1,164), top-5 finishes (555), top-10 finishes (712), poles (126), laps completed (307,836), laps led (52,194), races led (599), consecutive races won (10), consecutive years racing (35), and performance points (3,645). He has also won a record-tying seven Grand National/Winston Cup championships in his career (tied with Dale Earnhardt), and on most of the records, no one else is even close—David Pearson is second in career victories with 105, for example.

When was the **first NASCAR race held at night?**

With the popularity of racing booming, Charlotte Motor Speedway president Bruton Smith decided that racing was ready for prime-time. He brought in portable lights and staged the 1992 Winston Cup all-star race sport's at night, showcasing the sport's top drivers for a huge nationwide audience. The drivers did their part, as Davey Allison shot by Dale Earnhardt and Kyle Petty when the latter two collided on the last lap; Allison himself crashed shortly after crossing the finish line.

A good pit stop requires precision timing from every crew member.

What goes into a **good pit stop?**

In NASCAR, the difference between first and second place is often less than a tenth of a second. With that in mind, a driver's crew must get him in and out of the pit stops as soon as possible. A good pit stop today is one that is completed in less than 20 seconds—this includes a full tank of gas and four fresh tires. A pit stop works something like this:

When the driver pulls in, three men sprint around to the right (passenger) side of the car. One man lifts the car with a pneumatic jack, while the other two loosen the lug nuts, receive fresh tires from the tire carriers, and put the new tires in place. Sprinting, the three men shift to the left side of the car and repeat the procedure. While that is happening, the gas man is responsible for filling the gas tank using two 11-gallon dump cans that use aviation-style refueling nozzles. Finally, one man is responsible for cleaning the windshield and grill, and another crew member makes sure the driver gets a drink of water. Vroom! Less than 20 seconds, and the driver is back on the track.

Who is the only driver to run in the **Indianapolis 500 and a Winston Cup stock car race on the same day?**

In May 1994 John Andretti, nephew of racing legend Mario Andretti, finished 10th at the Indianapolis 500. Not content with running just one race that day, Andretti hopped in a waiting helicopter and flew to Charlotte, North Carolina, where he suited up for the Coca-Cola 600. His long day had an early finish when he crashed and ended up 36th at Charlotte.

NASCAR is full of father-son teams and other family connections. Who are some of the most **successful families in stock car racing?**

NASCAR has always seemed to draw its share of fathers and sons, brothers and cousins, nephews and uncles, and so on. One of the earliest families to take the track by storm was the Flocks—brothers Tim, Fonty, and Bob Flock all raced in the 1950s and early '60s. The Flocks

Lee Petty drapes his arm around his son Richard's shoulder. Together, the two of them won 254 races to form the greatest father-son combination in racing history.

were overshadowed, however, by the man who would become the patriarch of the greatest racing family of all-time—Lee Petty. Lee won his first race in 1949 and went on to win 53 more before he called it quits in the 1960s. By that time, he was racing side-by-side with son Richard, who of course went on to set the NASCAR record of 200 career victories. The latest addition to the Petty family album is Richard's son Kyle, who has won eight Winston Cup races and is still going strong today.

Other leading families include the Allisons—brothers Bobby and Donnie, and Bobby's sons Clifford and Davey, both of whom were tragically killed while in their prime; the Jarretts, father Ned and son Dale, who created a special moment in NASCAR history when Ned was the television color commentator at the Daytona 500 in 1993 when Dale took the checkered flag; Ralph Earnhardt and son Dale; Buck Baker and son Buddy; brothers Brett, Todd, and Geoff Bodine; brothers Rusty and Kenny Wallace; brothers Michael and Darrell Waltrip; brothers Bobby and Terry Labonte; Mario Andretti and nephew John; and brothers Jeff, Mark, and David Green.

What four tournaments make up the Grand Slam?

In the order of play during a calendar year, the Grand Slam comprises the Australian Open, French Open, Wimbledon, and U.S. Open. The Opens were collectively called the Big Four because only those host countries had won the Davis Cup for the first 73 years of its existence. Grand Slam is a sports term for major accomplishments: a bases-loaded home-run worth four runs in baseball, and a set of major golf tournaments—the Masters, British Open, U.S. Open, and PGA Championship.

TENNIS

GENERAL

OK, one more time: explain **the scoring in tennis.**

To win a game a player must score four points and win by at least two. Love is a term equivalent to zero points, 15 is equivalent to one point, 30 to two points, 40 to three points. The server's score is called or listed first, so a server who has scored three straight points at the beginning is ahead 40–Love. If one person leads 40–30, or 30–40, he/she can win by scoring the next point. If the other person ties the game at 40–40, the score is referred to as deuce, and the first person to score two straight points wins. The first to win a tiebreaker point is referred to has having "advantage," which is followed either by a win or by returning to deuce.

What are we talking about when we talk about **"love?"**

Love means zero score, in tennis. The term love is thought to have derived from the French word "l'oeuf," meaning "the egg"—implying the goose egg, which looks like an 0 and is a slang sports term for saying zero.

Who was the first woman to race in a NASCAR race?

While Janet Guthrie gained fame and notoriety when she competed on the Winston Cup circuit in the late 1970s and early '80s, she was far from the first woman to strap herself behind the wheel of a stock car. In fact, a woman started 13th and finished 14th in the very first NASCAR race ever run on June 19, 1949. Sarah Christian started in the No. 71 car, which was owned by her husband Frank, and drove the first 110 laps before turning the car over to Bob Flock, who drove the final 90 laps. Just three weeks later, Christian was joined by Louise Smith and Ethel Mobley in a 166-mile race at Daytona Beach, FL. Christian finished 6th in that race, Mobley 11th, and Smith 20th after surviving an early roll-over.

How many players have won **tennis' Grand Slam**?

Only two men, Don Budge (1938) and Rod Laver (twice—as an amateur in 1962 and as a professional in 1967), and three women, Maureen Connolly (1953), Margaret Smith Court (1970), and Steffi Graf (1988).

What is the **Federation Cup**?

The Federation Cup is the women's version of the Davis Cup. It began in 1963, established by the International Tennis Federation. 32 teams competed annually at one site over the course of a week until 1994, when the Fed Cup adopted the Davis Cup format. The U.S. has won 15 Fed Cups, Australia seven, Czechoslovakia five, Spain four, and Germany has won twice.

Which countries have **won the Davis Cup**?

The U.S. has won the Cup 31 times through 1997, Australia 20, France eight, Australasia (Australia and New Zealand competed as one from

313

What is the Davis Cup?

The Davis Cup is an international tournament established in 1900 by Dwight Davis, an American tennis player aged 20 at the time. The competition was originally called the International Lawn Tennis Challenge Trophy. Since 1981, the format for the Davis Cup has involved sixteen seeded nations competing in a series of one-match eliminations over the course of a year. Matches consist of two singles, one doubles, and two more singles contests competed over three days.

1920–24) six, British Isles and Sweden five, Great Britain four, and Germany three. Czechoslovakia won in 1980, Italy in 1976, South Africa in 1974.

What are the **dimensions of a tennis court** and net?

At the center point the net is three feet high and at either end, three-and-a-half feet. The court is 78 feet long and 27 feet wide. It is 21 feet from the service line to the net in tennis. The alley, an addition to the singles court on both sides that provides space for doubles play, is $4\frac{1}{2}$ feet. This area, widening the court by nine feet, is in use during doubles play following the serve.

What **three colors of tennis balls** are legal in most tournaments, and what is **the standard size and weight?**

White, orange, and yellow are the colors of the tournament tennis ball, which is two-and-a-half inches in diameter and weighs two ounces. Balls are pressurized, with the pressure varying slightly according to national origin. The American ball is generally livelier and more in use for the power game popular in the United States. The European ball is

What are the different surfaces on which tennis has been played?

Whether the playing surface is anthill grit (in Australia), dried cow dung (in India), wood, clay, grass, linoleum, canvas, concrete, asphalt or synthetic carpets, the dimensions are always the same. The game began on grass courts in England. That is an uncommon surface now, although the biggest tournament of all, Wimbledon, is still a grass event.

usually lower pressure, easier to control, yet harder to hit for an outright winning point. The nap of the ball also varies, depending on the surface on which it is played. It is thick for abrasive surfaces such as concrete and asphalt, medium for clay and indoor, and light for grass. Balls were uniformly white until 1972 when yellow, offering increased visibility, began to take over.

What other **good use for a tennis racket** is showcased in the 1960 movie, *The Apartment*?

Bachelor Jack Lemmon used his tennis racket to strain spaghetti.

Where is the **International Tennis Hall of Fame?**

Newport Casino, Newport, Rhode Island. The Hall of Fame was established to honor all-time greats of the game as well and to house a museum of tennis history and memorabilia. It was founded in 1953, conceived by tennis innovator Jimmy Van Alen as the National Tennis Hall of Fame, and until 1975 it enshrined only Americans. That year the name and scope went worldwide as the International Tennis Hall of Fame with the induction of Englishman Fred Perry. The first class of inductees was tapped in 1955.

Before which athletic showdown
did one player give the opposing player a live pig?

Before "The Battle of the Sexes" (Billie Jean King gave it to Bobby Riggs). This 1973 Houston Astrodome spectacle—equal parts tennis, carnival, and sociological phenomenon—captured the fancy of America as no pure tennis match ever had. The crowd of 30,472, paying as much as $100 a seat, was the largest ever to witness a tennis match. Some 50 million more watched on prime-time television. The whole gaudy promotion was worth supposedly $3 million, and the 29-year-old King collected a $100,000 winner-take-all purse, plus ancillary revenues, for squashing 55-year-old, self-proclaimed "king of male chauvinist pigs" Riggs, 6–4, 6–3, 6–3. He earned a substantial prize as well.

MEN'S

What was the **longest match** ever played?

Dick Leach and Dick Dell beat Tom Mozur and Len Schloss, 3–6, 49–47, 22–20—an astounding 147 games—in the 1967 Newport (Rhode Island) Invitation. This was prior to adoption of the tie-breaker—death to deuce sets—played at six games all. The longest singles match went 126 games, when Roger Taylor of Great Britain defeated Wieslaw Gasiorek of Poland, 27–29, 31–29, 6–4, in the King's Cup in Warsaw, Poland, 1966.

Who was the first **unseeded and youngest winner of Wimbledon** in 1985?

Boris Becker at age 17 years, 7 months. The redheaded phenomenon was the first German champ. A big man (6-foot-3, 180) playing a big carefree game of booming serves, heavy forehand, penetrating volleys, and diving saves, he was an immediate crowd favorite. Despite his

Billie Jean King and Bobby Riggs staged a "Battle of the Sexes" tennis match in 1973. King won, taking home $100,000 and bragging rights for her efforts.

youth, he showed sensitivity in rejecting an early, obvious nickname, "Boom Boom," considering it "too warlike."

Who was **Arthur Ashe?**

Ashe grew up in Richmond, Virginia, where he could not play in the usual junior tournaments due to racial segregation. He persisted and enjoyed a glorious career, ranking in the top 15 for tournaments won. He won the 1970 Australian Open and Wimbledon in 1975. In 1968, he won the U.S. Open and the U.S. Amateur Open, becoming the first African-American to win the U.S. men's national tennis title. He lent himself, his name, and his money to various social causes and entered the Hall of Fame in 1985.

In 1983, who was the **first Frenchman to win the French Open in 37 years?**

Yannick Noah.

What tennis player received No. 1 rankings in 1937 and 1938 and was the first to win the Grand Slam?

Don Budge. The red-haired young giant played a game of maximum power. His service was battering, his backhand considered perhaps the finest the game has known, his net play emphatic, his overhead drastic. Quick and rhythmic, he was truly the all-around player and, what is more, was temperamentally suited for the game. Affable and easygoing, he could not be shaken from the objective of winning with the utmost application of hitting power. He was elected to the Hall of Fame in 1964.

WOMEN'S

Who was the **first female to win the Grand Slam?**

Maureen "Little Mo" Connolly flashed briefly but brilliantly on the tennis scene. Nicknamed "Little Mo" for her big-gunning, unerring ground strokes (it was an allusion to "Big Mo," the U.S. battleship Missouri), she was devastating from the baseline, and seldom needed to go to the net. She lost only one set en route to scoring her Grand Slam in 1953.

Whose **only loss in 1983** was to Kathy Horvath?

Martina Navratilova, during the fourth round of the French Open. Born in Czechoslovakia, Martina became a U.S. citizen in 1981, after defecting six years earlier. The left-hander is the game's most prolific winner of the open era.

How old was **Tracy Austin** when she made her first Wimbledon appearance?

Fourteen. One of the game's prodigies, Tracy Ann Austin was meteoric, an iron-willed girl whose blaze was glorious though fleeting. A variety

Arthur Ashe was a champion on and off the court. He ranks in the top 15 in tournament wins and was well known for his work on behalf of humanitarian and charitable causes.

of injuries cut short what had promised to be one of the great careers. She and her brother, John, won the Wimbledon mixed in 1980, the only brother-sister pairing to do so. She entered the Hall of Fame in 1992 and works frequently as a TV tennis commentator.

ON WATER

What is the history of the America's Cup yacht races?

England's Royal Yacht Squadron organized a 60-mile regatta around the Isle of Wight in 1861 and offered a silver tropy—the Hundred Guinea Cup—to the winner. *America,* a 101-foot schooner from the New York Yacht Club, won the race and the trophy was deeded to the Club to defend it whenever challenged. Challenges have come in staggered time frames—from races held three consecutive years (1885-87) to having no competitions for seventeen (1903-20) and 21-year (1937-1958) periods.

319

Who was the first to win five straight Wimbledon singles tennis titles?

Bjorn Borg. Before he was 21, Bjorn Rune Borg had registered feats that would set him apart as one of the game's greats, and before he was 26, the head banded, golden-locked Swede was through. No male career of the modern era has been so brief and bright. Borg won six French Opens, Wimbledon five times, and was three-times runner-up at the U.S. Open.

From 1870-1937 the America's Cup was successfully defended 17 times in Schooners and J-Class boats; from 1958-1980, the America's Cup was successfully defended eight more times in 12-meter boats. *Australia II* broke American dominance in 1983 by winning four times in the best-of-seven format that had been in place since 1930. Four years later, *Stars & Stripes* of the San Diego Yacht Club won the trophy back, but they were immediately challenged the following year by Mercury Bay, a New Zealand crew. New Zealand planned to race with a 133 ft. Monohull, and defending skipper Dennis Connor countered with a 60 ft. Catamaran. After the Catamaran easily won two races, Mercury Bay protested use of the boat in court, leading to three years of legal wrangling. Since 1992, the America's Cup has been competed with 75-foot Monohulls with 110-foot masts. *America 3* won in 1992 and New Zealand's *Black Magic* won in 1995. Their defense is scheduled for the year 2000.

What is the **oldest American college sport** still held today?

Rowing. Harvard and Yale held the first U.S. collegiate regatta in 1852.

What are the different kinds of **rowing competitions**?

Regattas are competitions run in lanes where individual rowers and teams (referred to as shells) are eliminated over a series of races; Head Races are based on times, with boats going off at various intervals.

What tennis player's last name means "tall tree by still waters" in an Aboriginal language?

Goolagong, the surname of Evonne Fay Goolagong Cawley. She is the only native Australian to become an international tennis player. As one of eight children of an itinerant sheep-shearer and his wife, she spent her formative years in the small country town of Barellan. Her parents were convinced by a tennis school proprietor in Sydney to allow Evonne (at age 13) to live in his household, where he could coach her. She won six Grand Slam events: four Australian Opens (1974–77), the French Open (1971), and Wimbledon (1971). Londoners called her Sunshine Supergirl.

There are three kinds of Scull races—single scullers and double and quadruple teams; the scull is the type of boat and also refers to the oar, so in a Scull race scullers uses sculls to propel their sculls. Single sculls average about 27 feet in length, doubles about 34 feet in length, and quadruples about 44 feet in length.

In rowing contests the competitors use one oar, and a boat may or may not include a coxswain, or coach. Competitions include coxed and coxless pairs and fours and coxed eights. The coxless pair scull runs 34 feet in length, the coxed pair about 35 feet; the coxless four runs about 44 feet, the coxed four around 45; the coxed eight runs around 62 feet.

What about **canoe** competitions?

Canoe and kayak sprint racing is held on 500 meter, 1000 meter and 10,000 meter courses for men, 500 meter and 5000 meter for women, in one-, two-, and four-person events. The paddler in a kayak sits with their legs outstretched before them in a decked or covered boat and uses a double-bladed paddle; canoeists paddle a singe-bladed oar from a kneeling position in an open boat.

Martina Navratilova, the most prolific winner of the open era, lost only once in 1983.

The different races are distinguished by a K (denoting kayak) and C (denoting canoe) followed by the number of people in the boat. Men compete in K1 and K2 in the 500m 1000m and 10,000m events, but not in the 500m in K4. C1 and C2 are competed in each distance, but C4 competition does not include the 10,000m. Women compete only in Kayak competitions, but the women's K4 is not run at the 5000m distance.

Canoe slalom competiton contains a series of gates (at least 20) and various natural and artificial obstacles canoeists must negotiate. Men compete in K1, C1, and C2 events, women in K1. Each contestant is usually given one trial run on a course followed by one or two timed runs.

322

What is the history of the America's Cup Trophy?

The America's Cup trophy was originally called the Hundred Guinea's Cup when first contested for in 1851, but it was renamed to honor the first winner, the yacht *America*. It is 27 inches high and made of sterling silver and originally cost 100 guineas ($500); today it is valued at over $250,000. The trophy had to be restored after a Maori protester smashed it with a sledgehammer in 1997. The trophy is taken into possession by the winner of the America's Cup races who must defend the Cup when officially challenged.

BOXING

Who was the **first officially recognized heavyweight champion**?

On August 29, 1885, John L. Sullivan knocked out Dominick McAffrey in six rounds to claim the world championship. The International Boxing Hall of Fame considers Sullivan to be the first heavyweight champion. Sullivan held the title until 1892 when he lost the title to Gentleman James Corbett in an epic 21-round bare-knuckle bout. Corbett and Sullivan were the last of the great bare-knuckle fighters.

Who are the **oldest and youngest prizefight champions**?

Wilfred Benitez was 17 years, six months old when he became junior welterweight champion in 1976. George Foreman was 45 years, ten months old when he became heavyweight champion in 1994.

Who is the only boxer to **hold the title in three weight classes at the same time?**

"Hammerin' Hank" Armstrong owned the featherweight, lightweight,

> ## Why might a coxswain
> ## want his shell to lose a race on the Amazon?
>
> Traditionally, the winning team throws its coxswain overboard. Piranah's might makes a meal of the winning coach in the Amazon.

and welterweight titles—which ranged from 126 to 147 pounds—at the same time in 1938.

Who are the **three boxers Muhammad Ali defeated** to become world heavyweight champion an unprecedented three times?

On February 2, 1964, a young Cassius Clay knocked out Sonny Liston in seven rounds in Miami Beach, Florida to claim the heavyweight championship of the world. Ten years later, now known as Muhammad Ali, he reclaimed the title in the infamous "Rumble in the Jungle" in Zaire on the day before Halloween when he knocked out George Foreman in the eighth round. Finally, capping a remarkable career with a comeback nobody believed he could make, Ali defeated Leon Spinks in a 15-round decision in New Orleans on September 15, 1978.

Only two men have won both an Olympic gold medal and a world championship in the heavywieght division. Who are they?

Joe Frazier and George Foreman. Frazier won his gold medal at the Tokyo Olympics in 1964, while Foreman won his four years later in Mexico City. Four other men have won an Olympic gold medal outside the heavyweight division and then gone on to win the heavyweight world title—Floyd Patterson and Michael Spinks turned the trick in the middleweight division, while Cassius Clay (Muhammad Ali) and Leon Spinks earned medals as light heavyweights. It was Leon Spinks, of course,

John L. Sullivan, the first recognized heavyweight boxing champion.

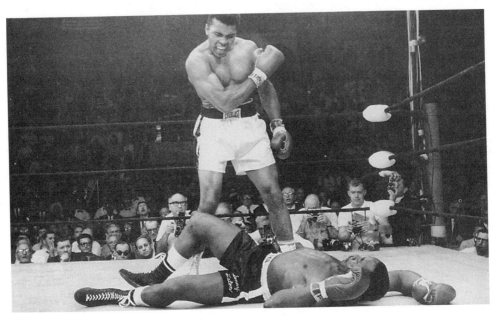

Muhammad Ali became World Heavyweight Champion three different times against three different opponents.

whom Ali defeated when he won the heavyweight title for an unprecedented third time in 1978.

Who are the only boxers to be inducted into the International Boxing Hall of Fame in their **first year of eligibility?**

In 1998, Matthew Saad Muhammed became the ninth fighter to gain entry in his first year of eligibility. The others are Sugar Ray Leonard, Alexis Arguello, Marvin Hagler, Michael Spinks, Carlos Zarate, Wilfredo Gomez, Wilfred Benitez, and Aaron Pryor.

Where is the **International Boxing Hall of Fame** and what does it take to be inducted?

The Hall is located in the small town of Canastota, New York. Eligible candidates must have been a professional boxer (he need not have been a champion) and must be retired from boxing for at least five years prior

Who is the only boxer to win titles in five different weight classes?

When the sport of boxing expanded during the 1980s—up to 17 weight classes from four different sanctioning bodies—the number of champions who won titles in multiple weight classes soared. Despite the fact that it became easier, only Sugar Ray Leonard has been able to pull off the feat in five different classes spanning 28 pounds. The five classes and the year he won the title in each: light heavyweight (1988), super middleweight (1988), middleweight (1987), junior middleweight (1981), and welterweight (1979). He actually won two of the titles on the same night in 1988 when the WBC allowed his fight against Donny Lalonde to count towards both the light heavyweight and the super middleweight titles.

to election. Nonparticipants will be chosen from among the following catagories: promoters, managers, trainers, journalists, announcers, commentators, rulemakers, executives, officals, patrons, and anyone else who was not a boxer. There is no retirement requirement for nonparticipants. The number of inductees is established each year by the International Boxing Hall of Fame Museum when ballots are sent out to members of the Boxing Writers Association of America and other select individuals.

What are boxing's **seventeen weight divisions?**

Class	Weight limit
Heaveyweight	over 190 lbs
Cruiserweight	up to 190 lbs
Light Heavyweight	up to 175 lbs
Super Middleweight	up to 168 lbs
Middleweight	up to 160 lbs

George Foreman is one of only two men to win an Olympic gold medal in the heavyweight division and a World Heavyweight Championship.

What fighters were named "Fighter of the Year" the most times by the Boxing Writers Association of America?

Three fighters each won the award three times: Muhammad Ali, in 1965, 1974, and 1975; Joe Frazier, in 1969, 1971, and 1975 (tied for the award with Ali); and Sugar Ray Leonard, in 1976, 1979, and 1981. Leonard's award in 1976 was part of a joint award to the five U.S. boxers who won gold medals at the Summer Olympics in Montreal—Leonard, Howard Davis, Leo Randolph, Michael Spinks, and Larry Spinks.

Junior Middleweight	up to 154 lbs
Welterweight	up to 147 lbs
Junior Welterweight	up to 140 lbs
Lightweight	up to 135 lbs
Junior Lightweight	up to 130 lbs
Featherweight	up to 126 lbs
Bantamweight	up to 118 lbs
Junior Bantamweight	up to 115 lbs
Flyweight	up to 112 lbs
Junior Flyweight	up to 108 lbs
Minimumweight	up to 105 lbs

FREESTYLING: GENERAL THINGS TO KNOW

What teams can't you bet on in Vegas?

You can't bet on Nevada college teams in Las Vegas or Reno.

Who is the only father-son combination enshrined in the Hall?

In 1998, Prof. Mike Donovan was inducted into the Hall in the Pioneer category (the Pioneer category is for bare-knuckle fighters whose last fight was held before 1892), joining his son, referee Arthur Donovan. Mike's grandson, Art Donovan Jr., played football for the Baltimore Colts and is enshrined in the Football Hall of Fame.

What are the **most popular participatory sports** in the United States?

According to a 1997 survey by the National Sporting Goods Association, exercise walking is most popular with over 70 million participants. Swimming is second with just over 60 million participants and bicycle riding third at over 50 million.

Exercising with equipment ranked fourth (over 47 million) and aerobics 13th (over 24 million). Fishing ranked fifth (over 45 million), overnight camping sixth (over 44 million), hiking 11th (over 26 million), backpacking 25th (over 11 million), and mountain biking 27th (over 11 million). Bowling was seventh (over 42 million), pool/billiards eighth (over 34 million), basketball ninth (over 33 million), and power boating 10th (over 28 million).

Others not mentioned above include In-line skating (12th, over 25 million), golf (14th, over 23 million), running/jogging (15th, over 22 million), darts (16th, over 21 million), softball (17th, just under 20 million), hunting with firearms (18th, over 19 million), volleyball (19th, 18½ million), and target shooting (20th, over 15 million). Soccer ranked 23rd with just under 14 million participants and tennis tied for 25th with 11½ million.

The survey involved Americans seven years of age and older.

What is the Tour de France?

The Tour de France is an endurance bicycle race covering about 2,300 miles in France and neighboring countries held over three weeks in June-July. Four bikers have won the race five times (Jacques Anquetil of France, Bernard Hinault of France, Miguel Indurain of Spain, and Eddie Merckx of Belgium). American Greg LeMond won the race three times. The Tour de France has been held annually since 1903.

What is the **top-grossing sports movie** of all-time

Through October 1, 1997, Tom Cruise's *Jerry McGuire* was the box office champ, pulling in $153,620,822. Sylvester Stallone is probably the undisputed heavyweight champ of the silver screen, however, as his five *Rocky* movies have combined to earn more than $510 million. *Rocky 4, Rocky 3,* and the original *Rocky* finished 2nd, 3rd, and 4th behind *McGuire,* respectively. Two sports movies—the original *Rocky* in 1976 and *Chariots of Fire* in 1981, won the Oscar for Best Picture.

What is the **International Women's Sports Hall of Fame**, and how are athletes chosen for inclusion?

The International Women's Sports Hall of Fame was founded in 1980 by the Women's Sports Foundation of East Meadow, New York. That organization selects honorees whose achievements and contributions are internationally recognized. Honorees are divided into two categories, Pioneers (those whose accomplishments pre-date 1960) and Contemporary. Auto racer Janet Guthrie, basketball stars Ann Meyers and Cheryl Miller, figure skater Peggy Fleming, gymnast Mary Lou Retton, tennis stars Chris Evert and Billie Jean King, track star Wilma Rudolph, and eight prominent golfers are among the Americans represented.

What are the teams of Japanese Baseball Leagues?

There are six teams in each of two leagues: The Central League has the Chunichi Dragons, the Hanshin Tigers, the Hiroshima Carp, the Yakult Swallows, the Yokahama BayStars, and the Yomiuri Giants; the Pacific League has the Chiba Lotte Marines, the Fukuoka Daiei Hawks, the Kintesu Buffaloes, the Nippon Ham Fighters, the Orix Blue Wave, and the Seibu Lions.

What is the **Women's Global Challenge**?

The Woman's Global Challenge is a biannual event beginning in 1999 that matches the world's top amateur and professional female athletes and women's teams in such events as basketball, beach volleyball, diving, figure skating, gymnastics, soccer, swimming, and track and field. The top ten athletes in each sport and the top four to eight teams will be invited to compete. The Women's Global Challenge was conceived by the Women's Sports Foundation.

Who was the first athlete whose **salary exceeded that of the President of the United States**?

Babe Ruth was the first athlete to have a contract with an annual salary higher than that of the president. When asked if he thought that was right, Ruth replied, "Yes. I had a better year."

Michael Jordan's 1997 salary was 16½ times higher than President Clinton's.

Has anyone ever **bowled a perfect series** (900 over three games)?

The only sanctioned 900 series occured in 1997, when Jeremy Sonnenfeld, a sophmore at Nebraska, rolled three perfect games in a row.

How did the Ivy League get its name?

Four schools—Harvard, Yale, Columbia, Princeton—formed an association called the League of IV; a sportswriter played with the name and turned it into the Ivy League.

What is the **triathlon?**

The triathlon, which will be an introduction sport at the 2000 Summer Olympic Games in Sydney, Australia, combines swimming, cycling, and running. For the 2000 Games, the longest Olympic swimming distance (1500 meters), cycling time trials (40 kilometers), and footrace (10,000 meters) will be used. The World Triathlon Championship, held annually since 1989, combines a 1.5 kilometer swim (.93 of a mile) a 40-kilometer bike (24.9 miles), and a 10-kilometer run (6.2 miles). Men have broken the 1 hour 40 minute mark for the competition, women the 1 hour 50 minute mark. The Ironman Triathlon Championship has been held since 1978 in Hawaii and features more grueling distances (2.4 mile swim, 112 mile bike, 26.2 mile run), with men challenging the 8-hour mark of total time, women challenging the 9-hour mark.

How do **Canadian Football and Australian Rules football** differ from their American cousin?

The Canadian football field runs 110 yards and end zones are 25 yards deep (as opposed to 100 and 10 yards, respectively in American); there are 12 offensive and defensive players on the field (as opposed to eleven); a team gets three downs to make 10 yards (as opposed to four); and there is no fair catch in Canadian football, as players returning kicks are allowed a five-yard free zone to catch the ball and begin their runback. In Canadian football players in the backfield are free to move in any direction before the ball is snapped, while in American football only one player can go in motion before the snap and he has to run parallel to the line of scrimmage or away from it. Canadian football has a 25 yard penalty in addition to the 5-, 10-, and 15-yard penalty distances it has in common with American football. In addition to a touchdown (6 points), field goal (3), safety and conversion (2), and extra point (1), Canadian football features the single, or rouge, worth one point if a team cannot advance a kicked ball beyond its own end zone; unlike American football, kicked balls are not allowed to roll dead, so the receiving team must retrieve the ball or else lose possession. A player who cannot return a kick from the end zone will concede a single, rather than risk getting tackled for a two-point safety.

The field in Australian Rules Football is oval shaped, 110 to 155 meters wide, 135 to 185 meters long. Teams of 18 players advance the ball towards sets of goal posts on either end of the oval: kicking or punching the ball through the center posts is worth a goal (six points), while kicking or punching the ball within two outer posts are called "behinds" (one point). Players can advance the ball toward the goals by running, but they must bounce the ball or touch it on the ground every 10 meters; ball handlers can kick, hand off, or punch the ball to another player, but passes are not allowed.

Who are those **guys in raincoats and shorts who occasionally wave flags** at either end of the oval in Australian Rules Football?

They're not bookies. They are game officials who signal whether a ball has passed through the center posts (worth six points) or the outer points (worth one point).

Index

335

Armstrong, Hank 323
Arnie's Army 187
Arsenal 289
Art Ross Trophy 205, 208-210, 212
Ashe, Arthur 317, 319
Ashland Junior College 92
Asian Cup 284
Asinof, Eliot 17
Assault 298
Associated Press (AP) 142-145, 160, 262
Association for Intercollegiate Athletics for Women (AIAW) 65
Atlanta Braves 23, 31, 49
Atlanta Falcons 137
Atlanta Hawks 60, 97
Auerbach, Red 74, 96-98
Augusta National 173, 179, 191, 196
Austin, Tracy 318
Australia II 320
Australian Open 312, 317
Australian Rules Football 333-334
Auto Racing 300-301, 304, 306-307
Automobile Club of America 303
Avco Cup 204
Avco Financial Services 204
Axe 157
Axel 273
Azinger, Paul 186

B

backpacking 330
backstroke 252-254
Badminton 246
Bagwell, Jeff 34
Bailey, Robert 137
Baja 500 302
Baker, Frank "Home Run" 6, 47
Baker, Buddy 311
Baker, Hobey 241

Baker, Buck 311
Balance Beam 257, 259
balata 176
Ballet 270
Baltimore Bullets 60, 75-76
Baltimore Colts 118, 124-125, 134-135, 330
Baltimore Ravens 137
bandy 200
Banks, Ernie 45
Banks, Gordon 287
Bannister, Roger 297
Barcelona (soccer team) 267, 286, 291
Barkley, Charles 71
Barksdale, Don 63
Barry, Jack 47
Barry, Rick 61, 71, 83, 102
baseball diamond 11
Baseball Writers Association of America (BBWAA) 30, 35, 42
Baseball Hall of Fame 4, 25, 27-30, 48
Basic Agreement 47
Basketball Association of America (BAA) 59-60, 78
Basketball Hall of Fame 62, 104
Baskins High School 95
Batistuta, Gabriel 289
Battle of the Sexes 316-317
Baugh, Sammy 122
Bay Hill Invitational 193
Bayern Munich 286
Baylor, Elgin 71, 80, 85
Beckenbauer, Franz 285, 287
Becker, Boris 316
Bednarik, Chuck 150
beech 175
Beer Barrel 157
behinds 334
Behrend, Mark 240
Beliveau, Jean 208, 236
Bell, Bobby 124, 150
Bell, Buddy 49

Bell, Gus 49
Bell, Jay 40
Belmont Park 298-300
Belmont Stakes 298-300
Bender, Bob 107
Benedict, Clint 239
Benitez, Wilfred 323, 326
Bennett, Cornelius 159
Bentley, Max 212
Berenson Abbott, Senda 65
Berenson, Red 240
Berg, Patty 170-171, 191
Bergkamp, Dennis 289
Bernebau 291
Berra, Yogi 24
Best, George 287
Bethea, Larry 130
Biathlon 271
bicycle riding 330
The Big House 157, 159
Big Man Era 82
Big Mo 318
Big Ten Conference 145
Bill Masterson Trophy 206
Billet 9
Bing, Dave 71
Bingham, Walter 259
Bird, Larry 67, 71, 85, 87-88, 105
Black Sox 7, 15, 17
Black, Joe 44, 51
Black Belt Hall of Fame 250
Black Magic 320
Blackpool 287
Blair, Andy 203-204
Blair, Bonnie 274-275
Blake, Toe 216
Blanchard, Doc 147, 151
Blanda, George 141-142
Blomberg, Ron 46
blue line 237
Blue, Vida 32
Blue Darter 53
Bobsledding 272
Bodine, Brett 311
Bodine, Geoff 311

National Basketball Association (NBA) 42, 59-64, 66, 68-72, 74-85, 87-89, 95-98, 101-102, 104, 108-109, 231, 249

National Basketball League (NBL) 59-60, 78, 80

National Broadcasting Company (NBC) 124, 126-127

National Collegiate Athletic Association (NCAA) 63-66, 69, 71-72, 74, 76, 78-80, 82, 85, 87-89, 91, 94-95, 98, 100, 102-103, 105-107, 115-116, 148, 155, 157-158, 194, 227, 239-241

National Football Foundation 157

National Football League (NFL) 42, 48, 117-125, 128-129, 134-137, 139-140, 142-143, 152-153, 158, 160-161, 231

National Hockey Association (NHA) 200-201

National Hockey League (NHL) 42, 200-202, 204-214, 216-219, 221, 223, 226-239, 266

National Hockey League Broadcasters' Association 206

National Invitational Tournament (NIT) 63-64, 69, 97

National League 5, 16-17, 23, 26, 31-34, 37, 41, 43-44, 47-48

National Sporting Goods Association (NSGA) 330

National Tennis Hall of Fame 315

Navratilova, Martina 318, 322

Navy 78, 143, 150, 157

NBA Championship 71-72, 74-81, 85, 89, 96-97, 108

NBA Rookie of the Year Award 71

NBA Sixth Man Award 76, 80

NCAA Tournament 63-64, 69, 91, 103, 106-107, 241

NCAA Tournament (Hockey) 239

Ndeti, Cosmas 295

neck guard 12

Nedved, Petr 226

Negro Leagues 13-14, 44-45

Nelson, Byron 96-97, 185

Nelson, Don 96-97, 185

New England Intercollegiate Basketball League 62

New England Whalers 204

New Jersey Devils 107, 228, 235

New Jersey Nets 61, 72, 89

New Orleans Jazz 61

New Orleans Saints 134, 137

New York Cosmos 289

New York Game 4

New York Giants 14, 17, 19, 24, 26-27, 32, 34, 44-45, 89, 119, 136, 142, 257, 332

New York Highlanders 17, 19

New York Islanders 210, 216, 219, 225-226, 228, 235

New York Jets 124-127, 142, 204, 208, 218

New York Knicks 60, 63, 72-77, 82, 96, 249

New York Nets 61, 72, 89

New York Rangers 200, 204, 206, 212, 214, 225-226, 228, 235

New York Renaissance 62

New York Times 147

New York Yacht Club 319

New York Yankees 16-17, 19, 21, 23-24, 26-27, 30, 34-35, 40, 46, 48, 51, 119

Newark Junior College 95

Newberry College 92

Newcastle United 289

Newcombe, Bob 27, 44, 51

Newport Casino 315

Newport Country Club 169

Newport Invitation 316

NFL Championship 119-121, 136

NHL Players' Association 206

NHL Governors 205

NHL Entry Draft 217

Nicaragua 29

Nicholson, Jack 53

Nicklaus, Jack 188, 192

Nippon Ham Fighters 332

no-hitter 24, 31-32

No-Name Defense 134-135

Noah, Yannick 317

Nobis, Tommy 150

Nomo, Hideo 51

Nordic skiing 270

Norman, Greg 185-186, 191

Norris Division 234

Norris, James 205, 207-208, 210-211, 214, 234

North American Soccer League (NASL) 289

Northwestern University 155-156

Notre Dame 91, 115, 143-148, 150-151, 154

Notre Dame Shift 146

Nou Camp 291

Nuxhall, Joe 13-14

O

Oakhurst Golf Club 166

Oakland A's 16-17, 32, 40, 50-51

Oakland Hills 174

Oakland Raiders 123, 126-127, 129, 136, 142

Oakley, Charles 85

Ocean Course 174

octopus 229

Oerter, Al 263

Oeschger, Joe 33

Off-Road Racing 302

offsides (hockey) 237

offsides (soccer) 280-281

347

Uecker, Bob 52-53
UEFA Cup 286
Underwood, Pat 50
Underwood, Tom 50
Uneven Bars 257, 259
Unitas, Johnny 125, 141
United Press International (UPI) 160
United States Air Force 94
United States Golf Association (USGA) 169, 171, 176, 182, 184
University of Alabama 143-145, 152, 266-267
University of Arizona 48, 137, 148, 193
University of California 31-32, 41, 47-48, 50-51, 94, 100, 124, 143-144, 154, 157, 179, 226, 234, 250, 302
University of California at Los Angeles (UCLA) 63, 67, 75, 79, 82, 95, 98, 100, 107, 157
University of Chicago 150
University of Cincinnati 91, 108
University of Colorado 60-240
University of Connecticut 65, 95
University of Denver
University of Georgia 144, 154-156, 160, 245
University of Houston 72, 75-76, 267
University of Illinois 118, 149, 152, 156-157, 303
University of Kansas 106
University of Maine 240
University of Maryland 116, 144, 159, 249, 298
University of Massachusetts 72
University of Miami (Florida) 102, 160
University of Michigan 85, 92, 102, 108, 145-146, 150-152, 155-157, 159, 174, 200-201, 239-240

University of Minnesota 150-151, 156-157, 240
University of Nebraska 139, 143-146, 150-151, 332
University of Nevada, Las Vegas 107-108
University of North Carolina 66, 87, 100, 102, 107-108, 169, 310
University of North Dakota 240
University of Northern Alabama 152
University of Oregon 63, 155, 200
University of St. Andrews 167
University of San Francisco 71, 79, 89, 96, 100, 102
University of Southern California (USC) 65, 143, 145-146
University of Southern Illinois 149
University of Texas 14, 48-49, 65, 102, 143, 145, 149-151, 191
University of Tulsa 148
University of Utah 48, 61, 75, 78-79, 98, 149
University of Virginia 66, 74, 80, 115, 144, 166, 317
University of Washington 107
University of Wisconsin 143, 155-157, 227, 240
Unseld, Wes 75-76, 79
Unser, Al 305
up and down 9, 171-172, 253
Uruguay Nacional 287
USA Basketball 64
Utah Jazz 61, 79
Utah Stars 48, 75, 78, 98

V

Valderrama, Carlos 289
Valenzuela, Fernando 51
Van Alen, Jimmy 315
Vancouver Canucks 217, 219
Vancouver Grizzlies 61

Vander Meer, Johnny 31
Vardon grip 173
Vardon, Harry 173, 183
Vatican 160-161
Vault 256, 259, 296
Veeck, Bill 12
Veterans Committee 30, 45, 104
Vezina, Georges 205, 209-212, 218, 239
Vezina Trophy 205, 209-212, 218, 239
Victory Bell 157
Victory Lane 307
Villanova 70, 106, 199
Vincent, Troy 137
Virginia Wesleyan College 115
Vogler, Matt 149
volleyball 95, 330, 332

W

Wagner, Honus 27
Walker, Chet 104
Walker Cup 184
Walker, Doak 143
Walker, Hershel 149
Walker, Larry 34
Walker, Moses Fleetwood 42
Walker, Welday 42
Wallace, Kenny 311
Wallace, Rusty 311
Walter Kennedy Citizenship Award 79
Walton, Bill 79
Waltrip, Darrell 307, 311
Waltrip, Michael 307, 311
War Admiral 298
Ward, Arch 41, 151
Warfield, Paul 134
Warner, Pop 147
Washington & Jefferson 144
Washington Bullets 60, 71, 75-76, 79
Washington Redskins 121, 135-136, 140